OLIVER GOLDSMITH

(SIR JOSHUA REYNOLDS)

OXFORD EDITION

THE COMPLETE
POETICAL WORKS
OF
OLIVER GOLDSMITH

EDITED WITH INTRODUCTION AND NOTES

BY

AUSTIN DOBSON
HON. LL.D. EDIN.

HENRY FROWDE
LONDON, EDINBURGH, GLASGOW
NEW YORK AND TORONTO
1911

PREFATORY NOTE

THIS volume is a reprint, extended and revised, of the *Selected Poems* of Goldsmith issued by the Clarendon Press in 1887. It is 'extended,' because it now contains the whole of Goldsmith's poetry : it is 'revised' because, besides the supplementary text, a good deal has been added in the way of annotation and illustration. In other words, the book has been substantially enlarged. Of the new editorial material, the bulk has been collected at odd times during the last twenty years ; but fresh Goldsmith facts are growing rare. I hope I have acknowledged obligation wherever it has been incurred ; I trust also, for the sake of those who come after me, that something of my own will be found to have been contributed to the literature of the subject.

AUSTIN DOBSON.

EALING, *September*, 1906.

CONTENTS

CONTENTS

NOTES

APPENDIXES

LIST OF ILLUSTRATIONS

INTRODUCTION

Two of the earlier, and, in some respects, more important *Memoirs* of Oliver Goldsmith open with a quotation from one of his minor works, in which he refers to the generally uneventful life of the scholar. His own
5 chequered career was a notable exception to this rule. He was born on the 10th of November, 1728, at Pallas, a village in the county of Longford in Ireland, his father, the Rev. Charles Goldsmith, being a clergyman of the Established Church. Oliver was the fifth of a
10 family of five sons and three daughters. In 1730, his father, who had been assisting the rector of the neighbouring parish of Kilkenny West, succeeded to that living, and moved to Lissoy, a hamlet in Westmeath, lying a little to the right of the road from Bally-
15 mahon to Athlone. Educated first by a humble relative named Elizabeth Delap, the boy passed subsequently to the care of Thomas Byrne, the village schoolmaster, an old soldier who had fought Queen Anne's battles in Spain, and had retained from those experiences a wandering and
20 unsettled spirit, which he is thought to have communicated to one at least of his pupils. After an attack of confluent small-pox, which scarred him for life, Oliver was transferred from the care of this not-uncongenial preceptor to a school at Elphin. From Elphin he passed
25 to Athlone; from Athlone to Edgeworthstown, where he remained until he was thirteen or fourteen years of age. The accounts of these early days are contradictory. By his schoolfellows he seems to have been regarded as stupid and heavy,—'little better than a fool'; but they

admitted that he was remarkably active and athletic, and
that he was an adept in all boyish sports. At home, notwithstanding a variable disposition, and occasional fits of
depression, he showed to greater advantage. He scrib-
bled verses early ; and sometimes startled those about
him by unexpected 'swallow-flights' of repartee. One of
these, an oft-quoted retort to a musical friend who had
likened his awkward antics in a hornpipe to the dancing
of Aesop,—

> Heralds ! proclaim aloud ! all saying,
> See *Aesop* dancing, and his *monkey* playing, —

reads more like a happily-adapted recollection than the
actual impromptu of a boy of nine. But another, in
which, after a painful silence, he replied to the brutal
enquiry of a ne'er-do-well relative as to when he meant
to grow handsome, by saying that he would do so when
the speaker grew good,—is characteristic of the easily-
wounded spirit and 'exquisite sensibility of contempt'
with which he was to enter upon the battle of life.

In June, 1744, after anticipating, in his own person, the
plot of his later play of *She Stoops to Conquer* by mistak-
ing the house of a gentleman at Ardagh for an inn, he
was sent to Trinity College, Dublin. The special dress
and semi-menial footing of a sizar or poor scholar—for
his father, impoverished by the imprudent portioning of
his eldest daughter, could not afford to make him a pen-
sioner—were scarcely calculated to modify his personal
peculiarities. Added to these, his tutor elect, Dr. Theaker
Wilder, was a violent and vindictive man, with whom his
ungainly and unhopeful pupil found little favour. Wilder
had a passion for mathematics which was not shared by
Goldsmith, who, indeed, spoke contemptuously enough
of that science in after life. He could, however, he told
Malone, ' turn an Ode of Horace into English better than
any of them.' But his academic career was not a success.

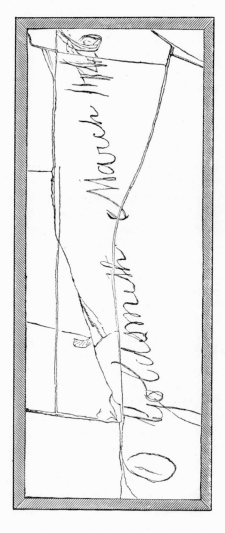

PANE OF GLASS WITH GOLDSMITH'S AUTOGRAPH

(TRINITY COLLEGE, DUBLIN)

In May, 1747, the year in which his father died,—an event
that further contracted his already slender means,—he became involved in a college riot, and was publicly admonished. From this disgrace he recovered to some extent in
5 the following month by obtaining a trifling money exhibition, a triumph which he unluckily celebrated by a party at
his rooms. Into these festivities, the heinousness of
which was aggravated by the fact that they included
guests of both sexes, the exasperated Wilder made irrup-
10 tion, and summarily terminated the proceedings by
knocking down the host. The disgrace was too much
for the poor lad. He forthwith sold his books and
belongings, and ran away, vaguely bound for America.
But after considerable privations, including the achieve-
15 ment of a destitution so complete that a handful of grey
peas, given him by a girl at a wake, seemed a banquet, he
turned his steps homeward, and, a reconciliation having
been patched up with his tutor, he was received once
more at college. In February, 1749, he took his
20 degree, a low one, as B.A., and quitted the university,
leaving behind him, for relics of that time, a scratched
signature upon a window-pane, a *folio* Scapula scored
liberally with ' promises to pay,' and a reputation for
much loitering at the college gates in the study of passing
25 humanity. Another habit which his associates recalled
was his writing of ballads when in want of funds. These
he would sell at five shillings apiece ; and would afterwards steal out in the twilight to hear them sung to the
indiscriminate but applauding audience of the Dublin
30 streets.

What was to be done with a genius so unstable, so
erratic ? Nothing, apparently, but to let him qualify for
orders, and for this he is too young. Thereupon ensues
a sort of ' Martin's summer ' in his changing life,—a dis-
35 engaged, delightful time when ' Master Noll ' wanders

irresponsibly from house to house, fishing and flute-playing, or, of winter evenings, taking the chair at the village inn. When at last the moment came for his presentation to the Bishop of Elphin, that prelate, sad to say, rejected him, perhaps because of his college repu- 5 tation, perhaps because of actual incompetence, perhaps even, as tradition affirms, because he had the bad taste to appear before his examiner in flaming scarlet breeches. After this rebuff, tutoring was next tried. But he had no sooner saved some thirty pounds by teach- 10 ing, than he threw up his engagement, bought a horse, and started once more for America, by way of Cork. In six weeks he had returned penniless, having substituted for his roadster a sorry jade, to which he gave the con-temptuous name of Fiddleback. He had also the simpli- 15 city to wonder, on this occasion, that his mother was not rejoiced to see him again. His next ambition was to be a lawyer; and, to this end, a kindly Uncle Contarine equipped him with fifty pounds for preliminary studies. But on his way to London he was decoyed into gambling, lost every 20 farthing, and came home once more in bitter self-abase-ment. Having now essayed both divinity and law, his next attempt was physic; and, in 1752, fitted out afresh by his long-suffering uncle, he started for, and succeeded in reaching, Edinburgh. Here more memories survive of 25 his social qualities than of his studies; and two years later he left the Scottish capital for Leyden, rather, it may be conjectured, from a restless desire to see the world than really to exchange the lectures of Monro for the lectures of Albinus. At Newcastle (according to his own 30 account) he had the good fortune to be locked up as a Jacobite, and thus escaped drowning, as the ship by which he was to have sailed to Bordeaux sank at the mouth of the Garonne. Shortly afterwards he arrived in Leyden. Gaubius and other Dutch professors figure 35 sonorously in his future works; but whether he had much experimental knowledge of their instructions may be doubted. What seems undeniable is, that the old seduction of play stripped him of every shilling ; so that, 5 like Holberg before him, he set out deliberately to make the tour of Europe on foot. '*Haud inexpertus loquor*,' he wrote in after days, when praising this mode of locomotion. He first visited Flanders. Thence he passed to France, Germany, Switzerland, and Italy, supporting himself 10 mainly by his flute, and by occasional disputations at convents or universities. 'Sir,' said Boswell to Johnson, 'he *disputed* his passage through Europe.' When, on the 1st February, 1756, he landed at Dover, it was with empty pockets. But he had sent home to his brother in Ireland 15 his first rough sketch for the poem of *The Traveller*.

He was now seven-and-twenty. He had seen and suffered much, but he was to have further trials before drifting definitely into literature. Between Dover and London, it has been surmised, he made a tentative appearance 20 as a strolling player. His next ascertained part was that of an apothecary's assistant on Fish Street Hill. From this, with the opportune aid of an Edinburgh friend, he proceeded—to use an eighteenth-century phrase—a poor physician in the Bankside, Southwark, where least of all, 25 perhaps, was London's fabled pavement to be found. So little of it, in fact, fell to Goldsmith's share, that we speedily find him reduced to the rank of reader and corrector of the press to Samuel Richardson, printer, of Salisbury Court, author of *Clarissa*. Later still he is 30 acting as help or substitute in Dr. Milner's 'classical academy' at Peckham. Here, at last, chance seemed to open to him the prospect of a literary life. He had already, says report, submitted a manuscript tragedy to Richardson's judgement; and something he said at 35 Dr. Milner's table attracted the attention of an occasional visitor there, the bookseller Griffiths, who was also proprietor of the *Monthly Review*. He invited Dr. Milner's usher to try his hand at criticism; and finally, in April, 1757, Goldsmith was bound over for a year to that venerable lady whom George Primrose dubs ' the *antiqua* 5 *mater* of Grub Street '—in other words, he was engaged for bed, board, and a fixed salary to supply copy-of-all-work to his master's magazine.

The arrangement thus concluded was not calculated to endure. After some five months of labour from nine till 10 two, and often later, it came suddenly to an end. No clear explanation of the breach is forthcoming, but mere incompatibility of temper would probably supply a sufficient ground for disagreement. Goldsmith, it is said, complained that the bookseller and his wife treated him 15 ill, and denied him ordinary comforts; added to which the lady, a harder taskmistress even than the *antiqua mater* above referred to, joined with her husband in ' editing ' his articles, a course which, hard though it may seem, is not unprecedented. However this may be, either in 20 September or October, 1757, he was again upon the world, existing precariously from hand to mouth. ' By a very little practice as a physician, and a very little reputation as a poet [a title which, as Prior suggests, possibly means no more than author], I make a shift to live.' So he 25 wrote to his brother-in-law in December. What his literary occupations were cannot be definitely stated ; but, if not prepared before, they probably included the translation of a remarkable work issued by Griffiths and others in the ensuing February. This was 30 the *Memoirs of a Protestant, condemned to the Galleys of France for his Religion*, being the authentic record of the sufferings of one Jean Marteilhe of Bergerac, a book of which Michelet has said that it is ' written as if between earth and heaven.' Marteilhe, who died at Cuylenberg 35

in 1777, was living in Holland in 1758; and it may be that
Goldsmith had seen or heard of him during his own stay
in that country. The translation, however, did not bear
Goldsmith's name, but that of James Willington, one of
5 his old class-fellows at Trinity College. Nevertheless,
Prior says distinctly that Griffiths (who should have
known) declared it to be by Goldsmith. Moreover,
the French original had been catalogued in Griffiths'
magazine in the second month of Goldsmith's servitude,
10 a circumstance which colourably supplies the reason for
its subsequent rendering into English.

The publication of Marteilhe's *Memoirs* had no influence
upon Goldsmith's fortunes, for, in a short time, he
was again installed at Peckham, in place of Dr. Milner
15 invalided, waiting hopefully for the fulfilment of a
promise by his old master to procure him a medical
appointment on a foreign station. It is probable that,
with a view to provide the needful funds for this expatri-
ation, he now began to sketch the little volume after-
20 wards published under the title of *An Enquiry into the
Present State of Polite Learning in Europe*, for towards
the middle of the year we find him addressing long letters
to his relatives in Ireland to enlist their aid in soliciting
subscriptions for this book. At length the desired
25 advancement was obtained,—a nomination as physician
and surgeon to one of the factories on the coast of Coromandel. But banishment to the East Indies was not to
be his destiny. For some unexplained reason the project
came to nothing; and then—like Roderick Random—he
30 presented himself at Surgeons' Hall for the more modest
office of a hospital mate. This was on the 21st of December, 1758. The curt official record states that he was
'found not qualified.' What made matters worse, the
necessity for a decent appearance before the examiners
35 had involved him in new obligations to Griffiths,

out of which arose fresh difficulties. To pay his landlady, whose husband was arrested for debt, he pawned the
suit he had procured by Griffiths' aid; and he also
raised money on some volumes which had been sent him
for review. Thereupon ensued an angry and humiliating 5
correspondence with the bookseller, as a result of which
Griffiths, nevertheless, appears to have held his hand.

By this time Goldsmith had moved into those historic
but now non-existent lodgings in 12 Green Arbour Court,
Old Bailey, which have been photographed for ever in 10
Irving's *Tales of a Traveller*. It was here that the foregoing incidents took place; and it was here also that,
early in 1759, 'in a wretched dirty room, in which there
was but one chair,' the Rev. Thomas Percy, afterwards
Bishop of Dromore, found him composing (or more prob- 15
ably correcting the proofs of) *The Enquiry*. 'At least spare
invective 'till my book with Mr. Dodsley shall be publish'd,'
—he had written not long before to the irate Griffiths—
' and then perhaps you may see the bright side of a mind
when my professions shall not appear the dictates of 20
necessity but of choice.' *The Enquiry* came out on the
2nd of April. It had no author's name, but it was an
open secret that Goldsmith had written it; and to this
day it remains to the critic one of the most interesting
of his works. Obviously, in a duodecimo of some two 25
hundred widely-printed pages, it was impossible to keep
the high-sounding promise of its title; and at best
its author's knowledge of the subject, notwithstanding his continental wanderings, can have been but that
of an external spectator. Still, in an age when critical 30
utterance was more than ordinarily full-wigged and
ponderous, it dared to be sprightly and epigrammatic.
Some of its passages, besides, bear upon the writer's
personal experiences, and serve to piece the imperfections
of his biography. If it brought him no sudden wealth, 35

it certainly raised his reputation with the book-selling world. A connexion already begun with Smollett's *Critical Review* was drawn closer; and the shrewd Sosii of the Row began to see the importance of securing so vivacious and unconventional a pen. Towards the end of the year he was writing for Wilkie the collection of periodical essays entitled *The Bee*; and contributing to the same publisher's *Lady's Magazine*, as well as to *The Busy Body* of one Pottinger. In these, more than ever, he was finding his distinctive touch; and ratifying anew, with every fresh stroke of his pen, his bondage to authorship as a calling.

He had still, however, to conquer the public. *The Bee*, although it contains one of his most characteristic essays (' A City Night-Piece '), and some of the most popular of his lighter verses (' The Elegy on Mrs. Mary Blaize '), never attained the circulation essential to healthy existence. It closed with its eighth number in November, 1759. In the following month two gentlemen called at Green Arbour Court to enlist the services of its author. One was Smollett, with a new serial, *The British Magazine*; the other was Johnson's ' Jack Whirler,' bustling Mr. John Newbery from the ' Bible and Sun' in St. Paul's Churchyard, with a new daily newspaper, *The Public Ledger*. For Smollett, Goldsmith wrote the ' Rêverie at the Boar's Head Tavern ' and the ' Adventures of a Strolling Player,' besides a number of minor papers. For Newbery, by a happy recollection of the *Lettres Persanes* of Montesquieu, or some of his imitators, he struck almost at once into that charming epistolary series, brimful of fine observation, kindly satire, and various fancy, which was ultimately to become the English classic known as *The Citizen of the World*. He continued to produce these letters periodically until the August of the following year, when they were an-

nounced for republication in ' two volumes of the usual
Spectator size.' In this form they appeared in May, 1762.

But long before this date a change for the better had
taken place in Goldsmith's life. Henceforth he was sure
of work,—mere journey-work though much of it must 5
have been;—and, had his nature been less improvi-
dent, of freedom from absolute want. The humble
lodgings in the Old Bailey were discarded for new premises
at No. 6 Wine Office Court, Fleet Street; and here, on the
31st of May, 1761, with Percy, came one whose name 10
was often in the future to be associated with Goldsmith's,
the great Dictator of London literary society, Samuel
Johnson. Boswell, who made Johnson's acquaintance
later, has not recorded the humours of that supper; but
it marks the beginning of Goldsmith's friendship with 15
the man who of all others (Reynolds excepted) loved him
most and understood him best.

During the remainder of 1761 he continued busily to
ply his pen. Besides his contributions to *The Ledger* and
The British Magazine, he edited *The Lady's Magazine*, 20
inserting in it the *Memoirs of Voltaire*, drawn up some
time earlier to accompany a translation of the *Henriade*
by his crony and compatriot Edward Purdon. Towards
the beginning of 1762 he was hard at work on several compilations for Newbery, for whom he wrote or edited a 25
History of Mecklenburgh, and a series of monthly volumes
of an abridgement of *Plutarch's Lives*. In October of the
same year was published the *Life of Richard Nash*, apparently the outcome of special holiday-visits to the then
fashionable watering-place of Bath, whence its fantastic 30
old Master of the Ceremonies had only very lately made
his final exit. It is a pleasantly gossiping, and not un-
edifying little book, which still holds a respectable place
among its author's minor works. But a recently discovered
entry in an old ledger shows that during the latter half 35

of 1762 he must have planned, if he had not, indeed,
already in part composed, a far more important effort,
The Vicar of Wakefield. For on the 28th of October in
this year he sold to one Benjamin Collins, printer, of
5 Salisbury, for £21, a third in a work with that title,
further described as ' 2 vols. 12ᵐᵒ.' How this little
circumstance, discovered by Mr. Charles Welsh when
preparing his Life of John Newbery, is to be brought
into agreement with the time-honoured story, related
10 (with variations) by Boswell and others, to the effect that
Johnson negotiated the sale of the manuscript for Goldsmith when the latter was arrested for rent by his incensed
landlady—has not yet been satisfactorily suggested.
Possibly the solution is a simple one, referable to some of
15 those intricate arrangements favoured by ' the Trade ' at
a time when not one but half a score publishers' names
figured in an imprint. At present, the fact that Collins
bought a third share of the book from the author for
twenty guineas, and the statement that Johnson trans-
20 ferred the entire manuscript to a bookseller for sixty
pounds, seem irreconcilable. That *The Vicar of Wakefield* was nevertheless written, or was being written, in
1762, is demonstrable from internal evidence.

About Christmas in the same year Goldsmith moved into
25 lodgings at Islington, his landlady being one Mrs. Elizabeth Fleming, a friend of Newbery, to whose generalship
this step seems attributable. From the curious accounts
printed by Prior and Forster, it is clear that the publisher
was Mrs. Fleming's paymaster, punctually deducting his
30 disbursements from the account current between himself and Goldsmith, an arrangement which as plainly
indicates the foresight of the one as it implies the improvidence of the other. Of the work which Goldsmith did
for the businesslike and not unkindly little man, there is
35 no very definite evidence ; but various prefaces, intro-

ductions, and the like, belong to this time; and he undoubtedly was the author of the excellent *History of England in a Series of Letters addressed by a Nobleman to his Son*, published anonymously in June, 1764, and long attributed, for the grace of its style, to Lyttelton, 5 Chesterfield, Orrery, and other patrician pens. Meanwhile his range of acquaintance was growing larger. The establishment, at the beginning of 1764, of the famous association known afterwards as the 'Literary Club' brought him into intimate relations with Beauclerk, 10 Reynolds, Langton, Burke, and others. Hogarth, too, is said to have visited him at Islington, and to have painted the portrait of Mrs. Fleming. Later in the same year, incited thereto by the success of Christopher Smart's *Hannah*, he wrote the Oratorio of *The Captivity*, now to 15 be found in most editions of his poems, but never set to music. Then, after the slow growth of months, was issued on the 19th December the elaboration of that fragmentary sketch which he had sent years before to his brother Henry from the Continent, the poem entitled *The Tra-* 20 *veller; or, A Prospect of Society*.

In the notes appended to *The Traveller* in the present volume, its origin and progress are sufficiently explained. Its success was immediate and enduring. The beauty of the descriptive passages, the subtle simplicity 25 of the language, the sweetness and finish of the versification, found ready admirers,—perhaps all the more because of the contrast they afforded to the rough and strenuous sounds with which Charles Churchill had lately filled the public ear. Johnson, who contributed a few 30 lines at the close, proclaimed *The Traveller* to be the best poem since the death of Pope; and it is certainly not easy to find its equal among the works of contemporary bards. It at once raised Goldsmith from the condition of a clever newspaper essayist, or—as men like Sir John 35

Hawkins would have said—a mere 'bookseller's drudge,'
to the foremost rank among the poets of the day. Another
result of its success was the revival of some of his earlier
work, which, however neglected by the author, had been
5 freely appropriated by the discerning pirate. In
June, 1765, Griffin and Newbery published a little volume
of *Essays by Mr. Goldsmith*, including some of the
best of his contributions to *The Bee, The Busy Body, The
Public Ledger*, and *The British Magazine*, besides ' The
10 Double Transformation ' and ' The Logicians Refuted,'
two pieces of verse in imitation of Prior and Swift, which
have not been traced to an earlier source. To the same
year belongs the first version of a poem which he himself
regarded as his best work, and which still retains some-
15 thing of its former popularity. This was the ballad of
Edwin and Angelina, otherwise known as *The Hermit*.
It originated in certain metrical discussions with
Percy, then engaged upon his famous *Reliques of
English Poetry*; and in 1765, Goldsmith, who through
20 his friend Nugent (afterwards Lord Clare) had made the
acquaintance of the Earl of Northumberland, printed it
privately for the amusement of the Countess. In a revised
and amended form it was subsequently given to the
world in *The Vicar of Wakefield*.

25 With the exception of an abortive attempt to resume
his practice as a medical man,—an attempt which seems to
have been frustrated by the preternatural strength of his
prescriptions,—the next memorable thing in Goldsmith's
life is the publication of *The Vicar of Wakefield* itself. It
30 made its appearance on the 27th of March, 1766. A
second edition followed in May, a third in August. Why,
having been sold (in part) to a Salisbury printer as far
back as October, 1762, it had remained unprinted so long;
and why, when published, it was published by Francis
35 Newbery and not by John Newbery, Goldsmith's em-

ployer,—are questions at present unsolved. But the
charm of this famous novel is as fresh as when it was
first issued. Its inimitable types, its happy mingling
of Christianity and character, its wholesome benevolence
and its practical wisdom, are still unimpaired. We 5
smile at the inconsistencies of the plot; but we are carried
onward in spite of them, captivated by the grace, the
kindliness, the gentle humour of the story. Yet it is a
mistake to suppose that its success was instantaneous.
Pirated it was, of course; but, according to expert 10
investigations, the authorized edition brought so little
gain to its first proprietors that the fourth issue of
1770 started with a loss. The fifth, published in April,
1774, was dated 1773; and had apparently been withheld
because the previous edition, which consisted of no more 15
than one thousand copies, was not exhausted. Five
years elapsed before the sixth edition made its tardy
appearance in 1779. These facts show that the writer's
contemporaries were not his most eager readers. But
he has long since appealed to the wider audience of pos- 20
terity; and his fame is not confined to his native country,
for he has been translated into most European languages.
Dr. Primrose and his family are now veritable ' citizens
of the world.'

A selection of *Poems for Young Ladies*, in the ' Moral ' 25
division of which he included his own *Edwin and Angelina*;
two volumes of *Beauties of English Poesy*, disfigured, with
strange heedlessness, by a couple of the most objectionable
pieces of Prior; a translation of a French history of
philosophy, and other occasional work, followed the 30
publication of the *Vicar*. But towards the middle of
1766, he was meditating a new experiment in that line
in which Farquhar, Steele, Southerne, and others of his
countrymen had succeeded before him. A fervent lover
of the stage, he detested the vapid and colourless 'genteel' 35

comedy which had gradually gained ground in England ;
and he determined to follow up *The Clandestine Marriage*,
then recently adapted by Colman and Garrick from
Hogarth's *Marriage A-la-Mode*, with another effort of the
5 same class, depending exclusively for its interest upon
humour and character. Early in 1767 it was completed,
and submitted to Garrick for Drury Lane. But Garrick,
perhaps too politic to traverse the popular taste,
temporized; and eventually, after many delays and dis-
10 appointments, *The Good Natur'd Man*, as it was called, was
produced at Covent Garden by Colman on the 29th of
January, 1768. Its success was only partial; and in
deference to the prevailing craze for the ' genteel,' an
admirable scene of low humour had to be omitted in the
15 representation. But the piece, notwithstanding, brought
the author £400, to which the sale of the book, with the
condemned passages restored, added another £100.
Furthermore, Johnson, whose 'Suspirius' in *The Rambler*
was, under the name of ' Croaker,' one of its most
20 prominent personages, pronounced it to be the best
comedy since Cibber's *Provok'd Husband*.

During the autumn of 1767, Goldsmith had again been
living at Islington. On this occasion he had a room in
Canonbury Tower, Queen Elizabeth's old hunting-lodge,
25 and perhaps occupied the very chamber generally used
by John Newbery, whose active life was, in this year, to
close. When in London he had modest housing
in the Temple. But the acquisition of £500 for *The
Good Natur'd Man* seemed to warrant a change of resi-
30 dence, and he accordingly expended four-fifths of that sum
for the lease of three rooms on the second floor of No. 2
Brick Court, which he straightway proceeded to decorate
sumptuously with mirrors, Wilton carpets, moreen curtains, and Pembroke tables. It was an unfortunate
35 step ; and he would have done well to remember the *Nil*

te quaesiveris extra with which his inflexible monitor, Johnson, had greeted his apologies for the shortcomings of some earlier lodgings. One of its natural results was to involve him in a new sequence of task-work, from which he never afterwards shook himself free. Hence, following hard upon a *Roman History* which he had already engaged to write for Davies of Russell Street, came a more ambitious project for Griffin, *A History of Animated Nature*; and after this again, another *History of England* for Davies. The pay was not inadequate; for the first he was to have 250 guineas, for the second 800 guineas, for the last £500. But as employment for the author of a unique novel, an excellent comedy, and a deservedly successful poem, it was surely—in his own words—' to cut blocks with a razor.'

And yet, apart from the anxieties of growing money troubles, his life could not have been wholly unhappy. There are records of pleasant occasional junketings—' shoe-maker's holidays ' he called them—in the still countrified suburbs of Hampstead and Edgware; there was the gathering at the Turk's Head, with its literary magnates, for his severer hours; and, for his more pliant moments, the genial ' free-and-easy ' or shilling whist-club of a less pretentious kind, where the student of mixed character might shine with something of the old supremacy of George Conway's inn at Ballymahon. And there must have been quieter and more chastened resting-places of memory, when, softening towards the home of his youth, with a sadness made more poignant by the death of his brother Henry in May, 1768, he planned and perfected his new poem of *The Deserted Village*.

In December, 1769, the recent appointment of his friend Reynolds as President of the Royal Academy brought him the honorary office of Professor of History to that institution ; and to Reynolds *The Deserted Village* was dedicated. It appeared on the 26th of May, 1770, with a success equal, if not superior, to that of *The Traveller*. It ran through five editions in the year of its publication ; and has ever since retained its reputation. If, as alleged, contemporary critics ranked it below its predecessor, the reason advanced by Washington Irving, that the poet had become his own rival, is doubtless correct ; and there is always a prejudice in favour of the first success. This, however, is not an obstacle which need disturb the reader now; and he will probably decide that in grace and tenderness of description *The Deserted Village* in no wise falls short of *The Traveller* ; and that its central idea, and its sympathy with humanity, give it a higher value as a work of art.

After *The Deserted Village* had appeared, Goldsmith made a short trip to Paris, in company with Mrs. and the two Miss Hornecks, the younger of whom, christened by the poet with the pretty pet-name of ' The Jessamy Bride,' is supposed to have inspired him with more than friendly feelings. Upon his return he had to fall again to the old ' book-building ' in order to recruit his exhausted finances. Since his last poem he had published a short *Life of Parnell* ; and Davies now engaged him on a *Life of Bolingbroke*, and an abridgement of the *Roman History*. Thus, with visits to friends, among others to Lord Clare, for whom he wrote the delightful occasional verses called *The Haunch of Venison*, the months wore on until, in December, 1770, the print-shops began to be full of the well-known mezzotint which Marchi had engraved from his portrait by Sir Joshua.

His chief publications in the next two years were the above-mentioned *History of England*, 1771 ; *Threnodia Augustalis*, a poetical lament-to-order on the death of the Princess Dowager of Wales, 1772 ; and the abridgement

of the *Roman History*, 1772. But in the former year he
had completed a new comedy, *She Stoops to Conquer ;
or, The Mistakes of a Night*, which, after the usual
vexatious negotiations, was brought out by Colman at
Covent Garden on Monday, the 15th of March, 1773. 5
The manager seems to have acted Goldsmith's own
creation of ' Croaker ' with regard to this piece, and even
to the last moment predicted its failure. But it was a
brilliant success. More skilful in construction than *The
Good Natur'd Man*, more various in its contrasts of char- 10
acter, richer and stronger in humour and *vis comica, She
Stoops to Conquer* has continued to provide an inex-
haustible fund of laughter to more than three generations
of playgoers, and still bids fair to retain the character
generally given to it, of being one of the three most popular 15
comedies upon the English stage. When published, it
was gratefully inscribed, in one of those admirable dedi-
cations of which its author above all men possessed the
secret, to Johnson, who had befriended it from the first.
' I do not mean,' wrote Goldsmith, ' so much to compli- 20
ment you as myself. It may do me some honour to
inform the public, that I have lived many years in in-
timacy with you. It may serve the interests of mankind also to inform them, that the greatest wit may be
found in a character, without impairing the most unaf- 25
fected piety.'

His gains from *She Stoops to Conquer* were considerable ;
but by this time his affairs had reached a stage of com-
plication which nothing short of a miracle could disen-
tangle ; and there is reason for supposing that his 30
involved circumstances preyed upon his mind. During
the few months of life that remained to him he published
nothing, being doubtless sufficiently occupied by the
undertakings to which he was already committed. The
last of his poetical efforts was the poem entitled *Retalia-* 35

tion, a group of epitaph-epigrams prompted by some similar *jeux d'esprit* directed against himself by Garrick and other friends, and left incomplete at his death. In March, 1774, the combined effects of work and worry, added to a local disorder, brought on a nervous fever, which he unhappily aggravated by the use of a patent medicine called 'James's Powder.' He had often relied upon this before, but in the present instance it was unsuited to his complaint. On Monday, the 4th of April, 1774, he died, in his forty-sixth year, and was buried on the 9th in the burying-ground of the Temple Church. Two years later a monument, with a medallion portrait by Nollekens, and a Latin inscription by Johnson, was erected to him in Westminster Abbey, at the expense of the Literary Club. But although the inscription contains more than one phrase of felicitous discrimination, notably the oft-quoted *affectuum potens, at lenis dominator*, it may be doubted whether the simpler words used by his rugged old friend in a letter to Langton are not a fitter farewell to Oliver Goldsmith,—' Let not his frailties be remembered : he was a very great man.'

In person Goldsmith was short and strongly built. His complexion was rather fair, but he was deeply scarred with small-pox ; and—if we may believe his own account —the vicissitudes and privations of his early life had not tended to diminish his initial disadvantages. 'You scarcely can conceive,' he writes to his brother in 1759, 'how much eight years of disappointment, anguish, and study, have worn me down. . . . Imagine to yourself a pale melancholy visage, with two great wrinkles between the eye-brows, with an eye disgustingly severe, and a big wig ; and you may have a perfect picture of my present appearance,' i. e. at thirty years of age. 'I can neither laugh nor drink,' he goes on ; 'have contracted an hesitating, disagreeable manner of speaking, and a visage that looks ill-nature itself ; in short, I have thought myself into a settled melancholy, and an utter disgust of all that life brings with it.' It is obvious that this description is largely coloured by passing depression. ' His features,' says one contemporary, ' were plain, but not repulsive,—certainly not so when lighted up by conversation.' Another witness—the ' Jessamy Bride '— declares that 'his benevolence was unquestionable, and his countenance bore every trace of it.' His true likeness would seem to lie midway between the grotesquely truthful sketch by Bunbury prefixed in 1776 to the *Haunch of Venison*, and the portrait, idealized by personal regard, which Reynolds painted in 1770. In this latter he is shown wearing, in place of his customary wig, his own scant brown hair, and, on this occasion, masquerades in a furred robe, and falling collar. But even through the disguise of a studio ' costume,' the finely-perceptive genius of Reynolds has managed to suggest much that is most appealing in his sitter's nature. Past suffering, present endurance, the craving to be understood, the mute deprecation of contempt, are all written legibly in this pathetic picture. It has been frequently copied, often very ineffectively, for so subtle is the art that the slightest deviation hopelessly distorts and vulgarizes what Reynolds has done supremely, once and for ever.

Goldsmith's character presents but few real complexities. What seems most to have impressed his contemporaries is the difference, emphasized by the happily-antithetic epigram of Garrick, between his written style and his conversation ; and collaterally, between his eminence as a literary man and his personal insignificance. Much of this is easily intelligible. He had started in life with few temporal or physical advantages, and with a native susceptibility that intensified his defects. Until

he became a middle-aged man, he led a life of which we
do not even now know all the degradations ; and these
had left their mark upon his manners. With the publication of *The Traveller*, he became at once the associate
of some of the best talent and intellect in England,—of
fine gentlemen such as Beauclerk and Langton, of artists
such as Reynolds and Garrick, of talkers such as Johnson
and Burke. Morbidly self-conscious, nervously anxious
to succeed, he was at once forced into a competition for
which neither his antecedents nor his qualifications had
prepared him. To this, coupled with the old habit of
poverty, must be attributed his oft-cited passion for fine
clothes, which surely arose less from vanity than from
a mistaken attempt to extenuate what he felt to be his
most obvious shortcomings. As a talker especially he
was ill-fitted to shine. He was easily disconcerted by
retort, and often discomfited in argument. To the end
of his days he never lost his native brogue ; and (as
he himself tells us) he had that most fatal of defects
to a narrator, a slow and hesitating manner. The
perspicuity which makes the charm of his writings
deserted him in conversation ; and his best things were
momentary flashes. But some of these were undoubtedly
very happy. His telling Johnson that he would make
the little fishes talk like whales; his affirmation of Burke
that he wound into a subject like a serpent; and half-a-
dozen other well-remembered examples—afford ample
proof of this. Something of the uneasy jealousy he is
said to have exhibited with regard to certain of his contemporaries may also be connected with the long proba-
tion of obscurity during which he had been a spectator of
the good fortune of others, to whom he must have known
himself superior. His improvidence seems to have been
congenital, since it is to be traced ' even from his boyish
days.' But though it cannot justly be ascribed to any

reaction from want to sufficiency, it can still less be supposed to have been diminished by that change. If he was careless of money, it must also be remembered that he gave much of it away; and fortune lingers little with those whose ears are always open to a plausible tale of distress. Of his sensibility and genuine kindheartedness there is no doubt. And it is well to remember that most of the tales to his disadvantage come, not from his more distinguished companions, but from such admitted detractors as Hawkins and Boswell. It could be no mean individuality that acquired the esteem, and deserved the regret, of Johnson and Reynolds.

In an edition of Goldsmith's poems, any extended examination of his remaining productions would be out of place. Moreover, the bulk of these is considerably reduced when all that may properly be classed as hackwork has been withdrawn. The histories of Greece, of Rome, and of England; the *Animated Nature*; the lives of Nash, Voltaire, Parnell, and Bolingbroke, are merely compilations, only raised to the highest level in that line because they proceeded from a man whose gift of clear and easy exposition lent a charm to everything he touched. With the work which he did for himself, the case is different. Into *The Citizen of the World*, *The Vicar of Wakefield*, and his two comedies, he put all the best of his knowledge of human nature, his keen sympathy with his kind, his fine common-sense and his genial humour. The same qualities, tempered by a certain grace and tenderness, also enter into the best of his poems. Avoiding the epigram of Pope and the austere couplet of Johnson, he yet borrowed something from each, which he combined with a delicacy and an amenity that he had learned from neither. He himself, in all probability, would have rested his fame on his three chief metrical efforts, *The Traveller*, *The Hermit*, and *The Deserted Village*. But, as is often the case, he is remembered even more favourably by some of those delightful familiar verses, unprinted during his lifetime, which he threw off with no other ambition than the desire to amuse his friends. *Retaliation,* *The Haunch of Venison,* the *Letter in Prose and Verse to Mrs. Bunbury,* all afford noteworthy exemplification of that playful touch and wayward fancy which constitute the chief attraction of this species of poetry. In his imitations of Swift and Prior, and his variations upon French suggestions, his personal note is scarcely so apparent; but the two Elegies and some of the minor pieces retain a deserved reputation. His ingenious prologues and epilogues also serve to illustrate the range and versatility of his talent. As a rule, the arrangement in the present edition is chronological; but it has not been thought necessary to depart from the practice which gives a time-honoured precedence to *The Traveller* and *The Deserted Village.* The true sequence of the poems, in their order of publication, is, however, exactly indicated in the table which follows this Introduction.

CHRONOLOGY OF GOLDSMITH'S LIFE AND POEMS.

1728. *November* 10.   Born at Pallas, near Ballymahon, in the county of Longford, Ireland.

1730.   Family remove to Lissoy, in the county of Westmeath.

1731.   Under Elizabeth Delap.

1734.   Under Mr. Thomas Byrne of the village school.

1736–44.   At school at Elphin (Mr. Griffin's), Athlone (Mr. Campbell's), Edgeworthstown (Mr. Hughes's).

1744.   *June* 11.   Admitted a sizar of Trinity College, Dublin, '*annum agens* 15.'

1747.   [Death of his father, the Rev. Charles Goldsmith.]
    May.   Takes part in a college riot.
    June 15.   Obtains a Smythe exhibition.
    Runs away from college.

1749.   *February* 27.   Takes his degree as Bachelor of Arts.

1751.   Rejected for orders by the Bishop of Elphin.
    Tutor to Mr. Flinn.
    Sets out for America (*viâ* Cork), but returns.   Letter to Mrs. Goldsmith (his mother).

1752.   Starts as a law student, but loses his all at play.
    Goes to Edinburgh to become a medical student.

1753.   *January* 13.   Admitted a member of the 'Medical Society' of Edinburgh.
    May 8.   Letter to his Uncle Contarine.
    September 26.   Letter to Robert Bryanton.
    Letter to his Uncle Contarine.

1754.   Goes to Leyden.   Letter to his Uncle Contarine.

1755.   *February.*   Leaves Leyden.
    Takes degree of Bachelor of Medicine at Louvain (?).
    Travels on foot in France, Germany, Switzerland, and Italy.
    Sketches *The Traveller.*

1756.   *February* 1.   Returns to Dover.
    Low comedian ; usher (?) ; apothecary's journeyman ; poor physician in Bankside, Southwark.

1757. Press corrector to Samuel Richardson, printer and novelist ; assistant at Peckham Academy (Dr. Milner's).
April. Bound over to Griffiths the bookseller.
Quarrels with Griffiths.
December 27. Letter to his brother-in-law, Daniel Hodson.

1758. *February.* Publishes *The Memoirs of a Protestant, condemned to the Galleys of France for his Religion.*
Gives up literature and returns to Peckham.
August. Leaves Peckham. Letters to Edward Mills, Bryanton, Mrs. Jane Lawder.
Appointed surgeon and physician to a factory on the Coast of Coromandel.
November (?). Letter to Hodson.
Moves into 12 Green Arbour Court, Old Bailey.
Coromandel appointment comes to nothing.
December 21. Rejected at Surgeons' Hall as ' not qualified ' for a hospital mate.

1759. *February* (?). Letter to Henry Goldsmith.
March. Visited by Percy at 12 Green Arbour Court.
April 2. *Enquiry into the Present State of Polite Learning in Europe* published. 'Prologue of Laberius' (*Enquiry*).
October 6. *The Bee* commenced. ' On a Beautiful Youth struck blind with Lightning ' (*Bee*).
October 13. ' The Gift ' (*Bee*).
   ,,   18. ' The Logicians Refuted ' (*Busy Body*).
   ,,   20. ' A Sonnet ' (*Bee*).
   ,,   22. ' Stanzas on the Taking of Quebec ' (*Busy Body*).
October 27. ' Elegy on Mrs. Mary Blaize ' (*Bee*).
November 24. *The Bee* closed.

1760. *January* 1. *The British Magazine* commenced.
   ,,   12. *The Public Ledger* commenced.
   ,,   24. First Chinese Letter published (*Citizen of the World*).
May 2. ' Description of an Author's Bedchamber ' (' Chinese Letter ' in *Public Ledger*).
October 21. ' On seeing Mrs. . . . perform,' &c. (' Chinese Letter ' in *Public Ledger*).
Editing *Lady's Magazine*. Compiling Prefaces.
Moves into 6 Wine Office Court, Fleet Street.

1761. *March* 4. 'On the Death of the Right Hon. . . . (' Chinese Letter' in *Public Ledger*).

April 4–14. 'An Epigram'; To G. C. and R. L. (' Chinese Letter in *Public Ledger*).

May 13. 'Translation of a South American Ode.' (' Chinese Letter' in *Public Ledger*)

May 31. Visited by Johnson at 6 Wine Office Court.

August 14. Last Chinese Letter published (*Citizen of the World*).

Memoirs of M. de Voltaire published in *Lady's Magazine*.

1762. *February* 23. Pamphlet on Cock Lane Ghost published.

    „   26. *History of Mecklenburgh* published.

May 1. *Citizen of the World* published.

May 1 to *Nov.* 1. *Plutarch's Lives*, vol. i to vii, published. At Bath and Tunbridge.

October 14. *Life of Richard Nash* published.

    „   28. Sells third share of *Vicar of Wakefield* to B. Collins, printer, Salisbury.

At Mrs. Fleming's at Islington.

1763 *March* 31. Agrees with James Dodsley to write a *Chronological History of the Lives of Eminent Persons of Great Britain and Ireland*. (Never done.)

1764. 'The Club,' afterwards the Literary Club, founded.

Moves into lodgings on the library staircase of the Temple.

June 26. *History of England, in a series of Letters from a Nobleman to his Son* published.

October 31. Oratorio of *The Captivity* sold to James Dodsley.

December 19. *The Traveller* published.

1765. *June* 4. *Essays by Mr. Goldsmith* published. 'The Double Transformation,' 'A New Simile' (*Essays*).

Edwin and Angelina (*The Hermit*) printed privately for the amusement of the Countess of Northumberland.

Resumes practice as a physician.

1766. *March* 27. *Vicar of Wakefield* published. 'Elegy on a Mad Dog'; 'Olivia's Song' (*Vicar of Wakefield*).

May 31. *Vicar of Wakefield*, 2nd edition.

June. Translation of Formey's *Concise History of Philosophy and Philosophers* published.

August 29. *Vicar of Wakefield*, 3rd edition.

December 15. *Poems for Young Ladies* published.

1766. *December* 28. *English Grammar* written.

1767. *April. Beauties of English Poesy* published.

    July 19. Living in Garden Court, Temple.

       ,, 25. Letter to the *St. James's Chronicle.*

    [*December* 22. Death of John Newbery.]

1768. *February* 5. Publishes *The Good Natur'd Man,* a Comedy, produced at Covent Garden, January 29. 'Epilogue to *The Good Natur'd Man.*'

    Moves to 2 Brick Court, Middle Temple.

    [*May.* Death of Henry Goldsmith.]

    Living at Edgware.

1769. *February* 18. 'Epilogue to Mrs. Lenox's *Sister.*'

       ,, 29. Agreement for 'a new Natural History of Animals' (*Animated Nature*).

    May 18. *Roman History* published.

    June 13. Agreement for *History of England.*

    December. Appointed Professor of History to the Royal Academy.

1770. *January.* Letter to Maurice Goldsmith.

    April 24–*May* 26. Portrait by Reynolds exhibited.

    May 26. *The Deserted Village* published.

    July 13. *Life of Thomas Parnell* published.

    July. On the Continent with the Hornecks. Letters to Reynolds.

    September 15. Agreement for abridgement of *Roman History.*

    December 1. Marchi's print from Reynolds's portrait published.

    December 19. *Life of Bolingbroke* published.

    Vicar of Wakefield, 4th edition.

1771. *Haunch of Venison* written. (?)

    August 6. *History of England* published.

    December 11. 'Prologue to Cradock's *Zobeide.*'

1772. *February* 20. *Threnodia Augustalis* published.

    Watson's Engraving of *Resignation* published.

    December. Abridgement of *Roman History* published.

1773. *March* 26. Publishes *She Stoops to Conquer; or, The Mistakes of a Night,* a Comedy, produced at Covent Garden, March 15. 'Song in *She Stoops to Conquer,*' 'Epilogue to *She Stoops to Conquer.*'

1773.   *March* 24.   Kenrick's libel in the *London Packet*.
         ,,   31.   Letter in the *Daily Advertiser*.
         May 8.   *The Grumbler* produced.
         Projects a *Dictionary of Arts and Sciences*.
1774.   *March* 25.   Illness.
         April 4.   Death.
         ,,   9.   ' Buried 9th April, Oliver Goldsmith, MB, late
         of Brick-court, Middle Temple ' (Register of Burials,
         Temple Church).
         April 19.   *Retaliation* published.
         April.   *Vicar of Wakefield*, 5th edition (dated 1773).
         June.   Song (' Ah me, when shall I marry me ? ') pub-
         lished.
         June 28.   Letters of Administration granted.
         June.   *An History of the Earth and Animated Nature* pub-
         lished. 'Translation from Addison.' (*History*, &c., 1774.)
1776.   *The Haunch of Venison* published.   ' Epitaph on Thomas
         Parnell,' and ' Two Songs from *The Captivity* ' (*Haunch
         of Venison*).
         Monument with medallion by Nollekens erected in the
         south transept of Westminster Abbey.
1777.   *Poems and Plays* published.   ' The Clown's Reply,'
         ' Epitaph on Edward Purdon ' (*Poems*, &c., 1777).
1779.   *Vicar of Wakefield*, 6th edition.
1780.   *Poetical and Dramatic Works*, Evans's edition, published.
         ' Epilogue for Lee Lewes ' (*Poetical*, &c., *Works*, 1780).
1801.   *Miscellaneous Works*, Percy's edition, published.   ' Epi-
         logues (unspoken) to *She Stoops to Conquer* ' (*Misc.
         Works*, 1801).
1820.   *Miscellaneous Works*, ' trade ' edition, published.   ' An
         Oratorio ' (*The Captivity*).   (*Misc. Works*, 1820.)
1837.   *Miscellaneous Works*, Prior's edition, published.   ' Verses
         in Reply to an Invitation to Dinner ' ; ' Letter in Prose
         and Verse to Mrs. Bunbury ' (*Misc. Works*, 1837).
         Tablet erected in the Temple Church.
1854.   *Goldsmith's Works*, Cunningham's edition, published.
         'Translation of Vida's *Game of Chess* ' (*Works*, 1854,
         vol. iv).
1864.   *January* 5.   J. H. Foley's statue placed in front of
         Dublin University.

DESCRIPTIVE POEMS

VIGNETTE TO 'THE TRAVELLER'

(SAMUEL WALE)

DESCRIPTIVE POEMS

THE TRAVELLER

OR

A PROSPECT OF SOCIETY

DEDICATION

TO THE REV. HENRY GOLDSMITH

DEAR SIR,

I am sensible that the friendship between us can acquire no new force from the ceremonies of a Dedication; 5 and perhaps it demands an excuse thus to prefix your name to my attempts, which you decline giving with your own. But as a part of this Poem was formerly written to you from Switzerland, the whole can now, with propriety, be only inscribed to you. It will also 10 throw a light upon many parts of it, when the reader understands, that it is addressed to a man, who, despising Fame and Fortune, has retired early to Happiness and Obscurity, with an income of forty pounds a year.

I now perceive, my dear brother, the wisdom of your 15 humble choice. You have entered upon a sacred office, where the harvest is great, and the labourers are but few; while you have left the field of Ambition, where the labourers are many, and the harvest not worth carrying away. But of all kinds of ambition, what from the refine- 20 ment of the times, from different systems of criticism, and from the divisions of party, that which pursues poetical fame is the wildest.

Poetry makes a principal amusement among unpolished nations; but in a country verging to the extremes of 25 refinement, Painting and Music come in for a share. As these offer the feeble mind a less laborious entertainment,

they at first rival Poetry, and at length supplant her ;
they engross all that favour once shown to her, and
though but younger sisters, seize upon the elder's birth- 30
right.

Yet, however this art may be neglected by the powerful, it is still in greater danger from the mistaken efforts
of the learned to improve it.   What criticisms have we
not heard of late in favour of blank verse, and Pindaric 35
odes, choruses, anapæsts and iambics, alliterative care
and happy negligence !   Every absurdity has now a
champion to defend it ;   and as he is generally much in
the wrong, so he has always much to say ;   for error is
ever talkative.   40

But there is an enemy to this art still more dangerous,
I mean Party.   Party entirely distorts the judgment,
and destroys the taste.   When the mind is once infected
with this disease, it can only find pleasure in what con-
tributes to increase the distemper.   Like the tiger, that 45
seldom desists from pursuing man after having once
preyed upon human flesh, the reader, who has once
gratified his appetite with calumny, makes, ever after,
the most agreeable feast upon murdered reputation.
Such readers generally admire some half-witted thing, 50
who wants to be thought a bold man, having lost the
character of a wise one.   Him they dignify with the name
of poet ;   his tawdry lampoons are called satires, his
turbulence is said to be force, and his frenzy fire.

What reception a Poem may find, which has neither 55
abuse, party, nor blank verse to support it, I cannot tell,
nor am I solicitous to know.   My aims are right.   Without espousing the cause of any party, I have attempted to
moderate the rage of all.   I have endeavoured to show,
that there may be equal happiness in states, that are 60
differently governed from our own ;   that every state has
a particular principle of happiness, and that this principle
in each may be carried to a mischievous excess.   There
are few can judge, better than yourself, how far these
positions are illustrated in this Poem.   65

I am, dear Sir,
Your most affectionate Brother,
OLIVER GOLDSMITH.

THE TRAVELLER

OR

A PROSPECT OF SOCIETY

REMOTE, unfriended, melancholy, slow,
Or by the lazy Scheldt, or wandering Po;
Or onward, where the rude Carinthian boor
Against the houseless stranger shuts the door;
Or where Campania's plain forsaken lies,   5
A weary waste expanding to the skies:
Where'er I roam, whatever realms to see,
My heart untravell'd fondly turns to thee;
Still to my brother turns with ceaseless pain,
And drags at each remove a lengthening chain.   10

Eternal blessings crown my earliest friend,
And round his dwelling guardian saints attend:
Bless'd be that spot, where cheerful guests retire
To pause from toil, and trim their ev'ning fire;
Bless'd that abode, where want and pain repair, 15
And every stranger finds a ready chair:
Bless'd be those feasts with simple plenty crown'd,

Where all the ruddy family around
Laugh at the jests or pranks that never fail,
Or sigh with pity at some mournful tale, 20
Or press the bashful stranger to his food,
And learn the luxury of doing good.

But me, not destin'd such delights to share,
My prime of life in wand'ring spent and care,
Impell'd, with steps unceasing, to pursue 25
Some fleeting good, that mocks me with the view;
That, like the circle bounding earth and skies,
Allures from far, yet, as I follow, flies;
My fortune leads to traverse realms alone,
And find no spot of all the world my own. 30

E'en now, where Alpine solitudes ascend,
I sit me down a pensive hour to spend;
And, plac'd on high above the storm's career,
Look downward where a hundred realms appear;
Lakes, forests, cities, plains, extending wide, 35
The pomp of kings, the shepherd's humbler pride.

When thus Creation's charms around combine,
Amidst the store, should thankless pride repine?
Say, should the philosophic mind disdain
That good, which makes each humbler bosom vain?
Let school-taught pride dissemble all it can, 41
These little things are great to little man;
And wiser he, whose sympathetic mind
Exults in all the good of all mankind.
Ye glitt'ring towns, with wealth and splendour crown'd,
Ye fields, where summer spreads profusion round, 46
Ye lakes, whose vessels catch the busy gale,
Ye bending swains, that dress the flow'ry vale,

For me your tributary stores combine ;
Creation's heir, the world, the world is mine !   50

As some lone miser visiting his store,
Bends at his treasure, counts, re-counts it o'er ;
Hoards after hoards his rising raptures fill,
Yet still he sighs, for hoards are wanting still :
Thus to my breast alternate passions rise,   55
Pleas'd with each good that heaven to man supplies :
Yet oft a sigh prevails, and sorrows fall,
To see the hoard of human bliss so small ;
And oft I wish, amidst the scene, to find
Some spot to real happiness consign'd,   60
Where my worn soul, each wand'ring hope at rest,
May gather bliss to see my fellows bless'd.

But where to find that happiest spot below,
Who can direct, when all pretend to know ?
The shudd'ring tenant of the frigid zone   65
Boldly proclaims that happiest spot his own,
Extols the treasures of his stormy seas,
And his long nights of revelry and ease ;
The naked negro, panting at the line,
Boasts of his golden sands and palmy wine,   70
Basks in the glare, or stems the tepid wave,
And thanks his gods for all the good they gave.
Such is the patriot's boast, where'er we roam,
His first, best country ever is, at home.
And yet, perhaps, if countries we compare,   75
And estimate the blessings which they share,
Though patriots flatter, still shall wisdom find
An equal portion dealt to all mankind,

As different good, by Art or Nature given,
To different nations makes their blessings even.   80

Nature, a mother kind alike to all,
Still grants her bliss at Labour's earnest call;
With food as well the peasant is supplied
On Idra's cliffs as Arno's shelvy side;
And though the rocky-crested summits frown,   85
These rocks, by custom, turn to beds of down.
From Art more various are the blessings sent;
Wealth, commerce, honour, liberty, content.
Yet these each other's power so strong contest,
That either seems destructive of the rest.   90
Where wealth and freedom reign, contentment fails,
And honour sinks where commerce long prevails.
Hence every state to one lov'd blessing prone,
Conforms and models life to that alone.
Each to the favourite happiness attends,   95
And spurns the plan that aims at other ends;
Till, carried to excess in each domain,
This favourite good begets peculiar pain.

But let us try these truths with closer eyes,
And trace them through the prospect as it lies: 100
Here for a while my proper cares resign'd,
Here let me sit in sorrow for mankind,
Like yon neglected shrub at random cast,
That shades the steep, and sighs at every blast.

Far to the right where Apennine ascends,   105
Bright as the summer, Italy extends;
Its uplands sloping deck the mountain's side,
Woods over woods in gay theatric pride;

THE TRAVELLER

(R. WESTALL)

While oft some temple's mould'ring tops between
With venerable grandeur mark the scene. 110

Could Nature's bounty satisfy the breast,
The sons of Italy were surely blest.
Whatever fruits in different climes were found,
That proudly rise, or humbly court the ground;
Whatever blooms in torrid tracts appear, 115
Whose bright succession decks the varied year;
Whatever sweets salute the northern sky
With vernal lives that blossom but to die;
These here disporting own the kindred soil,
Nor ask luxuriance from the planter's toil; 120
While sea-born gales their gelid wings expand
To winnow fragrance round the smiling land.

But small the bliss that sense alone bestows,
And sensual bliss is all the nation knows.
In florid beauty groves and fields appear, 125
Man seems the only growth that dwindles here.
Contrasted faults through all his manners reign;
Though poor, luxurious; though submissive, vain;
Though grave, yet trifling; zealous, yet untrue;
And e'en in penance planning sins anew. 130
All evils here contaminate the mind,
That opulence departed leaves behind;
For wealth was theirs, not far remov'd the date,
When commerce proudly flourish'd through the state;
At her command the palace learn'd to rise, 135
Again the long-fall'n column sought the skies;
The canvas glow'd beyond e'en Nature warm,
The pregnant quarry teem'd with human form;
Till, more unsteady than the southern gale,

Commerce on other shores display'd her sail;　140
While nought remain'd of all that riches gave,
But towns unmann'd, and lords without a slave;
And late the nation found, with fruitless skill,
Its former strength was but plethoric ill.

Yet still the loss of wealth is here supplied　145
By arts, the splendid wrecks of former pride;
From these the feeble heart and long-fall'n mind
An easy compensation seem to find.
Here may be seen, in bloodless pomp array'd,
The paste-board triumph and the cavalcade;　150
Processions form'd for piety and love,
A mistress or a saint in every grove.
By sports like these are all their cares beguil'd,
The sports of children satisfy the child;
Each nobler aim, repress'd by long control,　155
Now sinks at last, or feebly mans the soul;
While low delights, succeeding fast behind,
In happier meanness occupy the mind:
As in those domes, where Caesars once bore sway,
Defac'd by time and tottering in decay,　160
There in the ruin, heedless of the dead,
The shelter-seeking peasant builds his shed,
And, wond'ring man could want the larger pile,
Exults, and owns his cottage with a smile.

My soul, turn from them; turn we to survey　165
Where rougher climes a nobler race display,
Where the bleak Swiss their stormy mansions tread,
And force a churlish soil for scanty bread;
No product here the barren hills afford,
But man and steel, the soldier and his sword;　170

No vernal blooms their torpid rocks array,
But winter ling'ring chills the lap of May;
No Zephyr fondly sues the mountain's breast,
But meteors glare, and stormy glooms invest.

Yet still, e'en here, content can spread a charm,
Redress the clime, and all its rage disarm.　176
Though poor the peasant's hut, his feasts though small,
He sees his little lot the lot of all;
Sees no contiguous palace rear its head
To shame the meanness of his humble shed;　180
No costly lord the sumptuous banquet deal
To make him loathe his vegetable meal;
But calm, and bred in ignorance and toil,
Each wish contracting, fits him to the soil.
Cheerful at morn he wakes from short repose,　185
Breasts the keen air, and carols as he goes;
With patient angle trolls the finny deep,
Or drives his vent'rous plough-share to the steep;
Or seeks the den where snow-tracks mark the way,
And drags the struggling savage into day.　190
At night returning, every labour sped,
He sits him down the monarch of a shed;
Smiles by his cheerful fire, and round surveys
His children's looks, that brighten at the blaze;
While his lov'd partner, boastful of her hoard,　195
Displays her cleanly platter on the board:
And haply too some pilgrim, thither led,
With many a tale repays the nightly bed.

Thus every good his native wilds impart,
Imprints the patriot passion on his heart,　200

And e'en those ills, that round his mansion rise,
Enhance the bliss his scanty fund supplies.
Dear is that shed to which his soul conforms,
And dear that hill which lifts him to the storms ;
And as a child, when scaring sounds molest,   205
Clings close and closer to the mother's breast,
So the loud torrent, and the whirlwind's roar,
But bind him to his native mountains more.

Such are the charms to barren states assign'd ;
Their wants but few, their wishes all confin'd.   210
Yet let them only share the praises due,
If few their wants, their pleasures are but few ;
For every want that stimulates the breast,
Becomes a source of pleasure when redrest.
Whence from such lands each pleasing science flies,
That first excites desire, and then supplies ;   216
Unknown to them, when sensual pleasures cloy,
To fill the languid pause with finer joy ;
Unknown those powers that raise the soul to flame,
Catch every nerve, and vibrate through the frame.
Their level life is but a smould'ring fire,   221
Unquench'd by want, unfann'd by strong desire ;
Unfit for raptures, or, if raptures cheer
On some high festival of once a year,
In wild excess the vulgar breast takes fire,   225
Till, buried in debauch, the bliss expire.

But not their joys alone thus coarsely flow :
Their morals, like their pleasures, are but low ;
For, as refinement stops, from sire to son
Unalter'd, unimprov'd the manners run ;   230

And love's and friendship's finely pointed dart
Fall blunted from each indurated heart.
Some sterner virtues o'er the mountain's breast
May sit, like falcons cow'ring on the nest ;
But all the gentler morals, such as play 235
Through life's more cultur'd walks, and charm the way,
These far dispers'd, on timorous pinions fly,
To sport and flutter in a kinder sky.

To kinder skies, where gentler manners reign,
I turn ; and France displays her bright domain. 240
Gay sprightly land of mirth and social ease,
Pleas'd with thyself, whom all the world can please,
How often have I led thy sportive choir,
With tuneless pipe, beside the murmuring Loire !
Where shading elms along the margin grew, 245
And freshen'd from the wave the Zephyr flew ;
And haply, though my harsh touch falt'ring still,
But mock'd all tune, and marr'd the dancer's skill ;
Yet would the village praise my wondrous power,
And dance, forgetful of the noon-tide hour. 250
Alike all ages. Dames of ancient days
Have led their children through the mirthful maze,
And the gay grandsire, skill'd in gestic lore,
Has frisk'd beneath the burthen of threescore.

So bless'd a life these thoughtless realms display,
Thus idly busy rolls their world away : 256
Theirs are those arts that mind to mind endear,
For honour forms the social temper here :
Honour, that praise which real merit gains,
Or e'en imaginary worth obtains, 260

Here passes current ; paid from hand to hand,
It shifts in splendid traffic round the land :
From courts, to camps, to cottages it strays,
And all are taught an avarice of praise ; 264
They please, are pleas'd, they give to get esteem,
Till, seeming bless'd, they grow to what they seem.

But while this softer art their bliss supplies,
It gives their follies also room to rise ;
For praise too dearly lov'd, or warmly sought,
Enfeebles all internal strength of thought ; 270
And the weak soul, within itself unblest,
Leans for all pleasure on another's breast.
Hence ostentation here, with tawdry art,
Pants for the vulgar praise which fools impart ;
Here vanity assumes her pert grimace, 275
And trims her robes of frieze with copper lace ;
Here beggar pride defrauds her daily cheer,
To boast one splendid banquet once a year ;
The mind still turns where shifting fashion draws,
Nor weighs the solid worth of self-applause. 280

To men of other minds my fancy flies,
Embosom'd in the deep where Holland lies.
Methinks her patient sons before me stand,
Where the broad ocean leans against the land,
And, sedulous to stop the coming tide, 285
Lift the tall rampire's artificial pride.
Onward, methinks, and diligently slow,
The firm-connected bulwark seems to grow ;
Spreads its long arms amidst the wat'ry roar,
Scoops out an empire, and usurps the shore ; 290

While the pent ocean rising o'er the pile,
Sees an amphibious world beneath him smile ;
The slow canal, the yellow-blossom'd vale,
The willow-tufted bank, the gliding sail,
The crowded mart, the cultivated plain,   295
A new creation rescu'd from his reign.

Thus, while around the wave-subjected soil
Impels the native to repeated toil,
Industrious habits in each bosom reign,
And industry begets a love of gain.   300
Hence all the good from opulence that springs,
With all those ills superfluous treasure brings,
Are here displayed.   Their much-lov'd wealth imparts
Convenience, plenty, elegance, and arts ;
But view them closer, craft and fraud appear,   305
E'en liberty itself is barter'd here.
At gold's superior charms all freedom flies,
The needy sell it, and the rich man buys ;
A land of tyrants, and a den of slaves,
Here wretches seek dishonourable graves,   310
And calmly bent, to servitude conform,
Dull as their lakes that slumber in the storm.

Heavens ! how unlike their Belgic sires of old !
Rough, poor, content, ungovernably bold ;
War in each breast, and freedom on each brow; 315
How much unlike the sons of Britain now !

Fir'd at the sound, my genius spreads her wing,
And flies where Britain courts the western spring ;
Where lawns extend that scorn Arcadian pride,
And brighter streams than fam'd Hydaspes glide.

There all around the gentlest breezes stray,   321
There gentle music melts on ev'ry spray;
Creation's mildest charms are there combin'd,
Extremes are only in the master's mind!
Stern o'er each bosom reason holds her state,   325
With daring aims irregularly great;
Pride in their port, defiance in their eye,
I see the lords of human kind pass by,
Intent on high designs, a thoughtful band,
By forms unfashion'd, fresh from Nature's hand;
Fierce in their native hardiness of soul,   331
True to imagin'd right, above control,
While e'en the peasant boasts these rights to scan,
And learns to venerate himself as man.

Thine, Freedom, thine the blessings pictur'd here,
Thine are those charms that dazzle and endear;   336
Too bless'd, indeed, were such without alloy,
But foster'd e'en by Freedom, ills annoy:
That independence Britons prize too high,
Keeps man from man, and breaks the social tie;
The self-dependent lordlings stand alone,   341
All claims that bind and sweeten life unknown;
Here by the bonds of nature feebly held,
Minds combat minds, repelling and repell'd.
Ferments arise, imprison'd factions roar,   345
Repress'd ambition struggles round her shore,
Till over-wrought, the general system feels
Its motions stop, or frenzy fire the wheels.

Nor this the worst. As nature's ties decay,
As duty, love, and honour fail to sway,   350

Fictitious bonds, the bonds of wealth and law,
Still gather strength, and force unwilling awe.
Hence all obedience bows to these alone,
And talent sinks, and merit weeps unknown ;
Till time may come, when stripp'd of all her charms,
The land of scholars, and the nurse of arms,   356
Where noble stems transmit the patriot flame,
Where kings have toil'd, and poets wrote for fame,
One sink of level avarice shall lie,
And scholars, soldiers, kings, unhonour'd die.   360

Yet think not, thus when Freedom's ills I state,
I mean to flatter kings, or court the great ;
Ye powers of truth, that bid my soul aspire,
Far from my bosom drive the low desire ;
And thou, fair Freedom, taught alike to feel   365
The rabble's rage, and tyrant's angry steel ;
Thou transitory flower, alike undone
By proud contempt, or favour's fostering sun,
Still may thy blooms the changeful clime endure,
I only would repress them to secure :   370
For just experience tells, in every soil,
That those who think must govern those that toil ;
And all that freedom's highest aims can reach,
Is but to lay proportion'd loads on each.
Hence, should one order disproportion'd grow,   375
Its double weight must ruin all below.

O then how blind to all that truth requires,
Who think it freedom when a part aspires !
Calm is my soul, nor apt to rise in arms,
Except when fast-approaching danger warms :   380

But when contending chiefs blockade the throne,
Contracting regal power to stretch their own ;
When I behold a factious band agree
To call it freedom when themselves are free ;
Each wanton judge new penal statutes draw,　385
Laws grind the poor, and rich men rule the law ;
The wealth of climes, where savage nations roam,
Pillag'd from slaves to purchase slaves at home ;
Fear, pity, justice, indignation start,
Tear off reserve, and bare my swelling heart ;　390
Till half a patriot, half a coward grown,
I fly from petty tyrants to the throne.

　　Yes, brother, curse with me that baleful hour,
When first ambition struck at regal power ;
And thus polluting honour in its source,　395
Gave wealth to sway the mind with double force.
Have we not seen, round Britain's peopled shore,
Her useful sons exchang'd for useless ore ?
Seen all her triumphs but destruction haste,
Like flaring tapers bright'ning as they waste ;　400
Seen opulence, her grandeur to maintain,
Lead stern depopulation in her train,
And over fields where scatter'd hamlets rose,
In barren solitary pomp repose ?
Have we not seen, at pleasure's lordly call,　405
The smiling long-frequented village fall ?
Beheld the duteous son, the sire decay'd,
The modest matron, and the blushing maid,
Forc'd from their homes, a melancholy train,
To traverse climes beyond the western main ;　410

Where wild Oswego spreads her swamps around,
And Niagara stuns with thund'ring sound ?

E'en now, perhaps, as there some pilgrim strays
Through tangled forests, and through dangerous ways ;
Where beasts with man divided empire claim,   415
And the brown Indian marks with murd'rous aim ;
There, while above the giddy tempest flies,
And all around distressful yells arise,
The pensive exile, bending with his woe,
To stop too fearful, and too faint to go,   420
Casts a long look where England's glories shine,
And bids his bosom sympathise with mine.

Vain, very vain, my weary search to find
That bliss which only centres in the mind :
Why have I stray'd from pleasure and repose,   425
To seek a good each government bestows ?
In every government, though terrors reign,
Though tyrant kings, or tyrant laws restrain,
How small, of all that human hearts endure,
That part which laws or kings can cause or cure.
Still to ourselves in every place consign'd,   431
Our own felicity we make or find :
With secret course, which no loud storms annoy,
Glides the smooth current of domestic joy.
The lifted axe, the agonising wheel,   435
Luke's iron crown, and Damiens' bed of steel,
To men remote from power but rarely known,
Leave reason, faith, and conscience, all our own.

VIGNETTE TO 'THE DESERTED VILLAGE'

(ISAAC TAYLOR)

THE DESERTED VILLAGE

DEDICATION

TO SIR JOSHUA REYNOLDS

Dear Sir,

I can have no expectations in an address of this kind, either to add to your reputation, or to establish my own. You can gain nothing from my admiration, as I am ignorant of that art in which you are said to excel; and I may lose much by the severity of your judgment, as few have a juster taste in poetry than you. Setting interest therefore aside, to which I never paid much attention, I must be indulged at present in following my affections. The only dedication I ever made was to my brother, because I loved him better than most other men. He is since dead. Permit me to inscribe this Poem to you.

How far you may be pleased with the versification and mere mechanical parts of this attempt, I don't pretend to enquire; but I know you will object (and indeed several of our best and wisest friends concur in the opinion) that the depopulation it deplores is no where to be seen, and the disorders it laments are only to be found in the poet's own imagination. To this I can scarce make any other answer than that I sincerely believe what I have written; that I have taken all possible pains, in my country excursions, for these four or five years past, to be certain of what I allege; and that all my views and enquiries have led me to believe those miseries real, which I here attempt to display. But this is not the place to enter into an enquiry, whether the country be depopulating, or not; the discussion would take up much room, and I should prove myself, at best, an indifferent politician, to tire the reader with a long preface, when I want his unfatigued attention to a long poem.

In regretting the depopulation of the country, I inveigh against the increase of our luxuries ; and here also 35 I expect the shout of modern politicians against me. For twenty or thirty years past, it has been the fashion to consider luxury as one of the greatest national advantages ; and all the wisdom of antiquity in that particular, as erroneous. Still however, I must remain a professed 40 ancient on that head, and continue to think those luxuries prejudicial to states, by which so many vices are introduced, and so many kingdoms have been undone. Indeed so much has been poured out of late on the other side of the question, that, merely for the sake of novelty 45 and variety, one would sometimes wish to be in the right.

I am, Dear Sir,
Your sincere friend, and ardent admirer,
OLIVER GOLDSMITH.

THE DESERTED VILLAGE

SWEET AUBURN ! loveliest village of the plain,
Where health and plenty cheer'd the labouring swain,
Where smiling spring its earliest visit paid,
And parting summer's lingering blooms delay'd :
Dear lovely bowers of innocence and ease,　　5
Seats of my youth, when every sport could please,
How often have I loiter'd o'er thy green,
Where humble happiness endear'd each scene ;
How often have I paus'd on every charm,
The shelter'd cot, the cultivated farm,　　10
The never-failing brook, the busy mill,
The decent church that topp'd the neighbouring hill,
The hawthorn bush, with seats beneath the shade,
For talking age and whisp'ring lovers made ;
How often have I bless'd the coming day,　　15
When toil remitting lent its turn to play,
And all the village train, from labour free,
Led up their sports beneath the spreading tree ;
While many a pastime circled in the shade,
The young contending as the old survey'd ;　　20

And many a gambol frolick'd o'er the ground,
And sleights of art and feats of strength went round ;
And still as each repeated pleasure tir'd,
Succeeding sports the mirthful band inspir'd ;
The dancing pair that simply sought renown,   25
By holding out to tire each other down ;
The swain mistrustless of his smutted face,
While secret laughter titter'd round the place ;
The bashful virgin's side-long looks of love,   29
The matron's glance that would those looks reprove :
These were thy charms, sweet village ; sports like these,
With sweet succession, taught e'en toil to please ;
These round thy bowers their cheerful influence shed,
These were thy charms—But all these charms are fled.

Sweet smiling village, loveliest of the lawn,   35
Thy sports are fled, and all thy charms withdrawn ;
Amidst thy bowers the tyrant's hand is seen,
And desolation saddens all thy green :
One only master grasps the whole domain,
And half a tillage stints thy smiling plain :   40
No more thy glassy brook reflects the day,
But chok'd with sedges, works its weedy way.
Along thy glades, a solitary guest,
The hollow-sounding bittern guards its nest ;
Amidst thy desert walks the lapwing flies,   45
And tires their echoes with unvaried cries.
Sunk are thy bowers in shapeless ruin all,
And the long grass o'ertops the mould'ring wall ;
And trembling, shrinking from the spoiler's hand,
Far, far away, thy children leave the land.   50

Ill fares the land, to hast'ning ills a prey,
Where wealth accumulates, and men decay :
Princes and lords may flourish, or may fade ;
A breath can make them, as a breath has made ;
But a bold peasantry, their country's pride,   55
When once destroy'd, can never be supplied.

A time there was, ere England's griefs began,
When every rood of ground maintain'd its man ;
For him light labour spread her wholesome store,
Just gave what life requir'd, but gave no more : 60
His best companions, innocence and health ;
And his best riches, ignorance of wealth.

But times are alter'd ; trade's unfeeling train
Usurp the land and dispossess the swain ;
Along the lawn, where scatter'd hamlets rose,   65
Unwieldy wealth, and cumbrous pomp repose ;
And every want to opulence allied,
And every pang that folly pays to pride.
Those gentle hours that plenty bade to bloom,
Those calm desires that ask'd but little room,   70
Those healthful sports that grac'd the peaceful scene,
Liv'd in each look, and brighten'd all the green ;
These, far departing, seek a kinder shore,
And rural mirth and manners are no more.

Sweet AUBURN ! parent of the blissful hour,   75
Thy glades forlorn confess the tyrant's power.
Here as I take my solitary rounds,
Amidst thy tangling walks, and ruin'd grounds,
And, many a year elaps'd, return to view
Where once the cottage stood, the hawthorn grew,

Remembrance wakes with all her busy train,   81
Swells at my breast, and turns the past to pain.

In all my wand'rings round this world of care,
In all my griefs—and GOD has given my share—
I still had hopes my latest hours to crown,   85
Amidst these humble bowers to lay me down;
To husband out life's taper at the close,
And keep the flame from wasting by repose.
I still had hopes, for pride attends us still,
Amidst the swains to show my book-learn'd skill, 90
Around my fire an evening group to draw,
And tell of all I felt, and all I saw;
And, as a hare, whom hounds and horns pursue,
Pants to the place from whence at first she flew,
I still had hopes, my long vexations pass'd,   95
Here to return—and die at home at last.

O blest retirement, friend to life's decline,
Retreats from care, that never must be mine,
How happy he who crowns in shades like these,
A youth of labour with an age of ease;   100
Who quits a world where strong temptations try
And, since 'tis hard to combat, learns to fly!
For him no wretches, born to work and weep,
Explore the mine, or tempt the dangerous deep;
No surly porter stands in guilty state   105
To spurn imploring famine from the gate;
But on he moves to meet his latter end,
Angels around befriending Virtue's friend;
Bends to the grave with unperceiv'd decay,
While Resignation gently slopes the way;   110

THE WATER-CRESS GATHERER

(JOHN BEWICK)

And, all his prospects bright'ning to the last,
His Heaven commences ere the world be pass'd !

Sweet was the sound, when oft at evening's close
Up yonder hill the village murmur rose ;
There, as I pass'd with careless steps and slow, 115
The mingling notes came soften'd from below ;
The swain responsive as the milk-maid sung,
The sober herd that low'd to meet their young ;
The noisy geese that gabbled o'er the pool,
The playful children just let loose from school ; 120
The watchdog's voice that bay'd the whisp'ring wind,
And the loud laugh that spoke the vacant mind ;
These all in sweet confusion sought the shade,
And fill'd each pause the nightingale had made.
But now the sounds of population fail,   125
No cheerful murmurs fluctuate in the gale,
No busy steps the grass-grown foot-way tread,
For all the bloomy flush of life is fled.
All but yon widow'd, solitary thing
That feebly bends beside the plashy spring ;   130
She, wretched matron, forc'd, in age, for bread,
To strip the brook with mantling cresses spread,
To pick her wintry faggot from the thorn,
To seek her nightly shed, and weep till morn ;
She only left of all the harmless train,   135
The sad historian of the pensive plain.

Near yonder copse, where once the garden smil'd,
And still where many a garden flower grows wild ;
There, where a few torn shrubs the place disclose,
The village preacher's modest mansion rose.   140

A man he was to all the country dear,
And passing rich with forty pounds a year;
Remote from towns he ran his godly race,
Nor e'er had chang'd, nor wished to change his place;
Unpractis'd he to fawn, or seek for power,   145
By doctrines fashion'd to the varying hour;
Far other aims his heart had learned to prize,
More skill'd to raise the wretched than to rise.
His house was known to all the vagrant train,
He chid their wand'rings, but reliev'd their pain;
The long-remember'd beggar was his guest,   151
Whose beard descending swept his aged breast;
The ruin'd spendthrift, now no longer proud,
Claim'd kindred there, and had his claims allow'd;
The broken soldier, kindly bade to stay,   155
Sat by his fire, and talk'd the night away;
Wept o'er his wounds, or tales of sorrow done,
Shoulder'd his crutch, and show'd how fields were won.
Pleas'd with his guests, the good man learn'd to glow,
And quite forgot their vices in their woe;   160
Careless their merits, or their faults to scan,
His pity gave ere charity began.

Thus to relieve the wretched was his pride,
And e'en his failings lean'd to Virtue's side;
But in his duty prompt at every call,   165
He watch'd and wept, he pray'd and felt, for all.
And, as a bird each fond endearment tries
To tempt its new-fledg'd offspring to the skies,
He tried each art, reprov'd each dull delay,
Allur'd to brighter worlds, and led the way.   170

Beside the bed where parting life was laid,
And sorrow, guilt, and pain, by turns dismay'd,
The reverend champion stood. At his control,
Despair and anguish fled the struggling soul ;
Comfort came down the trembling wretch to raise,
And his last falt'ring accents whisper'd praise.   176

At church, with meek and unaffected grace,
His looks adorn'd the venerable place ;
Truth from his lips prevail'd with double sway,
And fools, who came to scoff, remain'd to pray. 180
The service pass'd, around the pious man,
With steady zeal, each honest rustic ran ;
Even children follow'd with endearing wile,
And pluck'd his gown, to share the good man's smile.
His ready smile a parent's warmth express'd,   185
Their welfare pleas'd him, and their cares distress'd;
To them his heart, his love, his griefs were given,
But all his serious thoughts had rest in Heaven.
As some tall cliff, that lifts its awful form,   189
Swells from the vale, and midway leaves the storm,
Though round its breast the rolling clouds are spread,
Eternal sunshine settles on its head.

Beside yon straggling fence that skirts the way,
With blossom'd furze unprofitably gay,
There, in his noisy mansion, skill'd to rule,   195
The village master taught his little school ;
A man severe he was, and stern to view ;
I knew him well, and every truant knew ;
Well had the boding tremblers learn'd to trace
The day's disasters in his morning face ;   200

Full well they laugh'd, with counterfeited glee,
At all his jokes, for many a joke had he ;
Full well the busy whisper, circling round,
Convey'd the dismal tidings when he frown'd ;
Yet he was kind ; or if severe in aught,　205
The love he bore to learning was in fault ;
The village all declar'd how much he knew ;
'Twas certain he could write, and cypher too ;
Lands he could measure, terms and tides presage,
And e'en the story ran that he could gauge.　210
In arguing too, the parson own'd his skill,
For e'en though vanquish'd, he could argue still ;
While words of learned length and thund'ring sound
Amazed the gazing rustics rang'd around,
And still they gaz'd, and still the wonder grew,　215
That one small head could carry all he knew.

But past is all his fame. The very spot
Where many a time he triumph'd, is forgot.
Near yonder thorn, that lifts its head on high,　219
Where once the sign-post caught the passing eye,
Low lies that house where nut-brown draughts inspir'd,
Where grey-beard mirth and smiling toil retir'd,
Where village statesmen talk'd with looks profound,
And news much older than their ale went round.
Imagination fondly stoops to trace　225
The parlour splendours of that festive place ;
The white-wash'd wall, the nicely sanded floor,
The varnish'd clock that click'd behind the door ;
The chest contriv'd a double debt to pay,
A bed by night, a chest of drawers by day ;　230

The pictures plac'd for ornament and use,
The twelve good rules, the royal game of goose ;
The hearth, except when winter chill'd the day,
With aspen boughs, and flowers, and fennel gay ;
While broken tea-cups, wisely kept for show,   235
Rang'd o'er the chimney, glisten'd in a row.

Vain, transitory splendours ! Could not all
Reprieve the tottering mansion from its fall !
Obscure it sinks, nor shall it more impart
An hour's importance to the poor man's heart ;   240
Thither no more the peasant shall repair
To sweet oblivion of his daily care ;
No more the farmer's news, the barber's tale,
No more the wood-man's ballad shall prevail ;
No more the smith his dusky brow shall clear,   245
Relax his pond'rous strength, and lean to hear ;
The host himself no longer shall be found
Careful to see the mantling bliss go round ;
Nor the coy maid, half willing to be press'd,
Shall kiss the cup to pass it to the rest.   250

Yes ! let the rich deride, the proud disdain,
These simple blessings of the lowly train ;
To me more dear, congenial to my heart,
One native charm, than all the gloss of art ;
Spontaneous joys, where Nature has its play,   255
The soul adopts, and owns their first-born sway ;
Lightly they frolic o'er the vacant mind,
Unenvied, unmolested, unconfin'd :
But the long pomp, the midnight masquerade,
With all the freaks of wanton wealth array'd,   260

In these, ere triflers half their wish obtain,
The toiling pleasure sickens into pain ;
And, e'en while fashion's brightest arts decoy,
The heart distrusting asks, if this be joy.

Ye friends to truth, ye statesmen, who survey
The rich man's joys increase, the poor's decay, 266
'Tis yours to judge, how wide the limits stand
Between a splendid and a happy land.
Proud swells the tide with loads of freighted ore,
And shouting Folly hails them from her shore ; 270
Hoards, e'en beyond the miser's wish abound,
And rich men flock from all the world around.
Yet count our gains. This wealth is but a name
That leaves our useful products still the same.
Not so the loss. The man of wealth and pride 275
Takes up a space that many poor supplied ;
Space for his lake, his park's extended bounds,
Space for his horses, equipage, and hounds ;
The robe that wraps his limbs in silken sloth
Has robb'd the neighbouring fields of half their growth,
His seat, where solitary sports are seen, 281
Indignant spurns the cottage from the green ;
Around the world each needful product flies,
For all the luxuries the world supplies :
While thus the land adorn'd for pleasure, all 285
In barren splendour feebly waits the fall.

As some fair female unadorn'd and plain,
Secure to please while youth confirms her reign,
Slights every borrow'd charm that dress supplies,
Nor shares with art the triumph of her eyes : 290

But when those charms are pass'd, for charms are frail,
When time advances, and when lovers fail,
She then shines forth, solicitous to bless,
In all the glaring impotence of dress.
Thus fares the land, by luxury betray'd,   295
In nature's simplest charms at first array'd;
But verging to decline, its splendours rise,
Its vistas strike, its palaces surprise;
While scourg'd by famine from the smiling land,
The mournful peasant leads his humble band;   300
And while he sinks, without one arm to save,
The country blooms—a garden, and a grave.

Where then, ah! where, shall poverty reside,
To 'scape the pressure of contiguous pride?
If to some common's fenceless limits stray'd,   305
He drives his flock to pick the scanty blade,
Those fenceless fields the sons of wealth divide,
And e'en the bare-worn common is denied.

If to the city sped—What waits him there?
To see profusion that he must not share;   310
To see ten thousand baneful arts combin'd
To pamper luxury, and thin mankind;
To see those joys the sons of pleasure know
Extorted from his fellow creature's woe.
Here, while the courtier glitters in brocade,   315
There the pale artist plies the sickly trade;
Here, while the proud their long-drawn pomps display,
There the black gibbet glooms beside the way.
The dome where Pleasure holds her midnight reign
Here, richly deck'd, admits the gorgeous train;   320

Tumultuous grandeur crowds the blazing square,
The rattling chariots clash, the torches glare.
Sure scenes like these no troubles e'er annoy !
Sure these denote one universal joy !
Are these thy serious thoughts ?—Ah, turn thine eyes
Where the poor houseless shiv'ring female lies.   326
She once, perhaps, in village plenty bless'd,
Has wept at tales of innocence distress'd ;
Her modest looks the cottage might adorn,
Sweet as the primrose peeps beneath the thorn ;   330
Now lost to all ; her friends, her virtue fled,
Near her betrayer's door she lays her head,
And, pinch'd with cold, and shrinking from the shower,
With heavy heart deplores that luckless hour,
When idly first, ambitious of the town,   335
She left her wheel and robes of country brown.

Do thine, sweet AUBURN, thine, the loveliest train,
Do thy fair tribes participate her pain ?
E'en now, perhaps, by cold and hunger led,
At proud men's doors they ask a little bread !   340

Ah, no. To distant climes, a dreary scene,
Where half the convex world intrudes between,
Through torrid tracts with fainting steps they go,
Where wild Altama murmurs to their woe.
Far different there from all that charm'd before,   345
The various terrors of that horrid shore ;
Those blazing suns that dart a downward ray,
And fiercely shed intolerable day ;
Those matted woods where birds forget to sing,
But silent bats in drowsy clusters cling ;   350

THE DEPARTURE

(THOMAS BEWICK)

Those pois'nous fields with rank luxuriance crown'd,
Where the dark scorpion gathers death around;
Where at each step the stranger fears to wake
The rattling terrors of the vengeful snake;
Where crouching tigers wait their hapless prey, 355
And savage men more murd'rous still than they;
While oft in whirls the mad tornado flies,
Mingling the ravag'd landscape with the skies.
Far different these from every former scene,
The cooling brook, the grassy-vested green, 360
The breezy covert of the warbling grove,
That only shelter'd thefts of harmless love.

Good heaven! what sorrows gloom'd that parting day,
That call'd them from their native walks away;
When the poor exiles, every pleasure pass'd, 365
Hung round their bowers, and fondly look'd their last,
And took a long farewell, and wish'd in vain
For seats like these beyond the western main;
And shudd'ring still to face the distant deep,
Return'd and wept, and still return'd to weep. 370
The good old sire, the first prepar'd to go
To new-found worlds, and wept for others' woe;
But for himself, in conscious virtue brave,
He only wish'd for worlds beyond the grave.
His lovely daughter, lovelier in her tears, 375
The fond companion of his helpless years,
Silent went next, neglectful of her charms,
And left a lover's for a father's arms.
With louder plaints the mother spoke her woes,
And bless'd the cot where every pleasure rose 380

And kiss'd her thoughtless babes with many a tear,
And clasp'd them close, in sorrow doubly dear;
Whilst her fond husband strove to lend relief
In all the silent manliness of grief.

O Luxury! thou curs'd by Heaven's decree, 385
How ill exchang'd are things like these for thee!
How do thy potions, with insidious joy
Diffuse their pleasures only to destroy!
Kingdoms, by thee, to sickly greatness grown,
Boast of a florid vigour not their own; 390
At every draught more large and large they grow,
A bloated mass of rank unwieldy woe;
Till sapp'd their strength, and every part unsound,
Down, down they sink, and spread a ruin round.

E'en now the devastation is begun, 395
And half the business of destruction done;
E'en now, methinks, as pond'ring here I stand,
I see the rural virtues leave the land:
Down where yon anchoring vessel spreads the sail,
That idly waiting flaps with ev'ry gale, 400
Downward they move, a melancholy band,
Pass from the shore, and darken all the strand.
Contented toil, and hospitable care,
And kind connubial tenderness, are there;
And piety, with wishes plac'd above, 405
And steady loyalty, and faithful love.
And thou, sweet Poetry, thou loveliest maid,
Still first to fly where sensual joys invade;
Unfit in these degenerate times of shame,
To catch the heart, or strike for honest fame; 410

Dear charming nymph, neglected and decried,
My shame in crowds, my solitary pride;
Thou source of all my bliss, and all my woe,
That found'st me poor at first, and keep'st me so;
Thou guide by which the nobler arts excel,   415
Thou nurse of every virtue, fare thee well!
Farewell, and Oh! where'er thy voice be tried,
On Torno's cliffs, or Pambamarca's side,
Whether where equinoctial fervours glow,
Or winter wraps the polar world in snow,   420
Still let thy voice, prevailing over time,
Redress the rigours of th' inclement clime;
Aid slighted truth; with thy persuasive strain
Teach erring man to spurn the rage of gain;
Teach him, that states of native strength possess'd,
Though very poor, may still be very bless'd;   426
That trade's proud empire hastes to swift decay,
As ocean sweeps the labour'd mole away;
While self-dependent power can time defy,
As rocks resist the billows and the sky.   430

LYRICAL AND MISCELLANEOUS
PIECES

LYRICAL AND MISCELLANEOUS PIECES

PART OF A PROLOGUE WRITTEN AND SPOKEN BY THE POET LABERIUS

A ROMAN KNIGHT, WHOM CAESAR FORCED UPON THE STAGE

PRESERVED BY MACROBIUS.

WHAT! no way left to shun th' inglorious stage,
And save from infamy my sinking age!
Scarce half alive, oppress'd with many a year,
What in the name of dotage drives me here?
A time there was, when glory was my guide,   5
Nor force nor fraud could turn my steps aside;
Unaw'd by pow'r, and unappall'd by fear,
With honest thrift I held my honour dear:
But this vile hour disperses all my store,
And all my hoard of honour is no more.   10
For ah! too partial to my life's decline,
Caesar persuades, submission must be mine;
Him I obey, whom heaven itself obeys,
Hopeless of pleasing, yet inclin'd to please.
Here then at once, I welcome every shame,   15
And cancel at threescore a life of fame;
No more my titles shall my children tell,
The old buffoon will fit my name as well;
This day beyond its term my fate extends,
For life is ended when our honour ends.   20

ON A BEAUTIFUL YOUTH STRUCK BLIND
WITH LIGHTNING

(Imitated from the Spanish.)

Sure 'twas by Providence design'd,
  Rather in pity, than in hate,
That he should be, like Cupid, blind,
  To save him from Narcissus' fate.

THE GIFT

TO IRIS, IN BOW STREET, COVENT GARDEN

SAY, cruel IRIS, pretty rake,
    Dear mercenary beauty,
What annual offering shall I make,
    Expressive of my duty?

My heart, a victim to thine eyes,   5
    Should I at once deliver,
Say, would the angry fair one prize
    The gift, who slights the giver?

A bill, a jewel, watch, or toy,
    My rivals give—and let 'em;   10
If gems, or gold, impart a joy,
    I'll give them—when I get 'em.

I'll give—but not the full-blown rose,
    Or rose-bud more in fashion;
Such short-liv'd offerings but disclose   15
    A transitory passion.

I'll give thee something yet unpaid,
    Not less sincere, than civil:
I'll give thee—Ah! too charming maid,
    I'll give thee—To the devil.   20

THE LOGICIANS REFUTED

IN IMITATION OF DEAN SWIFT

LOGICIANS have but ill defin'd
As rational, the human kind ;
Reason, they say, belongs to man,
But let them prove it if they can.
Wise Aristotle and Smiglecius,   5
By ratiocinations specious,
Have strove to prove with great precision,
With definition and division,
Homo est ratione praeditum,—
But for my soul I cannot credit 'em ;   10
And must in spite of them maintain,
That man and all his ways are vain ;
And that this boasted lord of nature
Is both a weak and erring creature ;
That instinct is a surer guide   15
Than reason-boasting mortals' pride ;
And that brute beasts are far before 'em,
Deus est anima brutorum.
Who ever knew an honest brute
At law his neighbour prosecute,   20
Bring action for assault and battery,
Or friend beguile with lies and flattery ?
O'er plains they ramble unconfin'd,
No politics disturb their mind ;
They eat their meals, and take their sport,   25
Nor know who 's in or out at court ;

They never to the levee go
To treat as dearest friend, a foe ;
They never importune his grace,
Nor ever cringe to men in place ;   30
Nor undertake a dirty job,
Nor draw the quill to write for B—b.
Fraught with invective they ne'er go
To folks at Pater-Noster-Row ;
No judges, fiddlers, dancing-masters,   35
No pick-pockets, or poetasters,
Are known to honest quadrupeds ;
No single brute his fellow leads.
Brutes never meet in bloody fray,
Nor cut each others' throats, for pay.   40
Of beasts, it is confess'd, the ape
Comes nearest us in human shape ;
Like man he imitates each fashion,
And malice is his ruling passion ;
But both in malice and grimaces   45
A courtier any ape surpasses.
Behold him humbly cringing wait
Upon a minister of state ;
View him soon after to inferiors,
Aping the conduct of superiors ;   50
He promises with equal air,
And to perform takes equal care.
He in his turn finds imitators ;
At court, the porters, lacqueys, waiters,
Their master's manners still contract,   55
And footmen, lords and dukes can act.
Thus at the court both great and small
Behave alike—for all ape all.

A SONNET

Weeping, murmuring, complaining,
  Lost to every gay delight;
Myra, too sincere for feigning,
  Fears th' approaching bridal night.

Yet, why impair thy bright perfection ?   5
  Or dim thy beauty with a tear ?
Had Myra followed my direction,
  She long had wanted cause of fear.

STANZAS

ON THE TAKING OF QUEBEC, AND DEATH OF GENERAL WOLFE

Amidst the clamour of exulting joys,
  Which triumph forces from the patriot heart,
Grief dares to mingle her soul-piercing voice,
  And quells the raptures which from pleasures start.

O Wolfe ! to thee a streaming flood of woe,   5
  Sighing we pay, and think e'en conquest dear ;
Quebec in vain shall teach our breast to glow,
  Whilst thy sad fate extorts the heart-wrung tear.

Alive, the foe thy dreadful vigour fled,
  And saw thee fall with joy-pronouncing eyes :   10
Yet they shall know thou conquerest, though dead—
  Since from thy tomb a thousand heroes rise !

AN ELEGY ON THAT GLORY OF HER SEX, MRS. MARY BLAIZE

GOOD people all, with one accord,
　　Lament for Madam BLAIZE,
Who never wanted a good word—
　　From those who spoke her praise.

The needy seldom pass'd her door,   5
　　And always found her kind;
She freely lent to all the poor,—
　　Who left a pledge behind.

She strove the neighbourhood to please,
　　With manners wond'rous winning,   10
And never follow'd wicked ways,—
　　Unless when she was sinning.

At church, in silks and satins new,
　　With hoop of monstrous size,
She never slumber'd in her pew,—   15
　　But when she shut her eyes.

Her love was sought, I do aver,
　　By twenty beaux and more;
The king himself has follow'd her,—
　　When she has walk'd before.   20

But now her wealth and finery fled,
　　Her hangers-on cut short all;
The doctors found, when she was dead,—
　　Her last disorder mortal.

Let us lament, in sorrow sore,   25
　　For Kent-street well may say,
That had she liv'd a twelve-month more,—
　　She had not died to-day.

DESCRIPTION OF AN AUTHOR'S BEDCHAMBER

WHERE the Red Lion flaring o'er the way,
Invites each passing stranger that can pay;
Where Calvert's butt, and Parsons' black champagne,
Regale the drabs and bloods of Drury-lane;
There in a lonely room, from bailiffs snug,   5
The Muse found Scroggen stretch'd beneath a rug;
A window, patch'd with paper, lent a ray,
That dimly show'd the state in which he lay;
The sanded floor that grits beneath the tread;
The humid wall with paltry pictures spread: 10
The royal game of goose was there in view,
And the twelve rules the royal martyr drew;
The seasons, fram'd with listing, found a place,
And brave prince William show'd his lamp-black face:
The morn was cold, he views with keen desire   15
The rusty grate unconscious of a fire;
With beer and milk arrears the frieze was scor'd,
And five crack'd teacups dress'd the chimney board;
A nightcap deck'd his brows instead of bay,
A cap by night—a stocking all the day!   20

ON SEEING MRS. ** PERFORM IN THE
CHARACTER OF ****

FOR you, bright fair, the nine address their lays,
And tune my feeble voice to sing thy praise.
The heartfelt power of every charm divine,
Who can withstand their all-commanding shine?
See how she moves along with every grace,   5
While soul-brought tears steal down each shining face.
She speaks! 'tis rapture all, and nameless bliss,
Ye gods! what transport e'er compared to this.
As when in Paphian groves the Queen of Love
With fond complaint addressed the listening Jove, 10
'Twas joy, and endless blisses all around,
And rocks forgot their hardness at the sound.
Then first, at last even Jove was taken in,
And felt her charms, without disguise, within.

OF THE DEATH OF THE RIGHT HON. ***

YE Muses, pour the pitying tear
   For Pollio snatch'd away ;
O ! had he liv'd another year !—
   He had not died to-day.

O ! were he born to bless mankind,   5
   In virtuous times of yore,
Heroes themselves had fallen behind !—
   Whene'er he went before.

How sad the groves and plains appear,
   And sympathetic sheep ;   10
Even pitying hills would drop a tear !—
   If hills could learn to weep.

His bounty in exalted strain
   Each bard might well display ;
Since none implor'd relief in vain !—   15
   That went reliev'd away.

And hark ! I hear the tuneful throng
   His obsequies forbid,
He still shall live, shall live as long !—
   As ever dead man did.   20

AN EPIGRAM

ADDRESSED TO THE GENTLEMEN REFLECTED ON IN THE ROSCIAD, A POEM, BY THE AUTHOR

Worried with debts and past all hopes of bail,
His pen he prostitutes t' avoid a gaol.

ROSCOM.

LET not the *hungry* Bavius' angry stroke
Awake resentment, or your rage provoke ;
But pitying his distress, let virtue shine,
And giving each your bounty, *let him dine ;*
For thus retain'd, as learned counsel can,   5
Each case, however bad, he'll new japan ;
And by a quick transition, plainly show
'Twas no defeat of yours, but *pocket low*,
That caused his *putrid kennel* to o'erflow.

TO G. C. AND R. L.

'TWAS you, or I, or he, or all together,
'Twas one, both, three of them, they know not
            whether ;
This, I believe, between us great or small,
You, I, he, wrote it not—'twas Churchill's all.

TRANSLATION OF A SOUTH AMERICAN ODE

IN all my Enna's beauties blest,
    Amidst profusion still I pine ;
For though she gives me up her breast,
    Its panting tenant is not mine.

THE DOUBLE TRANSFORMATION

A TALE

SECLUDED from domestic strife,
Jack Book-worm led a college life;
A fellowship at twenty-five
Made him the happiest man alive;
He drank his glass and crack'd his joke,   5
And freshmen wonder'd as he spoke.

Such pleasures, unalloy'd with care,
Could any accident impair?
Could Cupid's shaft at length transfix
Our swain, arriv'd at thirty-six?   10
O had the archer ne'er come down
To ravage in a country town!
Or Flavia been content to stop
At triumphs in a Fleet-street shop.
O had her eyes forgot to blaze!   15
Or Jack had wanted eyes to gaze.
O!——But let exclamation cease,
Her presence banish'd all his peace.
So with decorum all things carried;   19
Miss frown'd, and blush'd, and then was—married.

Need we expose to vulgar sight
The raptures of the bridal night?
Need we intrude on hallow'd ground,
Or draw the curtains clos'd around?
Let it suffice, that each had charms;   25
He clasp'd a goddess in his arms;

And, though she felt his usage rough,
Yet in a man 'twas well enough.

The honey-moon like lightning flew,
The second brought its transports too.   30
A third, a fourth, were not amiss,
The fifth was friendship mix'd with bliss :
But, when a twelvemonth pass'd away,
Jack found his goddess made of clay ;
Found half the charms that deck'd her face   35
Arose from powder, shreds, or lace ;
But still the worst remain'd behind,
That very face had robb'd her mind.

Skill'd in no other arts was she
But dressing, patching, repartee ;   40
And, just as humour rose or fell,
By turns a slattern or a belle :
'Tis true she dress'd with modern grace,
Half naked at a ball or race ;
But when at home, at board or bed,   45
Five greasy nightcaps wrapp'd her head.
Could so much beauty condescend
To be a dull domestic friend ?
Could any curtain-lectures bring
To decency so fine a thing ?   50
In short, by night, 'twas fits or fretting ;
By day, 'twas gadding or coquetting.
Fond to be seen, she kept a bevy
Of powder'd coxcombs at her levy ;
The 'squire and captain took their stations,   55
And twenty other near relations ;

Jack suck'd his pipe, and often broke
A sigh in suffocating smoke;
While all their hours were pass'd between
Insulting repartee or spleen.   60

Thus as her faults each day were known,
He thinks her features coarser grown;
He fancies every vice she shows,
Or thins her lip, or points her nose:
Whenever rage or envy rise,   65
How wide her mouth, how wild her eyes!
He knows not how, but so it is,
Her face is grown a knowing phiz;
And, though her fops are wond'rous civil,
He thinks her ugly as the devil.   70

Now, to perplex the ravell'd noose,
As each a different way pursues,
While sullen or loquacious strife,
Promis'd to hold them on for life,
That dire disease, whose ruthless power   75
Withers the beauty's transient flower:
Lo! the small-pox, whose horrid glare
Levell'd its terrors at the fair;
And, rifling ev'ry youthful grace,
Left but the remnant of a face.   80

The glass, grown hateful to her sight,
Reflected now a perfect fright:
Each former art she vainly tries
To bring back lustre to her eyes.
In vain she tries her paste and creams,   85
To smooth her skin, or hide its seams;

Her country beaux and city cousins,
Lovers no more, flew off by dozens :
The 'squire himself was seen to yield,
And e'en the captain quit the field.   90

Poor Madam, now condemn'd to hack
The rest of life with anxious Jack,
Perceiving others fairly flown,
Attempted pleasing him alone.
Jack soon was dazzl'd to behold   95
Her present face surpass the old ;
With modesty her cheeks are dy'd,
Humility displaces pride ;
For tawdry finery is seen
A person ever neatly clean :   100
No more presuming on her sway,
She learns good-nature every day ;
Serenely gay, and strict in duty,
Jack finds his wife a perfect beauty.

A NEW SIMILE

IN THE MANNER OF SWIFT

LONG had I sought in vain to find
A likeness for the scribbling kind;
The modern scribbling kind, who write
In wit, and sense, and nature's spite:
Till reading, I forget what day on,   5
A chapter out of Tooke's Pantheon,
I think I met with something there,
To suit my purpose to a hair;
But let us not proceed too furious,
First please to turn to god Mercurius;   10
You'll find him pictur'd at full length
In book the second, page the tenth:
The stress of all my proofs on him I lay,
And now proceed we to our simile.

Imprimis, pray observe his hat,   15
Wings upon either side—mark that.
Well! what is it from thence we gather?
Why these denote a brain of feather.
A brain of feather! very right,
With wit that's flighty, learning light;   20
Such as to modern bard's decreed:
A just comparison,—proceed.

In the next place, his feet peruse,
Wings grow again from both his shoes;
Design'd, no doubt, their part to bear,   25
And waft his godship through the air;

And here my simile unites,
For in a modern poet's flights,
I'm sure it may be justly said,
His feet are useful as his head.   30

Lastly, vouchsafe t' observe his hand,
Filled with a snake-encircl'd wand ;
By classic authors term'd caduceus,
And highly fam'd for several uses.
To wit—most wond'rously endu'd,   35
No poppy water half so good ;
For let folks only get a touch,
Its soporific virtue 's such,
Though ne'er so much awake before,
That quickly they begin to snore.   40
Add too, what certain writers tell,
With this he drives men's souls to hell.

Now to apply, begin we then ;
His wand 's a modern author's pen ;
The serpents round about it twin'd   45
Denote him of the reptile kind ;
Denote the rage with which he writes,
His frothy slaver, venom'd bites ;
An equal semblance still to keep,
Alike too both conduce to sleep.   50
This diff'rence only, as the god
Drove souls to Tart'rus with his rod,
With his goosequill the scribbling elf,
Instead of others, damns himself.

And here my simile almost tript,   55
Yet grant a word by way of postscript.

Moreover, Merc'ry had a failing :
Well ! what of that ? out with it—stealing ;
In which all modern bards agree,
Being each as great a thief as he :   60
But ev'n this deity's existence
Shall lend my simile assistance.
Our modern bards ! why what a pox
Are they but senseless stones and blocks ?

EDWIN AND ANGELINA

(T. STOTHARD)

EDWIN AND ANGELINA

A BALLAD

'Turn, gentle hermit of the dale,
　And guide my lonely way,
To where yon taper cheers the vale
　With hospitable ray.

'For here, forlorn and lost I tread,　　　　5
　With fainting steps and slow;
Where wilds immeasurably spread,
　Seem length'ning as I go.'

'Forbear, my son,' the hermit cries,
　'To tempt the dangerous gloom;　　　10
For yonder faithless phantom flies
　To lure thee to thy doom.

'Here to the houseless child of want
　My door is open still;
And though my portion is but scant,　　　15
　I give it with good will.

'Then turn to-night, and freely share
　Whate'er my cell bestows;
My rushy couch, and frugal fare,
　My blessing and repose.　　　　　　20

'No flocks that range the valley free
　To slaughter I condemn:
Taught by that power that pities me,
　I learn to pity them.

'But from the mountain's grassy side 25
  A guiltless feast I bring;
A scrip with herbs and fruits supplied,
  And water from the spring.

'Then, pilgrim, turn, thy cares forgo;
  All earth-born cares are wrong: 30
Man wants but little here below,
  Nor wants that little long.'

Soft as the dew from heav'n descends,
  His gentle accents fell:
The modest stranger lowly bends, 35
  And follows to the cell.

Far in a wilderness obscure
  The lonely mansion lay;
A refuge to the neighbouring poor
  And strangers led astray. 40

No stores beneath its humble thatch
  Requir'd a master's care;
The wicket, opening with a latch,
  Receiv'd the harmless pair.

And now, when busy crowds retire 45
  To take their evening rest,
The hermit trimm'd his little fire,
  And cheer'd his pensive guest:

And spread his vegetable store,
  And gaily press'd, and smil'd; 50
And, skill'd in legendary lore,
  The lingering hours beguil'd.

Around in sympathetic mirth
  Its tricks the kitten tries ;
The cricket chirrups in the hearth ;   55
  The crackling faggot flies.

But nothing could a charm impart
  To soothe the stranger's woe ;
For grief was heavy at his heart,
  And tears began to flow.   60

His rising cares the hermit spied,
  With answ'ring care oppress'd ;
' And whence, unhappy youth,' he cried,
  ' The sorrows of thy breast ?

' From better habitations spurn'd,   65
  Reluctant dost thou rove ;
Or grieve for friendship unreturn'd,
  Or unregarded love ?

' Alas ! the joys that fortune brings
  Are trifling, and decay ;   70
And those who prize the paltry things,
  More trifling still than they.

' And what is friendship but a name,
  A charm that lulls to sleep ;
A shade that follows wealth or fame,   75
  But leaves the wretch to weep ?

' And love is still an emptier sound,
  The modern fair one's jest :
On earth unseen, or only found
  To warm the turtle's nest.   80

'For shame, fond youth, thy sorrows hush,
    And spurn the sex,' he said :
But, while he spoke, a rising blush
    His love-lorn guest betray'd.

Surpris'd, he sees new beauties rise,   85
    Swift mantling to the view ;
Like colours o'er the morning skies,
    As bright, as transient too.

The bashful look, the rising breast,
    Alternate spread alarms :   90
The lovely stranger stands confess'd
    A maid in all her charms.

'And, ah ! forgive a stranger rude,
    A wretch forlorn,' she cried ;
'Whose feet unhallow'd thus intrude   95
    Where heaven and you reside.

'But let a maid thy pity share,
    Whom love has taught to stray ;
Who seeks for rest, but finds despair
    Companion of her way.   100

'My father liv'd beside the Tyne,
    A wealthy lord was he ;
And all his wealth was mark'd as mine,
    He had but only me.

'To win me from his tender arms   105
    Unnumber'd suitors came ;
Who prais'd me for imputed charms,
    And felt or feign'd a flame.

Each hour a mercenary crowd
   With richest proffers strove :   110
Amongst the rest young Edwin bow'd,
   But never talk'd of love.

' In humble, simplest habit clad,
   No wealth nor power had he ;
Wisdom and worth were all he had,   115
   But these were all to me.

' And when beside me in the dale
   He caroll'd lays of love ;
His breath lent fragrance to the gale,
   And music to the grove.   120

' The blossom opening to the day,
   The dews of heaven refin'd,
Could nought of purity display,
   To emulate his mind.

' The dew, the blossom on the tree,   125
   With charms inconstant shine ;
Their charms were his, but woe to me !
   Their constancy was mine.

' For still I tried each fickle art,
   Importunate and vain :   130
And while his passion touch'd my heart,
   I triumph'd in his pain.

' Till quite dejected with my scorn,
   He left me to my pride ;
And sought a solitude forlorn,   135
   In secret, where he died.

' But mine the sorrow, mine the fault,
    And well my life shall pay ;
I'll seek the solitude he sought,
    And stretch me where he lay.   140

' And there forlorn, despairing, hid,
    I'll lay me down and die ;
'Twas so for me that Edwin did,
    And so for him will I.'

' Forbid it, heaven ! ' the hermit cried,   145
    And clasp'd her to his breast :
The wondering fair one turn'd to chide,
    'Twas Edwin's self that prest.

' Turn, Angelina, ever dear,
    My charmer, turn to see   150
Thy own, thy long-lost Edwin here,
    Restor'd to love and thee.

' Thus let me hold thee to my heart,
    And ev'ry care resign ;
And shall we never, never part,   155
    My life—my all that 's mine ?

' No, never from this hour to part,
    We'll live and love so true ;
The sigh that rends thy constant heart
    Shall break thy Edwin's too.'   160

ELEGY ON THE DEATH OF A MAD DOG

GOOD people all, of every sort,
 Give ear unto my song;
And if you find it wond'rous short,
 It cannot hold you long.

In Islington there was a man,   5
 Of whom the world might say,
That still a godly race he ran,
 Whene'er he went to pray.

A kind and gentle heart he had,
 To comfort friends and foes;   10
The naked every day he clad,
 When he put on his clothes.

And in that town a dog was found,
 As many dogs there be,
Both mongrel, puppy, whelp, and hound,   15
 And curs of low degree.

This dog and man at first were friends;
 But when a pique began,
The dog, to gain some private ends,
 Went mad and bit the man.   20

Around from all the neighbouring streets
 The wond'ring neighbours ran,
And swore the dog had lost his wits,
 To bite so good a man.

GOLDSMITH   D

The wound it seem'd both sore and sad   25
  To every Christian eye ;
And while they swore the dog was mad,
  They swore the man would die.

But soon a wonder came to light,
  That show'd the rogues they lied :   30
The man recover'd of the bite,
  The dog it was that died.

SONG

FROM 'THE VICAR OF WAKEFIELD'

WHEN lovely woman stoops to folly,
    And finds too late that men betray,
What charm can soothe her melancholy,
    What art can wash her guilt away?

The only art her guilt to cover,   5
    To hide her shame from every eye,
To give repentance to her lover,
    And wring his bosom, is—to die.

EPILOGUE TO 'THE GOOD NATUR'D MAN'

As puffing quacks some caitiff wretch procure
To swear the pill, or drop, has wrought a cure ;
Thus on the stage, our play-wrights still depend
For Epilogues and Prologues on some friend,
Who knows each art of coaxing up the town,   5
And make full many a bitter pill go down.
Conscious of this, our bard has gone about,
And teas'd each rhyming friend to help him out.
' An Epilogue—things can't go on without it ;
It could not fail, would you but set about it.'   10
' Young man,' cries one—a bard laid up in clover—
' Alas, young man, my writing days are over ;
Let boys play tricks, and kick the straw ; not I :
Your brother Doctor there, perhaps, may try.'
' What I ? dear Sir,' the Doctor interposes ;   15
' What, plant my thistle, Sir, among his roses !
No, no ; I've other contests to maintain ;
To-night I head our troops at Warwick Lane :
Go, ask your manager.' ' Who, me ? Your pardon ;
Those things are not our forte at Covent Garden.'   20
Our Author's friends, thus plac'd at happy distance,
Give him good words indeed, but no assistance.
As some unhappy wight, at some new play,
At the Pit door stands elbowing a way,
While oft, with many a smile, and many a shrug,   25
He eyes the centre, where his friends sit snug ;

His simp'ring friends, with pleasure in their eyes,
Sink as he sinks, and as he rises rise ;
He nods, they nod ; he cringes, they grimace ;
But not a soul will budge to give him place.   30
Since then, unhelp'd, our bard must now conform
' To 'bide the pelting of this pitiless storm '—
Blame where you must, be candid where you can ;
And be each critic the *Good Natur'd Man*.

EPILOGUE TO 'THE SISTER'

WHAT! five long acts—and all to make us wiser!
Our authoress sure has wanted an adviser.
Had she consulted *me*, she should have made
Her moral play a speaking masquerade;
Warm'd up each bustling scene, and in her rage   5
Have emptied all the green-room on the stage.
My life on't, this had kept her play from sinking;
Have pleas'd our eyes, and sav'd the pain of thinking.
Well! since she thus has shown her want of skill,
What if I give a masquerade?—I will.   10
But how? ay, there's the rub! (*pausing*)—I've got my
    cue:
The world's a masquerade! the maskers, you, you, you.
                    (*To Boxes, Pit, and Gallery.*)
——, what a group the motley scene discloses!
False wits, false wives, false virgins, and false spouses!
Statesmen with bridles on; and, close beside 'em,   15
Patriots, in party-coloured suits, that ride 'em.
There Hebes, turn'd of fifty, try once more
To raise a flame in Cupids of threescore.
These in their turn, with appetites as keen,
Deserting fifty, fasten on fifteen,   20
Miss, not yet full fifteen, with fire uncommon,
Flings down her sampler, and takes up the woman:
The little urchin smiles, and spreads her lure,
And tries to kill, ere she's got power to cure.
Thus 'tis with all—their chief and constant care   25
Is to seem everything but what they are.

Yon broad, bold, angry spark, I fix my eye on,
Who seems to have robb'd his vizor from the lion ;
Who frowns, and talks, and swears, with round parade,
Looking, as who should say, D— —! who's afraid ? 30
(*Mimicking.*)
Strip but his vizor off, and sure I am
You'll find his lionship a very lamb.
Yon politician, famous in debate,
Perhaps, to vulgar eyes, bestrides the state ;
Yet, when he deigns his real shape t' assume, 35
He turns old woman, and bestrides a broom.
Yon patriot, too, who presses on your sight,
And seems to every gazer all in white,
If with a bribe his candour you attack,
He bows, turns round, and whip—the man's a black ! 40
Yon critic, too—but whither do I run ?
If I proceed, our bard will be undone !
Well then a truce, since she requests it too :
Do you spare her, and I'll for once spare you.

PROLOGUE TO 'ZOBEIDE'

In these bold times, when Learning's sons explore
The distant climate and the savage shore ;
When wise Astronomers to India steer,
And quit for Venus, many a brighter here ;
While Botanists, all cold to smiles and dimpling,   5
Forsake the fair, and patiently—go simpling ;
When every bosom swells with wond'rous scenes,
Priests, cannibals, and hoity-toity queens :
Our bard into the general spirit enters,
And fits his little frigate for adventures :   10
With Scythian stores, and trinkets deeply laden,
He this way steers his course, in hopes of trading—
Yet ere he lands he 'as ordered me before,
To make an observation on the shore.
Where are we driven ? our reck'ning sure is lost !   15
This seems a barren and a dangerous coast.
——— what a sultry climate am I under !
Yon ill foreboding cloud seems big with thunder.

                                   (*Upper Gallery.*)

There Mangroves spread, and larger than I've seen 'em—
                                   (*Pit.*)

Here trees of stately size—and turtles in 'em—   20
                                   (*Balconies.*)

Here ill-condition'd oranges abound——
                                   (*Stage.*)

And apples (*takes up one and tastes it*), bitter apples
    strew the ground.

The place is uninhabited, I fear !
I heard a hissing—there are serpents here !
O there the natives are—a dreadful race !   25
The men have tails, the women paint the face !
No doubt they're all barbarians.—Yes, 'tis so,
I'll try to make palaver with them though ;

(Making signs.)

'Tis best, however, keeping at a distance.
Good Savages, our Captain craves assistance ;   30
Our ship's well stor'd ;—in yonder creek we've laid her ;
His honour is no mercenary trader ;
This is his first adventure ; lend him aid,
Or you may chance to spoil a thriving trade.
His goods, he hopes, are prime, and brought from far, 35
Equally fit for gallantry and war.
What ! no reply to promises so ample ?
I'd best step back—and order up a sample.

THRENODIA AUGUSTALIS:

SACRED TO THE MEMORY OF HER LATE ROYAL HIGHNESS
THE PRINCESS DOWAGER OF WALES.

OVERTURE—A SOLEMN DIRGE.   AIR—TRIO.

ARISE, ye sons of worth, arise,
   And waken every note of woe ;
When truth and virtue reach the skies,
   'Tis ours to weep the want below !

CHORUS.

When truth and virtue, &c.   5

MAN SPEAKER.

The praise attending pomp and power,
   The incense given to kings,
Are but the trappings of an hour—
   Mere transitory things !
The base bestow them : but the good agree   10
To spurn the venal gifts as flattery.
   But when to pomp and power are join'd
   An equal dignity of mind—
When titles are the smallest claim—
     When wealth and rank and noble blood,   15
     But aid the power of doing good—
Then all their trophies last ; and flattery turns to
   fame.

   Bless'd spirit thou, whose fame, just born to bloom
Shall spread and flourish from the tomb,
   How hast thou left mankind for heaven !   20
Even now reproach and faction mourn,

And, wondering how their rage was borne,
   Request to be forgiven.
Alas! they never had thy hate:
   Unmov'd in conscious rectitude,   25
     Thy towering mind self-centred stood,
Nor wanted man's opinion to be great.
In vain, to charm thy ravish'd sight,
   A thousand gifts would fortune send;
In vain, to drive thee from the right,   30
   A thousand sorrows urg'd thy end:
Like some well-fashion'd arch thy patience stood,
And purchas'd strength from its increasing load.
Pain met thee like a friend that set thee free;
Affliction still is virtue's opportunity!   35
     Virtue, on herself relying,
       Ev'ry passion hush'd to rest,
   Loses ev'ry pain of dying
     In the hopes of being blest.
   Ev'ry added pang she suffers   40
     Some increasing good bestows,
   Ev'ry shock that malice offers
     Only rocks her to repose.

    SONG. BY A MAN—AFFETTUOSO.

Virtue, on herself relying,
   Ev'ry passion hush'd to rest,   45
Loses ev'ry pain of dying
   In the hopes of being blest.

Ev'ry added pang she suffers
   Some increasing good bestows,
Ev'ry shock that malice offers,   50
   Only rocks her to repose.

WOMAN SPEAKER.

Yet, ah! what terrors frowned upon her fate—
  Death, with its formidable band,
Fever and pain and pale consumptive care,
  Determin'd took their stand: 55
Nor did the cruel ravagers design
  To finish all their efforts at a blow;
  But, mischievously slow,
They robb'd the relic and defac'd the shrine.
  With unavailing grief,   60
  Despairing of relief,
Her weeping children round
  Beheld each hour
  Death's growing power,
And trembled as he frown'd.   65

As helpless friends who view from shore
The labouring ship, and hear the tempest roar,
  While winds and waves their wishes cross—
They stood, while hope and comfort fail,
Not to assist, but to bewail   70
  The inevitable loss.
Relentless tyrant, at thy call
How do the good, the virtuous fall!
Truth, beauty, worth, and all that most engage,
But wake thy vengeance and provoke thy rage.   75

SONG.   BY A MAN.—BASSO.—STACCATO.—SPIRITOSO.

When vice my dart and scythe supply,
How great a king of terrors I!
If folly, fraud, your hearts engage,
Tremble, ye mortals, at my rage!

Fall, round me fall, ye little things,   80
Ye statesmen, warriors, poets, kings ;
If virtue fail her counsel sage,
Tremble, ye mortals, at my rage !

MAN SPEAKER.

Yet let that wisdom, urged by her example,
Teach us to estimate what all must suffer ;   85
Let us prize death as the best gift of nature—
As a safe inn, where weary travellers,
When they have journeyed through a world of cares,
May put off life and be at rest for ever.
Groans, weeping friends, indeed, and gloomy sables,
May oft distract us with their sad solemnity: 91
The preparation is the executioner.
Death, when unmasked, shows me a friendly face,
And is a terror only at a distance ;
For as the line of life conducts me on   95
To Death's great court, the prospect seems more fair.
'Tis Nature's kind retreat, that's always open
To take us in when we have drained the cup
Of life, or worn our days to wretchedness.

      In that secure, serene retreat,   100
      Where all the humble, all the great,
         Promiscuously recline ;
      Where wildly huddled to the eye,
      The beggar's pouch and prince's purple lie,
         May every bliss be thine.   105
And ah ! bless'd spirit, wheresoe'er thy flight,
Through rolling worlds, or fields of liquid light,
May cherubs welcome their expected guest;
May saints with songs receive thee to their rest;

May peace that claimed while here thy warmest love,
May blissful endless peace be thine above!   111

SONG. BY A WOMAN.—AMOROSO.

Lovely, lasting Peace below,
Comforter of every woe,
Heav'nly born, and bred on high,
To crown the favourites of the sky—   115
Lovely, lasting Peace, appear;
This world itself, if thou art here,
Is once again with Eden blest,
And man contains it in his breast.

WOMAN SPEAKER.

Our vows are heard! Long, long to mortal eyes,
Her soul was fitting to its kindred skies: 121
Celestial-like her bounty fell,
Where modest want and patient sorrow dwell;
Want pass'd for merit at her door,
    Unseen the modest were supplied,   125
Her constant pity fed the poor—
    Then only poor, indeed, the day she died.
And oh! for this! while sculpture decks thy shrine,
    And art exhausts profusion round,
The tribute of a tear be mine,   130
    A simple song, a sigh profound.
There Faith shall come, a pilgrim gray,
To bless the tomb that wraps thy clay;
And calm Religion shall repair
To dwell a weeping hermit there.   135
Truth, Fortitude, and Friendship shall agree
To blend their virtues while they think of thee.

AIR. CHORUS.—POMPOSO.

Let us, let all the world agree,
To profit by resembling thee.

PART II

OVERTURE—PASTORALE

MAN SPEAKER.

FAST by that shore where Thames' translucent stream
　Reflects new glories on his breast,
Where, splendid as the youthful poet's dream,
　He forms a scene beyond Elysium blest—
Where sculptur'd elegance and native grace　　　　　5
Unite to stamp the beauties of the place,
　While sweetly blending still are seen
　The wavy lawn, the sloping green—
While novelty, with cautious cunning,
Through ev'ry maze of fancy running,　　　　　　　10
　From China borrows aid to deck the scene—
There, sorrowing by the river's glassy bed,
　Forlorn, a rural bard complain'd,
All whom Augusta's bounty fed,
　All whom her clemency sustain'd;　　　　　　　　15
The good old sire, unconscious of decay,
The modest matron, clad in homespun gray,
The military boy, the orphan'd maid,
The shatter'd veteran, now first dismay'd;

These sadly join beside the murmuring deep,   20
    And, as they view
    The towers of Kew,
Call on their mistress—now no more—and weep.

CHORUS.—AFFETTUOSO.—LARGO.

Ye shady walks, ye waving greens,
Ye nodding towers, ye fairy scenes—   25
Let all your echoes now deplore
That she who form'd your beauties is no more.

MAN SPEAKER.

First of the train the patient rustic came,
    Whose callous hand had form'd the scene,
Bending at once with sorrow and with age,   30
    With many a tear and many a sigh between;
'And where,' he cried, 'shall now my babes have
    bread,
    Or how shall age support its feeble fire?
No lord will take me now, my vigour fled,   34
    Nor can my strength perform what they require;
Each grudging master keeps the labourer bare—
A sleek and idle race is all their care.
My noble mistress thought not so:
    Her bounty, like the morning dew,
Unseen, though constant, used to flow;   40
    And as my strength decay'd, her bounty grew.'

WOMAN SPEAKER.

In decent dress, and coarsely clean,
The pious matron next was seen—

Clasp'd in her hand a godly book was borne,
By use and daily meditation worn ; 45
That decent dress, this holy guide,
Augusta's care had well supplied.
' And ah ! ' she cries, all woe-begone,
  ' What now remains for me ?
Oh ! where shall weeping want repair, 50
  To ask for charity ?
Too late in life for me to ask,
  And shame prevents the deed,
And tardy, tardy are the times
  To succour, should I need. 55
But all my wants, before I spoke,
  Were to my Mistress known ;
She still reliev'd, nor sought my praise,
  Contented with her own.
But ev'ry day her name I'll bless, 60
  My morning prayer, my evening song,
I'll praise her while my life shall last,
  A life that cannot last me long.'

SONG. BY A WOMAN.

Each day, each hour, her name I'll bless—
  My morning and my evening song ; 65
And when in death my vows shall cease,
  My children shall the note prolong.

MAN SPEAKER.

The hardy veteran after struck the sight,
  Scarr'd, mangled, maim'd in every part,
Lopp'd of his limbs in many a gallant fight, 70
  In nought entire—except his heart.

Mute for a while, and sullenly distress'd,
At last the impetuous sorrow fir'd his breast.
   ' Wild is the whirlwind rolling
      O'er Afric's sandy plain,   75
   And wild the tempest howling
      Along the billow'd main :
   But every danger felt before—
   The raging deep, the whirlwind's roar—
   Less dreadful struck me with dismay,   80
   Than what I feel this fatal day.
Oh, let me fly a land that spurns the brave,
Oswego's dreary shores shall be my grave ;
I'll seek that less inhospitable coast,
And lay my body where my limbs were lost.'   85

SONG. BY A MAN.—BASSO.—SPIRITOSO.

Old Edward's sons, unknown to yield,
Shall crowd from Crecy's laurell'd field,
   To do thy memory right ;
For thine and Britain's wrongs they feel,
Again they snatch the gleamy steel,   90
   And wish the avenging fight.

WOMAN SPEAKER.

In innocence and youth complaining,
   Next appear'd a lovely maid,
Affliction o'er each feature reigning,
   Kindly came in beauty's aid ;   95
Every grace that grief dispenses,
   Every glance that warms the soul,
In sweet succession charmed the senses,
   While pity harmonized the whole.   99

'The garland of beauty'—'tis thus she would say—
  ' No more shall my crook or my temples adorn,
I'll not wear a garland—Augusta's away,
  I'll not wear a garland until she return ;
But alas ! that return I never shall see,   104
  The echoes of Thames shall my sorrows proclaim,
There promised a lover to come—but, O me !
  'Twas death,—'twas the death of my mistress that
    came.
But ever, for ever, her image shall last,
  I'll strip all the spring of its earliest bloom ;   109
On her grave shall the cowslip and primrose be cast,
  And the new-blossomed thorn shall whiten her
    tomb.'

SONG.   BY A WOMAN.—PASTORALE.

With garlands of beauty the queen of the May
  No more will her crook or her temples adorn;
For who'd wear a garland when she is away,
  When she is remov'd, and shall never return. 115

On the grave of Augusta these garlands be plac'd,
  We'll rifle the spring of its earliest bloom,
And there shall the cowslip and primrose be cast,
  And the new-blossom'd thorn shall whiten her tomb.

CHORUS.—ALTRO MODO.

On the grave of Augusta this garland be plac'd, 120
  We'll rifle the spring of its earliest bloom,
And there shall the cowslip and primrose be cast,
  And the tears of her country shall water her tomb.

SONG

FROM 'SHE STOOPS TO CONQUER'

LET school-masters puzzle their brain,
  With grammar, and nonsense, and learning;
Good liquor, I stoutly maintain,
  Gives *genus* a better discerning.
Let them brag of their heathenish gods,   5
  Their Lethes, their Styxes, and Stygians:
Their Quis, and their Quaes, and their Quods,
  They're all but a parcel of Pigeons.
                    Toroddle, toroddle, toroll.

When Methodist preachers come down
  A-preaching that drinking is sinful,   10
I'll wager the rascals a crown
  They always preach best with a skinful.
But when you come down with your pence,
  For a slice of their scurvy religion,
I'll leave it to all men of sense,   15
  But you, my good friend, are the pigeon.
                    Toroddle, toroddle, toroll.

Then come, put the jorum about,
  And let us be merry and clever;
Our hearts and our liquors are stout;
  Here's the Three Jolly Pigeons for ever.   20
Let some cry up woodcock or hare,
  Your bustards, your ducks, and your widgeons;
But of all the birds in the air,
  Here's a health to the Three Jolly Pigeons.
                    Toroddle, toroddle, toroll.

EPILOGUE TO 'SHE STOOPS TO CONQUER'

WELL, having stoop'd to conquer with success,
And gain'd a husband without aid from dress,
Still, as a Bar-maid, I could wish it too,
As I have conquer'd him, to conquer you :
And let me say, for all your resolution,⁣   5
That pretty Bar-maids have done execution.
Our life is all a play, compos'd to please,
' We have our exits and our entrances.'
The First Act shows the simple country maid,
Harmless and young, of ev'ry thing afraid ;   10
Blushes when hir'd, and, with unmeaning action,
' I hopes as how to give you satisfaction.'
Her Second Act displays a livelier scene—
Th' unblushing Bar-maid of a country inn,
Who whisks about the house, at market caters,   15
Talks loud, coquets the guests, and scolds the waiters.
Next the scene shifts to town, and there she soars,
The chop-house toast of ogling connoisseurs.
On 'Squires and Cits she there displays her arts,
And on the gridiron broils her lovers' hearts :   20
And as she smiles, her triumphs to complete,
Even Common-Councilmen forget to eat.
The Fourth Act shows her wedded to the 'Squire,
And Madam now begins to hold it higher ;
Pretends to taste, at Operas cries *caro*,   25
And quits her *Nancy Dawson*, for *Che faro*,
Doats upon dancing, and in all her pride,
Swims round the room, the Heinel of Cheapside ;

Ogles and leers with artificial skill,
'Till having lost in age the power to kill,   30
She sits all night at cards, and ogles at spadille.
Such, through our lives, the eventful history—
The Fifth and Last Act still remains for me.
The Bar-maid now for your protection prays,
Turns Female Barrister, and pleads for Bayes.   35

PORTRAIT OF GOLDSMITH AFTER REYNOLDS

(VIGNETTE TO 'RETALIATION')

RETALIATION

A POEM

OF old, when Scarron his companions invited,
Each guest brought his dish, and the feast was united ;
If our landlord supplies us with beef, and with fish,
Let each guest bring himself, and he brings the best dish :
Our Dean shall be venison, just fresh from the plains ; 5
Our Burke shall be tongue, with a garnish of brains ;
Our Will shall be wild-fowl, of excellent flavour,
And Dick with his pepper shall heighten their savour :
Our Cumberland's sweet-bread its place shall obtain,
And Douglas is pudding, substantial and plain : 10
Our Garrick 's a salad ; for in him we see
Oil, vinegar, sugar, and saltness agree :
To make out the dinner, full certain I am,
That Ridge is anchovy, and Reynolds is lamb ;
That Hickey 's a capon, and by the same rule, 15
Magnanimous Goldsmith a gooseberry fool.
At a dinner so various, at such a repast,
Who'd not be a glutton, and stick to the last ?
Here, waiter ! more wine, let me sit while I'm able,
Till all my companions sink under the table ; 20
Then, with chaos and blunders encircling my head,
Let me ponder, and tell what I think of the dead.

Here lies the good Dean, re-united to earth,
Who mix'd reason with pleasure, and wisdom with
     mirth :
If he had any faults, he has left us in doubt, 25
At least, in six weeks, I could not find 'em out ;

Yet some have declar'd, and it can't be denied 'em,
That sly-boots was cursedly cunning to hide 'em.

Here lies our good Edmund, whose genius was such,
We scarcely can praise it, or blame it too much ; 30
Who, born for the Universe, narrow'd his mind,
And to party gave up what was meant for mankind.
Though fraught with all learning, yet straining his
    throat
To persuade Tommy Townshend to lend him a vote ;
Who, too deep for his hearers, still went on refining, 35
And thought of convincing, while they thought of
    dining ;
Though equal to all things, for all things unfit,
Too nice for a statesman, too proud for a wit :
For a patriot, too cool ; for a drudge, disobedient ;
And too fond of the *right* to pursue the *expedient*. 40
In short, 'twas his fate, unemploy'd, or in place, Sir,
To eat mutton cold, and cut blocks with a razor.

Here lies honest William, whose heart was a mint,
While the owner ne'er knew half the good that was in't ;
The pupil of impulse, it forc'd him along, 45
His conduct still right, with his argument wrong ;
Still aiming at honour, yet fearing to roam,
The coachman was tipsy, the chariot drove home ;
Would you ask for his merits ? alas ! he had none ;
What was good was spontaneous, his faults were his own. 50

Here lies honest Richard, whose fate I must sigh at ;
Alas, that such frolic should now be so quiet !
What spirits were his ! what wit and what whim !
Now breaking a jest, and now breaking a limb ;

Now wrangling and grumbling to keep up the ball, 55
Now teasing and vexing, yet laughing at all !
In short, so provoking a devil was Dick,
That we wish'd him full ten times a day at Old Nick ;
But, missing his mirth and agreeable vein,
As often we wish'd to have Dick back again.   60

Here Cumberland lies, having acted his parts,
The Terence of England, the mender of hearts ;
A flattering painter, who made it his care
To draw men as they ought to be, not as they are.
His gallants are all faultless, his women divine,   65
And comedy wonders at being so fine ;
Like a tragedy queen he has dizen'd her out,
Or rather like tragedy giving a rout.
His fools have their follies so lost in a crowd
Of virtues and feelings, that folly grows proud ;   70
And coxcombs, alike in their failings alone,
Adopting his portraits, are pleas'd with their own.
Say, where has our poet this malady caught ?
Or, wherefore his characters thus without fault ?
Say, was it that vainly directing his view   75
To find out men's virtues, and finding them few,
Quite sick of pursuing each troublesome elf,
He grew lazy at last, and drew from himself ?

Here Douglas retires, from his toils to relax,
The scourge of impostors, the terror of quacks :   80
Come, all ye quack bards, and ye quacking divines,
Come, and dance on the spot where your tyrant reclines :
When Satire and Censure encircl'd his throne,
I fear'd for your safety, I fear'd for my own ;

But now he is gone, and we want a detector,   85
Our Dodds shall be pious, our Kenricks shall lecture ;
Macpherson write bombast, and call it a style,
Our Townshend make speeches, and I shall compile ;
New Lauders and Bowers the Tweed shall cross over,
No countryman living their tricks to discover ;   90
Detection her taper shall quench to a spark,
And Scotchman meet Scotchman, and cheat in the
　　　dark.

Here lies David Garrick, describe me, who can,
An abridgment of all that was pleasant in man ;
As an actor, confess'd without rival to shine :   95
As a wit, if not first, in the very first line :
Yet, with talents like these, and an excellent heart,
The man had his failings, a dupe to his art.
Like an ill-judging beauty, his colours he spread,
And beplaster'd with rouge his own natural red.   100
On the stage he was natural, simple, affecting ;
'Twas only that when he was off he was acting.
With no reason on earth to go out of his way,
He turn'd and he varied full ten times a day.
Though secure of our hearts, yet confoundedly sick 105
If they were not his own by finessing and trick,
He cast off his friends, as a huntsman his pack,
For he knew when he pleas'd he could whistle them
　　　back.
Of praise a mere glutton, he swallow'd what came,
And the puff of a dunce he mistook it for fame ;   110
Till his relish grown callous, almost to disease,
Who pepper'd the highest was surest to please.

But let us be candid, and speak out our mind,
If dunces applauded, he paid them in kind.
Ye Kenricks, ye Kellys, and Woodfalls so grave,   115
What a commerce was yours, while you got and you
        gave !
How did Grub-street re-echo the shouts that you rais'd,
While he was be-Roscius'd, and you were be-prais'd !
But peace to his spirit, wherever it flies,
To act as an angel, and mix with the skies :   120
Those poets, who owe their best fame to his skill,
Shall still be his flatterers, go where he will.
Old Shakespeare, receive him, with praise and with love,
And Beaumonts and Bens be his Kellys above.

Here Hickey reclines, a most blunt, pleasant creature,
And slander itself must allow him good nature :   126
He cherish'd his friend, and he relish'd a bumper ;
Yet one fault he had, and that one was a thumper.
Perhaps you may ask if the man was a miser ?
I answer, no, no, for he always was wiser :   130
Too courteous, perhaps, or obligingly flat ?
His very worst foe can't accuse him of that :
Perhaps he confided in men as they go,
And so was too foolishly honest ? Ah no !   134
Then what was his failing? come, tell it, and, burn ye !
He was, could he help it ?—a special attorney.

Here Reynolds is laid, and, to tell you my mind,
He has not left a better or wiser behind :
His pencil was striking, resistless, and grand ;
His manners were gentle, complying, and bland ;   140

Still born to improve us in every part,
His pencil our faces, his manners our heart :
To coxcombs averse, yet most civilly steering,
When they judg'd without skill he was still hard of
    hearing :
When they talk'd of their Raphaels, Correggios, and
    stuff,   145
He shifted his trumpet, and only took snuff.

POSTSCRIPT

After the Fourth Edition of this Poem was printed, the
Publisher received an Epitaph on Mr. Whiteford, from
a friend of the late Doctor Goldsmith, inclosed in a letter,
of which the following is an abstract :—

' I have in my possession a sheet of paper, containing
near forty lines in the Doctor's own hand-writing : there
are many scattered, broken verses, on Sir Jos. Reynolds,
Counsellor Ridge, Mr. Beauclerk, and Mr. Whiteford.
The Epitaph on the last-mentioned gentleman is the only
one that is finished, and therefore I have copied it, that
you may add it to the next edition.   It is a striking proof
of Doctor Goldsmith's good-nature.   I saw this sheet of
paper in the Doctor's room, five or six days before he died;
and, as I had got all the other Epitaphs, I asked him if
I might take it.   " *In truth you may, my Boy,*" (replied
he,) " *for it will be of no use to me where I am going.*" '

HERE Whiteford reclines, and deny it who can,
Though he *merrily* liv'd, he is now a *grave* man ;
Rare compound of oddity, frolic, and fun !
Who relish'd a joke, and rejoic'd in a pun ;   150

Whose temper was generous, open, sincere ;
A stranger to flatt'ry, a stranger to fear ;
Who scatter'd around wit and humour at will ;
Whose daily *bons mots* half a column might fill ;
A Scotchman, from pride and from prejudice free ; 155
A scholar, yet surely no pedant was he.

What pity, alas ! that so lib'ral a mind
Should so long be to news-paper essays confin'd ;
Who perhaps to the summit of science could soar,
Yet content ' if the table he set on a roar ' ; 160
Whose talents to fill any station were fit,
Yet happy if Woodfall confess'd him a wit.

Ye news-paper witlings ! ye pert scribbling folks
Who copied his squibs, and re-echoed his jokes ;
Ye tame imitators, ye servile herd, come, 165
Still follow your master, and visit his tomb :
To deck it, bring with you festoons of the vine,
And copious libations bestow on his shrine :
Then strew all around it (you can do no less)
Cross-readings, *Ship-news*, and *Mistakes of the Press*.

Merry Whitefoord, farewell ! for *thy* sake I admit 171
That a Scot may have humour, I had almost said wit :
This debt to thy mem'ry I cannot refuse,
' Thou best humour'd man with the worst humour'd
    muse.'

SONG

INTENDED TO HAVE BEEN SUNG IN 'SHE STOOPS TO CONQUER'

AH, me! when shall I marry me?
  Lovers are plenty; but fail to relieve me:
He, fond youth, that could carry me,
  Offers to love, but means to deceive me.

But I will rally, and combat the ruiner: 5
  Not a look, not a smile shall my passion discover:
She that gives all to the false one pursuing her,
  Makes but a penitent, loses a lover.

TRANSLATION

CHASTE are their instincts, faithful is their fire,
No foreign beauty tempts to false desire;
The snow-white vesture, and the glittering crown,
The simple plumage, or the glossy down
Prompt not their loves :—the patriot bird pursues   5
His well acquainted tints, and kindred hues.
Hence through their tribes no mix'd polluted flame,
No monster-breed to mark the groves with shame;
But the chaste blackbird, to its partner true,
Thinks black alone is beauty's favourite hue.   10
The nightingale, with mutual passion blest,
Sings to its mate, and nightly charms the nest;
While the dark owl to court its partner flies,
And owns its offspring in their yellow eyes.

THE HAUNCH OF VENISON

A POETICAL EPISTLE TO LORD CLARE

THANKS, my Lord, for your venison, for finer or fatter
Never rang'd in a forest, or smok'd in a platter;
The haunch was a picture for painters to study,
The fat was so white, and the lean was so ruddy.
Though my stomach was sharp, I could scarce help
    regretting   5
To spoil such a delicate picture by eating;
I had thoughts, in my chambers, to place it in view,
To be shown to my friends as a piece of *virtù*;
As in some Irish houses, where things are so so,
One gammon of bacon hangs up for a show: 10
But for eating a rasher of what they take pride in,
They'd as soon think of eating the pan it is fried in.
But hold—let me pause—Don't I hear you pronounce
This tale of the bacon a damnable bounce?
Well, suppose it a bounce—sure a poet may try,   15
By a bounce now and then, to get courage to fly.

But, my Lord, it's no bounce: I protest in my turn,
It's a truth—and your Lordship may ask Mr. Byrne.
To go on with my tale—as I gaz'd on the haunch,
I thought of a friend that was trusty and staunch; 20
So I cut it, and sent it to Reynolds undress'd,
To paint it, or eat it, just as he lik'd best.
Of the neck and the breast I had next to dispose;
'Twas a neck and a breast—that might rival M—r—'s:

But in parting with these I was puzzled again,   25
With the how, and the who, and the where, and the
    when.
There's H—d, and C—y, and H—rth, and H—ff,
I think they love venison—I know they love beef;
There's my countryman H—gg—ns—Oh! let him
    alone,
For making a blunder, or picking a bone.   30
But hang it—to poets who seldom can eat,
Your very good mutton's a very good treat;
Such dainties to them, their health it might hurt,
It's like sending them ruffles, when wanting a shirt.
While thus I debated, in reverie centred,   35
An acquaintance, a friend as he call'd himself, enter'd;
An under-bred, fine-spoken fellow was he,
And he smil'd as he look'd at the venison and me.
" What have we got here?—Why, this is good eating!
Your own, I suppose—or is it in waiting?'   40
' Why, whose should it be?' cried I with a flounce,
' I get these things often;'—but that was a bounce:
' Some lords, my acquaintance, that settle the nation,
Are pleas'd to be kind—but I hate ostentation.'

' If that be the case, then,' cried he, very gay,   45
' I'm glad I have taken this house in my way.
To-morrow you take a poor dinner with me;
No words—I insist on't—precisely at three:
We'll have Johnson, and Burke; all the wits will be
    there;
My acquaintance is slight, or I'd ask my Lord Clare.   50
And now that I think on't, as I am a sinner!
We wanted this venison to make out the dinner.

What say you—a pasty ? it shall, and it must,
And my wife, little Kitty, is famous for crust.
Here, porter !—this venison with me to Mile-end ;   55
No stirring—I beg—my dear friend—my dear friend !
Thus snatching his hat, he brush'd off like the wind,
And the porter and eatables follow'd behind.

Left alone to reflect, having emptied my shelf,
'And nobody with me at sea but myself' ;   60
Though I could not help thinking my gentleman hasty,
Yet Johnson, and Burke, and a good venison pasty,
Were things that I never dislik'd in my life,
Though clogg'd with a coxcomb, and Kitty his wife.
So next day, in due splendour to make my approach,   65
I drove to his door in my own hackney coach.

When come to the place where we all were to dine,
(A chair-lumber'd closet just twelve feet by nine :)
My friend bade me welcome, but struck me quite dumb,
With tidings that Johnson and Burke would not come ; 70
' For I knew it,' he cried, ' both eternally fail,
The one with his speeches, and t'other with Thrale ;
But no matter, I'll warrant we'll make up the party
With two full as clever, and ten times as hearty.
The one is a Scotchman, the other a Jew,   75
They['re] both of them merry and authors like you ;
The one writes the *Snarler*, the other the *Scourge* ;
Some think he writes *Cinna*—he owns to *Panurge*.'
While thus he describ'd them by trade, and by name,
They enter'd, and dinner was serv'd as they came. 80

At the top a fried liver and bacon were seen,
At the bottom was tripe in a swinging tureen ;

At the sides there was spinach and pudding made hot ;
In the middle a place where the pasty—was not.
Now, my Lord, as for tripe, it's my utter aversion, 85
And your bacon I hate like a Turk or a Persian ;
So there I sat stuck, like a horse in a pound,
While the bacon and liver went merrily round.
But what vex'd me most was that d—'d Scottish rogue,
With his long-winded speeches, his smiles and his
    brogue ;   90
And, ' Madam,' quoth he, ' may this bit be my poison,
A prettier dinner I never set eyes on ;
Pray a slice of your liver, though may I be curs'd,
But I've eat of your tripe till I'm ready to burst.'
' The tripe,' quoth the Jew, with his chocolate cheek, 95
' I could dine on this tripe seven days in the week :
I like these here dinners so pretty and small ;
But your friend there, the Doctor, eats nothing at
    all.'
' O—Oh ! ' quoth my friend, ' he'll come on in a trice,
He's keeping a corner for something that's nice : 100
There's a pasty '—' A pasty ! ' repeated the Jew,
' I don't care if I keep a corner for 't too.'
' What the de'il, mon, a pasty ! ' re-echoed the Scot,
' Though splitting, I'll still keep a corner for thot.'
' We'll all keep a corner,' the lady cried out ;   105
' We'll all keep a corner,' was echoed about.
While thus we resolv'd, and the pasty delay'd,
With looks that quite petrified, enter'd the maid ;
A visage so sad, and so pale with affright,
Wak'd Priam in drawing his curtains by night.   110
But we quickly found out, for who could mistake her ?
That she came with some terrible news from the baker :

And so it fell out, for that negligent sloven
Had shut out the pasty on shutting his oven
Sad Philomel thus—but let similes drop—   115
And now that I think on 't, the story may stop.
To be plain, my good Lord, it 's but labour misplac'd
To send such good verses to one of your taste ;
You've got an odd something—a kind of discerning—
A relish—a taste—sicken'd over by learning ;   120
At least, it 's your temper, as very well known,
That you think very slightly of all that 's your own :
So, perhaps, in your habits of thinking amiss,
You may make a mistake, and think slightly of this.

EPITAPH ON THOMAS PARNELL

THIS tomb, inscrib'd to gentle Parnell's name,
May speak our gratitude, but not his fame.
What heart but feels his sweetly-moral lay,
That leads to truth through pleasure's flowery way !
Celestial themes confess'd his tuneful aid ;   5
And Heaven, that lent him genius, was repaid.
Needless to him the tribute we bestow—
The transitory breath of fame below :
More lasting rapture from his works shall rise,
While converts thank their poet in the skies.   10

THE CLOWN'S REPLY

JOHN TROTT was desired by two witty peers
To tell them the reason why asses had ears ?
'An't please you,' quoth John, 'I'm not given to letters,
Nor dare I pretend to know more than my betters ;
Howe'er, from this time I shall ne'er see your graces,   5
As I hope to be saved ! without thinking on asses.'

EPITAPH ON EDWARD PURDON

HERE lies poor Ned Purdon, from misery freed,
    Who long was a bookseller's hack ;
He led such a damnable life in this world,—
    I don't think he'll wish to come back.

EPILOGUE FOR MR. LEE LEWES

HOLD ! Prompter, hold ! a word before your nonsense ;
I'd speak a word or two, to ease my conscience.
My pride forbids it ever should be said,
My heels eclips'd the honours of my head ;
That I found humour in a piebald vest,   5
Or ever thought that jumping was a jest.

(Takes off his mask.)

Whence, and what art thou, visionary birth ?
Nature disowns, and reason scorns thy mirth,
In thy black aspect every passion sleeps,
The joy that dimples, and the woe that weeps.   10
How hast thou fill'd the scene with all thy brood,
Of fools pursuing, and of fools pursu'd !
Whose ins and outs no ray of sense discloses,
Whose only plot it is to break our noses ;
Whilst from below the trap-door Demons rise,   15
And from above the dangling deities ;
And shall I mix in this unhallow'd crew ?
May rosined lightning blast me, if I do !
No—I will act, I'll vindicate the stage :
Shakespeare himself shall feel my tragic rage.   20
Off ! off ! vile trappings ! a new passion reigns !
The madd'ning monarch revels in my veins.
Oh ! for a Richard's voice to catch the theme :
' Give me another horse ! bind up my wounds !—soft—
    'twas but a dream.'
Aye, 'twas but a dream, for now there 's no retreating : 25
If I cease Harlequin, I cease from eating.

'Twas thus that Aesop's stag, a creature blameless,
Yet something vain, like one that shall be nameless,
Once on the margin of a fountain stood,
And cavill'd at his image in the flood.   30
' The deuce confound,' he cries, ' these drumstick
    shanks,
They never have my gratitude nor thanks ;
They're perfectly disgraceful ! strike me dead !
But for a head, yes, yes, I have a head.
How piercing is that eye ! how sleek that brow ! 35
My horns ! I'm told horns are the fashion now.'
Whilst thus he spoke, astonish'd, to his view,
Near, and more near, the hounds and huntsmen drew.
' Hoicks ! hark forward ! ' came thund'ring from
    behind,
He bounds aloft, outstrips the fleeting wind :   40
He quits the woods, and tries the beaten ways ;
He starts, he pants, he takes the circling maze.
At length his silly head, so priz'd before,
Is taught his former folly to deplore ;
Whilst his strong limbs conspire to set him free, 45
And at one bound he saves himself,—like me.

(Taking a jump through the stage door.)

EPILOGUE

INTENDED TO HAVE BEEN SPOKEN FOR 'SHE STOOPS
TO CONQUER'

Enter MRS. BULKLEY, *who curtsies very low as beginning
to speak. Then enter* MISS CATLEY, *who stands full
before her, and curtsies to the audience.*

MRS. BULKLEY.

HOLD, Ma'am, your pardon. What's your business
here ?

MISS CATLEY.

The Epilogue.

MRS. BULKLEY.

The Epilogue ?

MISS CATLEY.

Yes, the Epilogue, my dear.

MRS. BULKLEY.

Sure you mistake, Ma'am. The Epilogue, *I* bring it.

MISS CATLEY.

Excuse me, Ma'am. The Author bid *me* sing it.

Recitative.

Ye beaux and belles, that form this splendid ring, 5
Suspend your conversation while I sing.

MRS. BULKLEY.

Why, sure the girl's beside herself : an Epilogue of
singing,
A hopeful end indeed to such a blest beginning.

Besides, a singer in a comic set !—
Excuse me, Ma'am, I know the etiquette.   10

MISS CATLEY.

What if we leave it to the House ?

MRS. BULKLEY.

The House !—Agreed.

MISS CATLEY.

Agreed.

MRS. BULKLEY.

And she, whose party's largest, shall proceed.
And first I hope, you'll readily agree
I've all the critics and the wits for me.
They, I am sure, will answer my commands :   15
Ye candid-judging few, hold up your hands.
What ! no return ? I find too late, I fear,
That modern judges seldom enter here.

MISS CATLEY.

I'm for a different set.—Old men, whose trade is
Still to gallant and dangle with the ladies ;—   20

Recitative.

Who mump their passion, and who, grimly smiling,
Still thus address the fair with voice beguiling :—

Air—Cotillon.

Turn, my fairest, turn, if ever
    Strephon caught thy ravish'd eye ;
Pity take on your swain so clever,   25
    Who without your aid must die.

Yes, I shall die, hu, hu, hu, hu!
Yes, I must die, ho, ho, ho, ho!

(Da capo.)

MRS. BULKLEY.

Let all the old pay homage to your merit;
Give me the young, the gay, the men of spirit.　　30
Ye travell'd tribe, ye macaroni train,
Of French friseurs, and nosegays, justly vain,
Who take a trip to Paris once a year
To dress, and look like awkward Frenchmen here,
Lend me your hands.—Oh! fatal news to tell:　　35
Their hands are only lent to the Heinel.

MISS CATLEY.

Ay, take your travellers, travellers indeed!
Give me my bonny Scot, that travels from the Tweed.
Where are the chiels? Ah! Ah, I well discern
The smiling looks of each bewitching bairn.　　40

Air—A bonny young lad is my Jockey.

I'll sing to amuse you by night and by day,
And be unco merry when you are but gay;
When you with your bagpipes are ready to play,
My voice shall be ready to carol away
　　With Sandy, and Sawney, and Jockey,　　45
　　With Sawney, and Jarvie, and Jockey.

MRS. BULKLEY.

Ye gamesters, who, so eager in pursuit,
Make but of all your fortune one *va toute*;

E 3

Ye jockey tribe, whose stock of words are few,
' I hold the odds.—Done, done, with you, with you;' 50
Ye barristers, so fluent with grimace,
' My Lord,—your Lordship misconceives the case;'
Doctors, who cough and answer every misfortuner,
' I wish I'd been called in a little sooner:'
Assist my cause with hands and voices hearty; 55
Come, end the contest here, and aid my party.

MISS CATLEY.

Air—Ballinamony.

Ye brave Irish lads, hark away to the crack,
Assist me, I pray, in this woful attack;
For sure I don't wrong you, you seldom are slack,
When the ladies are calling, to blush and hang back; 60
      For you're always polite and attentive,
      Still to amuse us inventive,
      And death is your only preventive:
      Your hands and your voices for me.

MRS. BULKLEY.

Well, Madam, what if, after all this sparring, 65
We both agree, like friends, to end our jarring?

MISS CATLEY.

And that our friendship may remain unbroken,
What if we leave the Epilogue unspoken?

MRS. BULKLEY.

Agreed.

MISS CATLEY.

Agreed.

MRS. BULKLEY.

And now with late repentance,
Un-epilogued the Poet waits his sentence.   70
Condemn the stubborn fool who can't submit
To thrive by flattery, though he starves by wit.

(*Exeunt.*)

EPILOGUE

INTENDED TO HAVE BEEN SPOKEN FOR 'SHE STOOPS TO CONQUER'

THERE is a place, so Ariosto sings,
A treasury for lost and missing things ;
Lost human wits have places there assign'd them,
And they, who lose their senses, there may find them.
But where's this place, this storehouse of the age ? 5
The Moon, says he :—but *I* affirm the Stage :
At least in many things, I think, I see
His lunar, and our mimic world agree.
Both shine at night, for, but at Foote's alone,
We scarce exhibit till the sun goes down.   10
Both prone to change, no settled limits fix,
And sure the folks of both are lunatics.
But in this parallel my best pretence is,
That mortals visit both to find their senses.
To this strange spot, Rakes, Macaronies, Cits,   15
Come thronging to collect their scatter'd wits.
The gay coquette, who ogles all the day,
Comes here at night, and goes a prude away.
Hither the affected city dame advancing,
Who sighs for operas, and dotes on dancing,   20
Taught by our art her ridicule to pause on,
Quits the *Ballet*, and calls for *Nancy Dawson*.
The Gamester too, whose wit's all high or low,
Oft risks his fortune on one desperate throw,
Comes here to saunter, having made his bets,   25
Finds his lost senses out, and pay his debts.

The Mohawk too—with angry phrases stored,
As ' D— —, Sir,' and ' Sir, I wear a sword ';
Here lesson'd for a while, and hence retreating,
Goes out, affronts his man, and takes a beating. 30
Here come the sons of scandal and of news,
But find no sense—for they had none to lose.
Of all the tribe here wanting an adviser
Our Author's the least likely to grow wiser ;
Has he not seen how you your favour place, 35
On sentimental Queens and Lords in lace ?
Without a star, a coronet or garter,
How can the piece expect or hope for quarter ?
No high-life scenes, no sentiment :—the creature
Still stoops among the low to copy nature. 40
Yes, he's far gone :—and yet some pity fix,
The English laws forbid to punish lunatics.

THE CAPTIVITY

AN

ORATORIO

THE PERSONS.

FIRST ISRAELITISH PROPHET.
SECOND ISRAELITISH PROPHET.
ISRAELITISH WOMAN.
FIRST CHALDEAN PRIEST.
SECOND CHALDEAN PRIEST.
CHALDEAN WOMAN.
CHORUS OF YOUTHS AND VIRGINS.

SCENE—The Banks of the River Euphrates, near Babylon.

THE CAPTIVITY

ACT I—Scene I.

Israelites sitting on the Banks of the Euphrates.

FIRST PROPHET.

RECITATIVE.

Ye captive tribes, that hourly work and weep
Where flows Euphrates murmuring to the deep,
Suspend awhile the task, the tear suspend,
And turn to God, your Father and your Friend.
Insulted, chain'd, and all the world a foe,   5
Our God alone is all we boast below.

FIRST PROPHET.

AIR.

Our God is all we boast below,
    To him we turn our eyes;
And every added weight of woe
    Shall make our homage rise.   10

SECOND PROPHET.

And though no temple richly drest,
    Nor sacrifice is here;
We'll make his temple in our breast,
    And offer up a tear.
        [*The first stanza repeated by the Chorus.*

SECOND PROPHET.

RECITATIVE.

That strain once more ; it bids remembrance rise,
And brings my long-lost country to mine eyes.   16
Ye fields of Sharon, dress'd in flow'ry pride,
Ye plains where Jordan rolls its glassy tide,
Ye hills of Lebanon, with cedars crown'd,
Ye Gilead groves, that fling perfumes around,   20
These hills how sweet ! those plains how wond'rous
    fair,
But sweeter still, when Heaven was with us there !

AIR.

O Memory, thou fond deceiver,
    Still importunate and vain ;
To former joys recurring ever,   25
    And turning all the past to pain ;

Hence, intruder, most distressing,
    Seek the happy and the free :
The wretch who wants each other blessing,
    Ever wants a friend in thee.   30

FIRST PROPHET.

RECITATIVE.

Yet, why complain ? What, though by bonds confin'd,
Should bonds repress the vigour of the mind ?
Have we not cause for triumph when we see
Ourselves alone from idol-worship free ?
Are not this very morn those feasts begun,   35
Where prostrate error hails the rising sun ?
Do not our tyrant lords this day ordain
For superstitious rites and mirth profane ?

And should we mourn ? should coward virtue fly,
When impious folly rears her front on high ?   40
No ; rather let us triumph still the more,
And as our fortune sinks, our wishes soar.

AIR.

The triumphs that on vice attend
Shall ever in confusion end ;
The good man suffers but to gain,   45
And every virtue springs from pain :

As aromatic plants bestow
No spicy fragrance while they grow ;
But crush'd, or trodden to the ground,
Diffuse their balmy sweets around.   50

SECOND PROPHET.

RECITATIVE.

But hush, my sons, our tyrant lords are near;
The sounds of barb'rous pleasure strike mine ear ;
Triumphant music floats along the vale;
Near, nearer still, it gathers on the gale ;
The growing sound their swift approach declares ;—
Desist, my sons, nor mix the strain with theirs.   56

Enter CHALDEAN PRIESTS *attended.*

FIRST PRIEST.

AIR.

Come on, my companions, the triumph display;
    Let rapture the minutes employ ;
The sun calls us out on this festival day,
    And our monarch partakes in the joy.   60

SECOND PRIEST.

Like the sun, our great monarch all rapture supplies,
   Both similar blessings bestow ;
The sun with his splendour illumines the skies,
   And our monarch enlivens below.

A CHALDEAN WOMAN.

AIR.

Haste, ye sprightly sons of pleasure ;   65
Love presents the fairest treasure,
   Leave all other joys for me.

A CHALDEAN ATTENDANT.

Or rather, Love's delights despising,
Haste to raptures ever rising :
   Wine shall bless the brave and free.   70

FIRST PRIEST.

Wine and beauty thus inviting,
Each to different joys exciting,
   Whither shall my choice incline ?

SECOND PRIEST.

I'll waste no longer thought in choosing ;
But, neither this nor that refusing,   75
   I'll make them both together mine.

RECITATIVE.

But whence, when joy should brighten o'er the land,
This sullen gloom in Judah's captive band ?
Ye sons of Judah, why the lute unstrung ?
Or why those harps on yonder willows hung ?   80
Come, take the lyre, and pour the strain along,
The day demands it ; sing us Sion's song.

Dismiss your griefs, and join our warbling choir,
For who like you can wake the sleeping lyre ?

SECOND PROPHET.

Bow'd down with chains, the scorn of all mankind,
To want, to toil, and every ill consign'd,   86
Is this a time to bid us raise the strain,
Or mix in rites that Heaven regards with pain ?
No, never ! May this hand forget each art
That speeds the power of music to the heart,   90
Ere I forget the land that gave me birth,
Or join with sounds profane its sacred mirth !

FIRST PRIEST.

Insulting slaves ! if gentler methods fail,
The whips and angry tortures shall prevail.

[Exeunt Chaldeans

FIRST PROPHET.

Why, let them come, one good remains to cheer ;
We fear the Lord, and know no other fear.   96

CHORUS.

Can whips or tortures hurt the mind
On God's supporting breast reclin'd ?
Stand fast, and let our tyrants see
That fortitude is victory.   *[Exeunt.*

ACT II.

Scene as before.

CHORUS OF ISRAELITES.

O PEACE of mind, angelic guest !
Thou soft companion of the breast !
    Dispense thy balmy store.
Wing all our thoughts to reach the skies,
Till earth, receding from our eyes,   5
    Shall vanish as we soar.

FIRST PRIEST.

RECITATIVE.

No more ! Too long has justice been delay'd,
The king's commands must fully be obey'd ;
Compliance with his will your peace secures,
Praise but our gods, and every good is yours.   10
But if, rebellious to his high command,
You spurn the favours offer'd from his hand,
Think, timely think, what terrors are behind ;
Reflect, nor tempt to rage the royal mind.

SECOND PRIEST.

AIR.

Fierce is the whirlwind howling   15
    O'er Afric's sandy plain,
And fierce the tempest rolling
    Along the furrow'd main :
        But storms that fly,
        To rend the sky,   20

To the last moment of his breath
  On Hope the wretch relies
And even the pang preceding death
  Bids Expectation rise.

Hope like the gleaming taper's light
  Adorns and cheers our way
And stile as darker grows the night
  Emits a brighter ray

  Oliver Goldsmith

October 31st 1764.

GOLDSMITH'S AUTOGRAPH

(STANZAS FROM 'THE CAPTIVITY')

Every ill presaging,
  Less dreadful show
  To worlds below
Than angry monarch's raging.

ISRAELITISH WOMAN.

RECITATIVE.

Ah, me ! what angry terrors round us grow ;   25
How shrinks my soul to meet the threaten'd blow !
Ye prophets, skill'd in Heaven's eternal truth,
Forgive my sex's fears, forgive my youth !
If, shrinking thus, when frowning power appears,
I wish for life, and yield me to my fears.   30
Let us one hour, one little hour obey ;
To-morrow's tears may wash our stains away.

AIR.

To the last moment of his breath
  On hope the wretch relies ;
And e'en the pang preceding death   35
  Bids expectation rise.

Hope, like the gleaming taper's light,
  Adorns and cheers our way ;
And still, as darker grows the night,
  Emits a brighter ray.   40

SECOND PRIEST.

RECITATIVE.

Why this delay ? at length for joy prepare ;
I read your looks, and see compliance there.
Come on, and bid the warbling rapture rise,
Our monarch's fame the noblest theme supplies.

Begin, ye captive bands, and strike the lyre,   45
The time, the theme, the place, and all conspire.

CHALDEAN WOMAN.

AIR.

See the ruddy morning smiling,
Hear the grove to bliss beguiling ;
Zephyrs through the woodland playing,
Streams along the valley straying.   50

FIRST PRIEST.

While these a constant revel keep,
Shall Reason only teach to weep ?
Hence, intruder ! we'll pursue
Nature, a better guide than you.

SECOND PRIEST.

Every moment, as it flows,   55
Some peculiar pleasure owes ;
Then let us, providently wise,
Seize the debtor as it flies.

Think not to-morrow can repay
The pleasures that we lose to-day ;   60
To-morrow's most unbounded store
Can but pay its proper score.

FIRST PRIEST.

RECITATIVE.

But hush ! see, foremost of the captive choir,
The master-prophet grasps his full-ton'd lyre.
Mark where he sits, with executing art,   65
Feels for each tone, and speeds it to the heart ;

See how prophetic rapture fills his form,
Awful as clouds that nurse the growing storm ;
And now his voice, accordant to the string,
Prepares our monarch's victories to sing.   70

FIRST PROPHET.

AIR.

From north, from south, from east, from west,
    Conspiring nations come ;
Tremble, thou vice-polluted breast ;
    Blasphemers, all be dumb.

The tempest gathers all around,   75
    On Babylon it lies ;
Down with her ! down—down to the ground ;
    She sinks, she groans, she dies.

SECOND PROPHET.

Down with her, Lord, to lick the dust,
    Ere yonder setting sun ;   80
Serve her as she hath served the just !
    'Tis fixed—it shall be done.

FIRST PRIEST.

RECITATIVE.

No more ! when slaves thus insolent presume,
The king himself shall judge, and fix their doom.
Unthinking wretches ! have not you, and all,   85
Beheld our power in Zedekiah's fall ?
To yonder gloomy dungeon turn your eyes ;
See where dethron'd your captive monarch lies,
Depriv'd of sight and rankling in his chain ;   89
See where he mourns his friends and children slain.

Yet know, ye slaves, that still remain behind
More ponderous chains, and dungeons more confin'd.

CHORUS OF ALL.

Arise, all potent ruler, rise,
    And vindicate thy people's cause;
Till every tongue in every land   95
    Shall offer up unfeign'd applause.

[*Exeunt.*

ACT III.

Scene as before.

FIRST PRIEST.

RECITATIVE.

YES, my companions, Heaven's decrees are past,
And our fix'd empire shall for ever last;
In vain the madd'ning prophet threatens woe,
In vain rebellion aims her secret blow;
Still shall our fame and growing power be spread,
And still our vengeance crush the traitor's head. 6

AIR.

Coeval with man
Our empire began,
And never shall fail
Till ruin shakes all;   10
When ruin shakes all,
Then shall Babylon fall.

FIRST PROPHET.

RECITATIVE.

'Tis thus that pride triumphant rears the head,
A little while, and all their power is fled;
But ha! what means yon sadly plaintive train, 15
That this way slowly bend along the plain?
And now, methinks, to yonder bank they bear
A palled corse, and rest the body there.
Alas! too well mine eyes indignant trace
The last remains of Judah's royal race: 20
Our monarch falls, and now our fears are o'er,
Unhappy Zedekiah is no more!

AIR.

Ye wretches who, by fortune's hate,
  In want and sorrow groan;
Come ponder his severer fate, 25
  And learn to bless your own.

You vain, whom youth and pleasure guide,
  Awhile the bliss suspend;
Like yours, his life began in pride,
  Like his, your lives shall end. 30

SECOND PROPHET.

RECITATIVE.

Behold his wretched corse with sorrow worn,
His squalid limbs with pond'rous fetters torn;
Those eyeless orbs that shock with ghastly glare,
Those ill-becoming rags—that matted hair!
And shall not Heaven for this its terrors show, 35
Grasp the red bolt, and lay the guilty low?

How long, how long, Almighty God of all,
Shall wrath vindictive threaten ere it fall!

ISRAELITISH WOMAN.

AIR.

As panting flies the hunted hind,
   Where brooks refreshing stray;   40
And rivers through the valley wind,
   That stop the hunter's way:

Thus we, O Lord, alike distrest,
   For streams of mercy long;
Those streams which cheer the sore opprest,
   And overwhelm the strong.   46

FIRST PROPHET.

RECITATIVE.

But, whence that shout? Good heavens! amazement
   all!
See yonder tower just nodding to the fall:
See where an army covers all the ground,
Saps the strong wall, and pours destruction round;
The ruin smokes, destruction pours along;   51
How low the great, how feeble are the strong!
The foe prevails, the lofty walls recline—
O God of hosts, the victory is thine!

CHORUS OF ISRAELITES.

Down with them, Lord, to lick the dust;   55
   Thy vengeance be begun:
Serve them as they have serv'd the just,
   And let thy will be done.

FIRST PRIEST.

FIRST PRIEST.

RECITATIVE.

All, all is lost. The Syrian army fails,
Cyrus, the conqueror of the world, prevails,   60
The ruin smokes, the torrent pours along ;
How low the proud, how feeble are the strong !
Save us, O Lord ! to thee, though late, we pray,
And give repentance but an hour's delay.

FIRST AND SECOND PRIEST.

AIR.

Thrice happy, who in happy hour   65
  To Heaven their praise bestow,
And own his all-consuming power
  Before they feel the blow !

FIRST PROPHET.

RECITATIVE.

Now, now 's our time ! ye wretches bold and blind,
Brave but to God, and cowards to mankind,   70
Too late you seek that power unsought before,
Your wealth, your pride, your kingdom, are no more.

AIR.

O Lucifer, thou son of morn,
  Alike of Heaven and man the foe ;
    Heaven, men, and all,   75
    Now press thy fall,
  And sink thee lowest of the low.

FIRST PROPHET.

O Babylon, how art thou fallen!
  Thy fall more dreadful from delay!
    Thy streets forlorn   80
    To wilds shall turn,
  Where toads shall pant, and vultures prey.

SECOND PROPHET.

RECITATIVE.

Such be her fate.   But listen! from afar
The clarion's note proclaims the finish'd war!
Cyrus, our great restorer, is at hand,   85
And this way leads his formidable band.
Give, give your songs of Sion to the wind,
And hail the benefactor of mankind:
He comes pursuant to divine decree,
To chain the strong, and set the captive free.   90

CHORUS OF YOUTHS.

Rise to transports past expressing,
  Sweeter from remember'd woes;
Cyrus comes, our wrongs redressing,
  Comes to give the world repose.

CHORUS OF VIRGINS.

Cyrus comes, the world redressing,   95
  Love and pleasure in his train;
Comes to heighten every blessing,
  Comes to soften every pain.

SEMI-CHORUS.

Hail to him with mercy reigning,
  Skilled in every peaceful art ;   100
Who from bonds our limbs unchaining,
  Only binds the willing heart.

THE LAST CHORUS.

But chief to Thee, our God, defender, friend,
  Let praise be given to all eternity ;
O Thou, without beginning, without end,   105
  Let us, and all, begin and end, in Thee !

VERSES IN REPLY TO AN INVITATION TO DINNER AT DR. BAKER'S

'This *is* a poem ! This *is* a copy of verses !'

YOUR mandate I got,
You may all go to pot ;
Had your senses been right,
You'd have sent before night ;
As I hope to be saved,   5
I put off being shaved ;
For I could not make bold,
While the matter was cold,
To meddle in suds,
Or to put on my duds ;   10
So tell Horneck and Nesbitt,
And Baker and his bit,
And Kauffmann beside,
And the Jessamy Bride,
With the rest of the crew,   15
The Reynoldses two,
Little Comedy's face,
And the Captain in lace,
(By-the-bye you may tell him,
I have something to sell him ;   20
Of use I insist,
When he comes to enlist.
Your worships must know
That a few days ago,
An order went out,   25
For the foot guards so stout

To wear tails in high taste,
Twelve inches at least :
Now I've got him a scale
To measure each tail,   30
To lengthen a short tail,
And a long one to curtail.)—
    Yet how can I when vext,
Thus stray from my text ?
Tell each other to rue   35
Your Devonshire crew,
For sending so late
To one of my state.
But 'tis Reynolds's way
From wisdom to stray,   40
And Angelica's whim
To be frolick like him,
But, alas ! your good worships, how could they be wiser,
When both have been spoil'd in to-day's *Advertiser* ?

                OLIVER GOLDSMITH.

LETTER IN PROSE AND VERSE TO
MRS. BUNBURY

MADAM,

I read your letter with all that allowance which
critical candour could require, but after all find so much
to object to, and so much to raise my indignation, that I
cannot help giving it a serious answer.

I am not so ignorant, Madam, as not to see there are
many sarcasms contained in it, and solecisms also.
(Solecism is a word that comes from the town of Soleis in
Attica, among the Greeks, built by Solon, and applied as
we use the word Kidderminster for curtains, from a town
also of that name ;—but this is learning you have no
taste for !)—I say, Madam, there are sarcasms in it, and
solecisms also. But not to seem an ill-natured critic,
I'll take leave to quote your own words, and give you
my remarks upon them as they occur. You begin as
follows :—

> 'I hope, my good Doctor, you soon will be here,
> And your spring-velvet coat very smart will appear,
> To open our ball the first day of the year.'

Pray, Madam, where did you ever find the epithet
'good,' applied to the title of Doctor ? Had you called
me 'learned Doctor,' or 'grave Doctor,' or 'noble Doctor,'
it might be allowable, because they belong to the profession. But, not to cavil at trifles, you talk of my
'spring-velvet coat,' and advise me to wear it the first
day in the year,—that is, in the middle of winter !—a
spring-velvet in the middle of winter !!! That would be

a solecism indeed ! and yet, to increase the inconsistence, in another part of your letter you call me a beau. Now, on one side or other, you must be wrong. If I am a beau, I can never think of wearing a spring-velvet in winter : and if I am not a beau, why then, that explains itself. But let me go on to your two next strange lines :—

> 'And bring with you a wig, that is modish and gay,
> To dance with the girls that are makers of hay.'

The absurdity of making hay at Christmas, you yourself seem sensible of : you say your sister will laugh ; and so indeed she well may ! The Latins have an expression for a contemptuous sort of laughter, ' Naso contemnere adunco ' ; that is, to laugh with a crooked nose. She may laugh at you in the manner of the ancients if she thinks fit. But now I come to the most extraordinary of all extraordinary propositions, which is, to take your and your sister's advice in playing at loo. The presumption of the offer raises my indignation beyond the bounds of prose ; it inspires me at once with verse and resentment. I take advice ! and from whom ? You shall hear.

First let me suppose, what may shortly be true,
The company set, and the word to be, Loo ;
All smirking, and pleasant, and big with adventure,
And ogling the stake which is fix'd in the centre.
Round and round go the cards, while I inwardly damn   5
At never once finding a visit from Pam.
I lay down my stake, apparently cool,
While the harpies about me all pocket the pool.

I fret in my gizzard, yet, cautious and sly,
I wish all my friends may be bolder than I :   10
Yet still they sit snug, not a creature will aim
By losing their money to venture at fame.
'Tis in vain that at niggardly caution I scold,
'Tis in vain that I flatter the brave and the bold :
All play their own way, and they think me an ass,—   15
' What does Mrs. Bunbury ? ' ' I, Sir ? I pass.'
' Pray what does Miss Horneck ? take courage, come
        do,'—
' Who, I ? let me see, Sir, why I must pass too.'
Mr. Bunbury frets, and I fret like the devil,
To see them so cowardly, lucky, and civil.   20
Yet still I sit snug, and continue to sigh on,
Till made by my losses as bold as a lion,
I venture at all,—while my avarice regards
The whole pool as my own—' Come, give me five
        cards.'
' Well done ! ' cry the ladies ; ' Ah, Doctor, that's
        good !   25
The pool's very rich—ah ! the Doctor is loo'd ! '
Thus foil'd in my courage, on all sides perplex'd,
I ask for advice from the lady that's next :
' Pray, Ma'am, be so good as to give your advice ;
Don't you think the best way is to venture for 't twice?' 30
' I advise,' cries the lady, ' to try it, I own.—
Ah ! the Doctor is loo'd ! Come, Doctor, put down.'
Thus, playing, and playing, I still grow more eager,
And so bold, and so bold, I'm at last a bold beggar.
Now, ladies, I ask, if law-matters you're skill'd in,   35
Whether crimes such as yours should not come before
        Fielding ?

For giving advice that is not worth a straw,
May well be call'd picking of pockets in law;
And picking of pockets, with which I now charge ye,
Is, by quinto Elizabeth, Death without Clergy.   40
What justice, when both to the Old Bailey brought!
By the gods, I'll enjoy it; though 'tis but in thought!
Both are plac'd at the bar, with all proper decorum,
With bunches of fennel, and nosegays before 'em;
Both cover their faces with mobs and all that ;   45
But the judge bids them, angrily, take off their hat.
When uncover'd, a buzz of enquiry runs round,—
' Pray what are their crimes ? '—' They've been pilfering
    found.'
' But, pray, whom have they pilfer'd ? '—' A Doctor,
    I hear.'
'What, yon solemn-faced, odd-looking man that stands
    near ! '   50
'The same.'—'What a pity! how does it surprise one !
Two handsomer culprits I never set eyes on ! '
Then their friends all come round me with cringing and
    leering,
To melt me to pity, and soften my swearing.
First Sir Charles advances with phrases well strung,   55
'Consider, dear Doctor, the girls are but young.'
' The younger the worse,' I return him again,
'It shows that their habits are all dyed in grain.'
'But then they're so handsome, one's bosom it grieves.'
'What signifies *handsome*, when people are thieves ? '   60
'But where is your justice ? their cases are hard.'
'What signifies *justice* ? I want the *reward*.

There's the parish of Edmonton offers forty pounds;

there's the parish of St. Leonard, Shoreditch, offers forty
pounds; there's the parish of Tyburn, from the Hog-in-
the-Pound to St. Giles's watchhouse, offers forty pounds,
—I shall have all that if I convict them!'—

'But consider their case,—it may yet be your own!
And see how they kneel! Is your heart made of stone?'
This moves:—so at last I agree to relent,   65
For ten pounds in hand, and ten pounds to be spent.

I challenge you all to answer this: I tell you, you cannot.
It cuts deep;—but now for the rest of the letter: and
next—but I want room—so I believe I shall battle the
rest out at Barton some day next week.

> I don't value you all!
>   O. G.

VIDA'S GAME OF CHESS

TRANSLATED

ARMIES of box that sportively engage
And mimic real battles in their rage,
Pleased I recount ; how, smit with glory's charms,
Two mighty Monarchs met in adverse arms,
Sable and white ; assist me to explore,   5
Ye Serian Nymphs, what ne'er was sung before.
No path appears : yet resolute I stray
Where youth undaunted bids me force my way.
O'er rocks and cliffs while I the task pursue,
Guide me, ye Nymphs, with your unerring clue.   10
For you the rise of this diversion know,
You first were pleased in Italy to show
This studious sport ; from Scacchis was its name,
The pleasing record of your Sister's fame.

When Jove through Ethiopia's parch'd extent   15
To grace the nuptials of old Ocean went,
Each god was there ; and mirth and joy around
To shores remote diffused their happy sound.
Then when their hunger and their thirst no more
Claim'd their attention, and the feast was o'er ;   20
Ocean, with pastime to divert the thought,
Commands a painted table to be brought.
Sixty-four spaces fill the chequer'd square ;
Eight in each rank eight equal limits share.

Alike their form, but different are their dyes,   25
They fade alternate, and alternate rise,
White after black; such various stains as those
The shelving backs of tortoises disclose.
Then to the gods that mute and wondering sate,
You see (says he) the field prepared for fate.   30
Here will the little armies please your sight,
With adverse colours hurrying to the fight:
On which so oft, with silent sweet surprise,
The Nymphs and Nereids used to feast their eyes,
And all the neighbours of the hoary deep,   35
When calm the sea, and winds were lull'd asleep
But see, the mimic heroes tread the board;
He said, and straightway from an urn he pour'd
The sculptured box, that neatly seem'd to ape
The graceful figure of a human shape :—   40
Equal the strength and number of each foe,
Sixteen appear'd like jet, sixteen like snow.
As their shape varies various is the name,
Different their posts, nor is their strength the same.
There might you see two Kings with equal pride 45
Gird on their arms, their Consorts by their side;
Here the Foot-warriors glowing after fame,
There prancing Knights and dexterous Archers came
And Elephants, that on their backs sustain
Vast towers of war, and fill and shake the plain. 50
    And now both hosts, preparing for the storm
Of adverse battle, their encampments form.
In the fourth space, and on the farthest line,
Directly opposite the Monarchs shine;
The swarthy on white ground, on sable stands   55
The silver King; and thence they send commands.

Nearest to these the Queens exert their might;
One the left side, and t'other guards the right:
Where each, by her respective armour known.
Chooses the colour that is like her own.　　　　60
Then the young Archers, two that snowy-white
Bend the tough yew, and two as black as night;
(Greece call'd them Mars's favourites heretofore,
From their delight in war, and thirst of gore).
These on each side the Monarch and his Queen　65
Surround obedient; next to these are seen
The crested Knights in golden armour gay;
Their steeds by turns curvet, or snort or neigh.
In either army on each distant wing
Two mighty Elephants their castles bring,　　　70
Bulwarks immense! and then at last combine
Eight of the Foot to form the second line,
The vanguard to the King and Queen; from far
Prepared to open all the fate of war.
So moved the boxen hosts, each double-lined,　75
Their different colours floating in the wind:
As if an army of the Gauls should go,
With their white standards, o'er the Alpine snow
To meet in rigid fight on scorching sands
The sun-burnt Moors and Memnon's swarthy
　　　　bands.　　　　　　　　　　　　　　　80
　Then Father Ocean thus; you see them here,
Celestial powers, what troops, what camps appear.
Learn now the sev'ral orders of the fray,
For e'en these arms their stated laws obey.
To lead the fight, the Kings from all their bands
Choose whom they please to bear their great com-
　　　　mands.　　　　　　　　　　　　　　86

Should a black hero first to battle go,
Instant a white one guards against the blow ;
But only one at once can charge or shun the foe.
Their gen'ral purpose on one scheme is bent,   90
So to besiege the King within the tent,
That there remains no place by subtle flight
From danger free ; and that decides the fight.
Meanwhile, howe'er, the sooner to destroy
Th' imperial Prince, remorseless they employ   95
Their swords in blood ; and whosoever dare
Oppose their vengeance, in the ruin share.
Fate thins their camp ; the parti-coloured field
Widens apace, as they o'ercome or yield,
But the proud victor takes the captive's post ;   100
There fronts the fury of th' avenging host
One single shock : and (should he ward the blow),
May then retire at pleasure from the foe.
The Foot alone (so their harsh laws ordain)
When they proceed can ne'er return again.   105
  But neither all rush on alike to prove
The terror of their arms : the Foot must move
Directly on, and but a single square ;
Yet may these heroes, when they first prepare
To mix in combat on the bloody mead,   110
Double their sally, and two steps proceed ;
But when they wound, their swords they subtly
    guide
With aim oblique, and slanting pierce his side.
But the great Indian beasts, whose backs sustain
Vast turrets arm'd, when on the redd'ning plain 115
They join in all the terror of the fight,
Forward or backward, to the left or right,

Run furious, and impatient of confine
Scour through the field, and threat the farthest line.
Yet must they ne'er obliquely aim their blows ;
That only manner is allow'd to those   121
Whom Mars has favour'd most, who bend the stub-
    born bows.

These glancing sidewards in a straight career,
Yet each confin'd to their respective sphere,
Or white or black, can send th' unerring dart   125
Wing'd with swift death to pierce through ev'ry part.
The fiery steed, regardless of the reins,
Comes prancing on ; but sullenly disdains
The path direct, and boldly wheeling round,
Leaps o'er a double space at ev'ry bound :   130
And shifts from white or black to diff'rent colour'd
    ground.

But the fierce Queen, whom dangers ne'er dismay,
The strength and terror of the bloody day,
In a straight line spreads her destruction wide,
To left or right, before, behind, aside.   135
Yet may she never with a circling course
Sweep to the battle like the fretful Horse ;
But unconfin'd may at her pleasure stray,
If neither friend nor foe block up the way ;
For to o'erleap a warrior, 'tis decreed   140
Those only dare who curb the snorting steed.
With greater caution and majestic state
The warlike Monarchs in the scene of fate
Direct their motions, since for these appear
Zealous each hope, and anxious ev'ry fear.   145
While the King 's safe, with resolution stern
They clasp their arms ; but should a sudden turn

Make him a captive, instantly they yield,
Resolved to share his fortune in the field.
He moves on slow ; with reverence profound   150
His faithful troops encompass him around,
And oft, to break some instant fatal scheme,
Rush to their fates, their sov'reign to redeem ;
While he, unanxious where to wound the foe,
Need only shift and guard against a blow.   155
But none, however, can presume t' appear
Within his reach, but must his vengeance fear ;
For he on ev'ry side his terror throws ;
But when he changes from his first repose,
Moves but one step, most awfully sedate,   160
Or idly roving, or intent on fate.
These are the sev'ral and establish'd laws :
Now see how each maintains his bloody cause.

Here paused the god, but (since whene'er they wage
War here on earth the gods themselves engage   165
In mutual battle as they hate or love,
And the most stubborn war is oft above),
Almighty Jove commands the circling train
Of gods from fav'ring either to abstain,
And let the fight be silently survey'd ;   170
And added solemn threats if disobey'd.
Then call'd he Phœbus from among the Powers
And subtle Hermes, whom in softer hours
Fair Maia bore : youth wanton'd in their face ;
Both in life's bloom, both shone with equal grace.
Hermes as yet had never wing'd his feet ;   176
As yet Apollo in his radiant seat
Had never driv'n his chariot through the air,
Known by his bow alone and golden hair.

These Jove commission'd to attempt the fray,   180
And rule the sportive military day ;
Bid them agree which party each maintains,
And promised a reward that 's worth their pains.
The greater took their seats ; on either hand
Respectful the less gods in order stand,   185
But careful not to interrupt their play,
By hinting when t' advance or run away.

   Then they examine, who shall first proceed
To try their courage, and their army lead.
Chance gave it for the White, that he should go   190
First with a brave defiance to the foe.
Awhile he ponder'd which of all his train
Should bear his first commission o'er the plain ;
And then determined to begin the scene
With him that stood before to guard the Queen.   195
He took a double step : with instant care
Does the black Monarch in his turn prepare
The adverse champion, and with stern command
Bid him repel the charge with equal hand.
There front to front, the midst of all the field,   200
With furious threats their shining arms they wield ;
Yet vain the conflict, neither can prevail
While in one path each other they assail.
On ev'ry side to their assistance fly
Their fellow soldiers, and with strong supply   205
Crowd to the battle, but no bloody stain
Tinctures their armour ; sportive in the plain
Mars plays awhile, and in excursion slight
Harmless they sally forth, or wait the fight.

   But now the swarthy Foot, that first appear'd   210
To front the foe, his pond'rous jav'lin rear'd

Leftward aslant, and a pale warrior slays,
Spurns him aside, and boldly takes his place.
Unhappy youth, his danger not to spy !
Instant he fell, and triumph'd but to die.   215
At this the sable King with prudent care
Removed his station from the middle square,
And slow retiring to the farthest ground,
There safely lurk'd, with troops entrench'd around.
Then from each quarter to the war advance   220
The furious Knights, and poise the trembling lance :
By turns they rush, by turns the victors yield,
Heaps of dead Foot choke up the crimson'd field :
They fall unable to retreat ; around
The clang of arms and iron hoofs resound.   225
    But while young Phœbus pleased himself to view
His furious Knight destroy the vulgar crew,
Sly Hermes long'd t' attempt with secret aim
Some noble act of more exalted fame.
For this, he inoffensive pass'd along   230
Through ranks of Foot, and midst the trembling throng
Sent his left Horse, that free without confine
Rov'd o'er the plain, upon some great design
Against the King himself.   At length he stood,
And having fix'd his station as he would,   235
Threaten'd at once with instant fate the King
And th' Indian beast that guarded the right wing.
Apollo sigh'd, and hast'ning to relieve
The straiten'd Monarch, griev'd that he must leave
His martial Elephant expos'd to fate,   240
And view'd with pitying eyes his dang'rous state.
First in his thoughts however was his care
To save his King, whom to the neighbouring square

On the right hand, he snatch'd with trembling flight ;
At this with fury springs the sable Knight,   245
Drew his keen sword, and rising to the blow,
Sent the great Indian brute to shades below.
O fatal loss ! for none except the Queen
Spreads such a terror through the bloody scene.
Yet shall you ne'er unpunish'd boast your prize,
The Delian god with stern resentment cries ;   251
And wedg'd him round with Foot, and pour'd in
          fresh supplies.
Thus close besieg'd trembling he cast his eye
Around the plain, but saw no shelter nigh,
No way for flight ; for here the Queen oppos'd,   255
The Foot in phalanx there the passage clos'd :
At length he fell ; yet not unpleas'd with fate,
Since victim to a Queen's vindictive hate.
With grief and fury burns the whiten'd host,
One of their Tow'rs thus immaturely lost.   260
As when a bull has in contention stern
Lost his right horn, with double vengeance burn
His thoughts for war, with blood he 's cover'd o'er,
And the woods echo to his dismal roar,
So look'd the flaxen host, when angry fate   265
O'erturn'd the Indian bulwark of their state.
Fired at this great success, with double rage
Apollo hurries on his troops t' engage,
For blood and havoc wild ; and, while he leads
His troops thus careless, loses both his steeds :   270
For if some adverse warriors were o'erthrown,
He little thought what dangers threat his own.
But slyer Hermes with observant eyes
March'd slowly cautious, and at distance spies

What moves must next succeed, what dangers next
    arise.   275
Often would he, the stately Queen to snare,
The slender Foot to front her arms prepare,
And to conceal his scheme he sighs and feigns
Such a wrong step would frustrate all his pains.
Just then an Archer, from the right-hand view,   280
At the pale Queen his arrow boldly drew,
Unseen by Phœbus, who, with studious thought,
From the left side a vulgar hero brought.
But tender Venus, with a pitying eye,
Viewing the sad destruction that was nigh,   285
Wink'd upon Phœbus (for the Goddess sat
By chance directly opposite) ; at that
Roused in an instant, young Apollo threw
His eyes around the field his troops to view :
Perceiv'd the danger, and with sudden fright   290
Withdrew the Foot that he had sent to fight,
And sav'd his trembling Queen by seasonable
    flight.
But Maia's son with shouts fill'd all the coast :
The Queen, he cried, the important Queen is lost.
Phœbus, howe'er, resolving to maintain   295
What he had done, bespoke the heavenly train.

    What mighty harm, in sportive mimic flight,
Is it to set a little blunder right,
When no preliminary rule debarr'd ?
If you henceforward, Mercury, would guard   300
Against such practice, let us make the law :
And whosoe'er shall first to battle draw,
Or white, or black, remorseless let him go
At all events, and dare the angry foe.

He said, and this opinion pleased around :   305
Jove turn'd aside, and on his daughter frown'd,
Unmark'd by Hermes, who, with strange surprise,
Fretted and foam'd, and roll'd his ferret eyes,
And but with great reluctance could refrain
From dashing at a blow all off the plain.   310
Then he resolved to interweave deceits,—
To carry on the war by tricks and cheats.
Instant he call'd an Archer from the throng,
And bid him like the courser wheel along :
Bounding he springs, and threats the pallid Queen,
The fraud, however, was by Phœbus seen ;   316
He smiled, and, turning to the Gods, he said :
Though, Hermes, you are perfect in your trade,
And you can trick and cheat to great surprise,
These little sleights no more shall blind my eyes ;
Correct them if you please, the more you thus dis-
        guise.   321
The circle laugh'd aloud ; and Maia's son
(As if it had but by mistake been done)
Recall'd his Archer, and with motion due,
Bid him advance, the combat to renew.   325
But Phœbus watch'd him with a jealous eye,
Fearing some trick was ever lurking nigh,
For he would oft, with sudden sly design,
Send forth at once two combatants to join
His warring troops, against the law of arms,   330
Unless the wary foe was ever in alarms.
    Now the white Archer with his utmost force
Bent the tough bow against the sable Horse,
And drove him from the Queen, where he had stood
Hoping to glut his vengeance with her blood.   335

Then the right Elephant with martial pride
Roved here and there, and spread his terrors wide :
Glittering in arms from far a courser came,
Threaten'd at once the King and Royal Dame ;
Thought himself safe when he the post had seized,
And with the future spoils his fancy pleased.   341
Fired at the danger a young Archer came,
Rush'd on the foe, and levell'd sure his aim ;
(And though a Pawn his sword in vengeance draws,
Gladly he'd lose his life in glory's cause).   345
The whistling arrow to his bowels flew,
And the sharp steel his blood profusely drew ;
He drops the reins, he totters to the ground,
And his life issued murm'ring through the wound.
Pierced by the Foot, this Archer bit the plain ;
The Foot himself was by another slain ;   351
And with inflamed revenge, the battle burns again.
Towers, Archers, Knights, meet on the crimson ground,
And the field echoes to the martial sound.
Their thoughts are heated, and their courage fired,
Thick they rush on with double zeal inspired ;   356
Generals and Foot, with different colour'd mien,
Confusedly warring in the camps are seen,—
Valour and Fortune meet in one promiscuous scene.
Now these victorious, lord it o'er the field ;   360
Now the foe rallies, the triumphant yield :
Just as the tide of battle ebbs or flows.
As when the conflict more tempestuous grows
Between the winds, with strong and boisterous sweep
They plough th' Ionian or Atlantic deep !   365
By turns prevail the mutual blustering roar,
And the big waves alternate lash the shore.

But in the midst of all the battle raged
The snowy Queen, with troops at once engaged ;
She fell'd an Archer as she sought the plain,—   370
As she retired an Elephant was slain :
To right and left her fatal spears she sent,
Burst through the ranks, and triumph'd as she went ;
Through arms and blood she seeks a glorious fate,
Pierces the farthest lines, and nobly great   375
Leads on her army with a gallant show,
Breaks the battalions, and cuts through the foe.
At length the sable King his fears betray'd,
And begg'd his military consort's aid :
With cheerful speed she flew to his relief,   380
And met in equal arms the female chief.

Who first, great Queen, and who at last did bleed ?
How many Whites lay gasping on the mead ?
Half dead, and floating in a bloody tide,
Foot, Knights, and Archer lie on every side.   385
Who can recount the slaughter of the day ?
How many leaders threw their lives away ?
The chequer'd plain is fill'd with dying box,
Havoc ensues, and with tumultuous shocks
The different colour'd ranks in blood engage,   390
And Foot and Horse promiscuously rage.
With nobler courage and superior might
The dreadful Amazons sustain the fight,
Resolved alike to mix in glorious strife,
Till to imperious fate they yield their life.   395

Meanwhile each Monarch, in a neighbouring cell,
Confined the warriors that in battle fell,
There watch'd the captives with a jealous eye,
Lest, slipping out again, to arms they fly.

But Thracian Mars, in stedfast friendship join'd   400
To Hermes, as near Phœbus he reclined,
Observed each chance, how all their motions
    bend,
Resolved if possible to serve his friend.
He a Foot-soldier and a Knight purloin'd
Out from the prison that the dead confined ;   405
And slyly push'd 'em forward on the plain ;   ⎫
Th' enliven'd combatants their arms regain,   ⎬
Mix in the bloody scene, and boldly war again.   ⎭

So the foul hag, in screaming wild alarms
O'er a dead carcase muttering her charms,   410
(And with her frequent and tremendous yell
Forcing great Hecate from out of hell)
Shoots in the corpse a new fictitious soul ;   ⎫
With instant glare the supple eyeballs roll,   ⎬
Again it moves and speaks, and life informs the⎬
    whole.   415 ⎭

Vulcan alone discern'd the subtle cheat ;
And wisely scorning such a base deceit,
Call'd out to Phœbus. Grief and rage assail
Phœbus by turns ; detected Mars turns pale.
Then awful Jove with sullen eye reproved   420
Mars, and the captives order'd to be moved
To their dark caves ; bid each fictitious spear
Be straight recall'd, and all be as they were.

And now both Monarchs with redoubled rage
Led on their Queens, the mutual war to wage.   425
O'er all the field their thirsty spears they send,
Then front to front their Monarchs they defend.
But lo ! the female White rush'd in unseen,
And slew with fatal haste the swarthy Queen ;

Yet soon, alas ! resign'd her royal spoils,   430
Snatch'd by a shaft from her successful toils.
Struck at the sight, both hosts in wild surprise
Pour'd forth their tears, and fill'd the air with cries ;
They wept and sigh'd, as pass'd the fun'ral train,
As if both armies had at once been slain.   435

And now each troop surrounds its mourning chief,
To guard his person, or assuage his grief.
One is their common fear ; one stormy blast
Has equally made havoc as it pass'd.
Not all, however, of their youth are slain ;   440
Some champions yet the vig'rous war maintain.
Three Foot, an Archer, and a stately Tower,
For Phœbus still exert their utmost power.
Just the same number Mercury can boast,
Except the Tower, who lately in his post   445
Unarm'd inglorious fell, in peace profound,
Pierced by an Archer with a distant wound ;
But his right Horse retain'd its mettled pride,—
The rest were swept away by war's strong tide.

But fretful Hermes, with despairing moan,   450
Griev'd that so many champions were o'erthrown,
Yet reassumes the fight ; and summons round
The little straggling army that he found,—
All that had 'scaped from fierce Apollo's rage,—
Resolved with greater caution to engage   455
In future strife, by subtle wiles (if fate
Should give him leave) to save his sinking state.
The sable troops advance with prudence slow,
Bent on all hazards to distress the foe.
More cheerful Phœbus, with unequal pace,   460
Rallies his arms to lessen his disgrace.

But what strange havoc everywhere has been ! ⎫
A straggling champion here and there is seen ; ⎬
And many are the tents, yet few are left within. ⎭

Th' afflicted Kings bewail their consorts dead,   465
And loathe the thoughts of a deserted bed ;
And though each monarch studies to improve
The tender mem'ry of his former love,
Their state requires a second nuptial tie.
Hence the pale ruler with a love-sick eye   470
Surveys th' attendants of his former wife,
And offers one of them a royal life.
These, when their martial mistress had been slain,
Weak and despairing tried their arms in vain ;
Willing, howe'er, amidst the Black to go,   475
They thirst for speedy vengeance on the foe.
Then he resolves to see who merits best,
By strength and courage, the imperial vest ;
Points out the foe, bids each with bold design
Pierce through the ranks, and reach the deepest line :
For none must hope with monarchs to repose   481
But who can first, through thick surrounding foes,
Through arms and wiles, with hazardous essay,
Safe to the farthest quarters force their way.
Fired at the thought, with sudden, joyful pace   485
They hurry on ; but first of all the race
Runs the third right-hand warrior for the prize,—
The glitt'ring crown already charms her eyes.
Her dear associates cheerfully give o'er ⎫
The nuptial chase ; and swift she flies before,   490 ⎬
And Glory lent her wings, and the reward in store. ⎭
Nor would the sable King her hopes prevent,
For he himself was on a Queen intent,

Alternate, therefore, through the field they go.
Hermes led on, but by a step too slow,   495
His fourth left Pawn : and now th' advent'rous White
Had march'd through all, and gain'd the wish'd for
          site.
Then the pleased King gives orders to prepare
The crown, the sceptre, and the royal chair,
And owns her for his Queen : around exult   500
The snowy troops, and o'er the Black insult.

Hermes burst into tears,—with fretful roar
Fill'd the wide air, and his gay vesture tore.
The swarthy Foot had only to advance
One single step ; but oh ! malignant chance !   505
A tower'd Elephant, with fatal aim,
Stood ready to destroy her when she came :
He keeps a watchful eye upon the whole,
Threatens her entrance, and protects the goal.
Meanwhile the royal new-created bride,   510
Pleased with her pomp, spread death and terror wide ;
Like lightning through the sable troops she flies,
Clashes her arms, and seems to threat the skies.
The sable troops are sunk in wild affright,   514
And wish th' earth op'ning snatch'd 'em from her sight.
In burst the Queen, with vast impetuous swing :
The trembling foes come swarming round the King,
Where in the midst he stood, and form a valiant ring.
So the poor cows, straggling o'er pasture land,
When they perceive the prowling wolf at hand,   520
Crowd close together in a circle full,
And beg the succour of the lordly bull ;
They clash their horns, they low with dreadful sound,
And the remotest groves re-echo round.

But the bold Queen, victorious, from behind   525
Pierces the foe ; yet chiefly she design'd
Against the King himself some fatal aim,
And full of war to his pavilion came.
Now here she rush'd, now there ; and had she been
But duly prudent, she had slipp'd between,   530
With course oblique, into the fourth white square,
And the long toil of war had ended there,
The King had fallen, and all his sable state ;
And vanquish'd Hermes cursed his partial fate.
For thence with ease the championess might go,   535
Murder the King, and none could ward the blow.

With silence, Hermes, and with panting heart,
Perceived the danger, but with subtle art,
(Lest he should see the place) spurs on the foe,   539
Confounds his thoughts, and blames his being slow.
For shame ! move on ; would you for ever stay ?
What sloth is this, what strange perverse delay ?—
How could you e'er my little pausing blame ?—
What ! you would wait till night shall end the game ?
Phœbus, thus nettled, with imprudence slew   545
A vulgar Pawn, but lost his nobler view.
Young Hermes leap'd, with sudden joy elate ;
And then, to save the monarch from his fate,
Led on his martial Knight, who stepp'd between,
Pleased that his charge was to oppose the Queen—
Then, pondering how the Indian beast to slay,   551
That stopp'd the Foot from making farther way,—
From being made a Queen ; with slanting aim
An archer struck him ; down the monster came,
And dying shook the earth : while Phœbus tries   555
Without success the monarch to surprise.

The Foot, then uncontroll'd with instant pride,
Seized the last spot, and moved a royal bride.
And now with equal strength both war again,
And bring their second wives upon the plain ;   560
Then, though with equal views each hop'd and fear'd,
Yet, as if every doubt had disappear'd,
As if he had the palm, young Hermes flies
Into excess of joy ; with deep disguise,   564
Extols his own Black troops, with frequent spite
And with invective taunts disdains the White.
Whom Phœbus thus reproved with quick return—
As yet we cannot the decision learn
Of this dispute, and do you triumph now ?
Then your big words and vauntings I'll allow,   570
When you the battle shall completely gain ;
At present I shall make your boasting vain.
He said, and forward led the daring Queen ;
Instant the fury of the bloody scene
Rises tumultuous, swift the warriors fly   575
From either side to conquer or to die.
They front the storm of war : around 'em Fear,
Terror, and Death, perpetually appear.
All meet in arms, and man to man oppose,
Each from their camp attempts to drive their foes ;
Each tries by turns to force the hostile lines ;   581
Chance and impatience blast their best designs.
The sable Queen spread terror as she went
Through the mid ranks : with more reserved intent
The adverse dame declined the open fray,   585
And to the King in private stole away :
Then took the royal guard, and bursting in,
With fatal menace close besieged the King.

Alarm'd at this, the swarthy Queen, in haste,
From all her havoc and destructive waste   590
Broke off, and her contempt of death to show,
Leap'd in between the Monarch and the foe,
To save the King and state from this impending
        blow.
But Phœbus met a worse misfortune here :
For Hermes now led forward, void of fear,   595
His furious Horse into the open plain,
That onward chafed, and pranced, and pawed amain.
Nor ceased from his attempts until he stood
On the long-wished-for spot, from whence he could
Slay King or Queen. O'erwhelm'd with sudden fears,
Apollo saw, and could not keep from tears.   601
Now all seem'd ready to be overthrown ;
His strength was wither'd, ev'ry hope was flown.
Hermes, exulting at this great surprise,
Shouted for joy, and fill'd the air with cries ;   605
Instant he sent the Queen to shades below,
And of her spoils made a triumphant show.
But in return, and in his mid career,
Fell his brave Knight, beneath the Monarch's spear.
    Phœbus, however, did not yet despair,   610
But still fought on with courage and with care.
He had but two poor common men to show,
And Mars's favourite with his iv'ry bow.
The thoughts of ruin made 'em dare their best
To save their King, so fatally distress'd.   615
But the sad hour required not such an aid ;
And Hermes breathed revenge where'er he stray'd.
Fierce comes the sable Queen with fatal threat,
Surrounds the Monarch in his royal seat ;

Rushed here and there, nor rested till she slew
The last remainder of the whiten'd crew.   621
Sole stood the King, the midst of all the plain,
Weak and defenceless, his companions slain.
As when the ruddy morn ascending high
Has chased the twinkling stars from all the sky,
Your star, fair Venus, still retains its light,   626
And, loveliest, goes the latest out of sight.
No safety 's left, no gleams of hope remain ;
Yet did he not as vanquish'd quit the plain,
But tried to shut himself between the foe,—   630
Unhurt through swords and spears he hoped to
      go,
Until no room was left to shun the fatal blow.
For if none threaten'd his immediate fate,
And his next move must ruin all his state,
All their past toil and labour is in vain,   635
Vain all the bloody carnage of the plain,—
Neither would triumph then, the laurel neither gain.
Therefore through each void space and desert
      tent,
By different moves his various course he bent :
The Black King watch'd him with observant eye, 640
Follow'd him close, but left him room to fly.
Then when he saw him take the farthest line,
He sent the Queen his motions to confine,
And guard the second rank, that he could go
No farther now than to that distant row.   645
The sable monarch then with cheerful mien
Approach'd, but always with one space between.
But as the King stood o'er against him there,
Helpless, forlorn, and sunk in his despair,

The martial Queen her lucky moment knew,
Seized on the farthest seat with fatal view,
Nor left th' unhappy King a place to flee unto.
At length in vengeance her keen sword she draws,
Slew him, and ended thus the bloody cause :
And all the gods around approved it with applause.

The victor could not from his insults keep,   656
But laugh'd and sneer'd to see Apollo weep.
Jove call'd him near, and gave him in his hand
The powerful, happy, and mysterious wand
By which the Shades are call'd to purer day,   660
When penal fire has purged their sins away ;
By which the guilty are condemn'd to dwell
In the dark mansions of the deepest hell ;
By which he gives us sleep, or sleep denies,
And closes at the last the dying eyes.   665
Soon after this, the heavenly victor brought
The game on earth, and first th' Italians taught.

For (as they say) fair Scacchis he espied
Feeding her cygnets in the silver tide,
(Scacchis, the loveliest Seriad of the place)   670
And as she stray'd, took her to his embrace.
Then, to reward her for her virtue lost,
Gave her the men and chequer'd board, emboss'd
With gold and silver curiously inlay'd ;
And taught her how the game was to be play'd.   675
Ev'n now 'tis honour'd with her happy name ;
And Rome and all the world admire the game.
All which the Seriads told me heretofore,
When my boy-notes amused the Serian shore.

NOTES.

NOTES.

INTRODUCTION

P. ix, l. 6. *He was born . . . at Pallas.* This is the usual account. But it was maintained by the family of the poet's mother, and has been contended (by Dr. Michael F. Cox in a Lecture on 'The Country and Kindred of Oliver Goldsmith,' published in vol. i, pt. 2, of the *Journal* of the 'National Literary Society of Ireland,' 1900) that his real birth-place was the residence of Mrs. Goldsmith's parents, Smith-Hill House, Elphin, Roscommon, to which she was in the habit of paying frequent visits. Meanwhile, in 1897, a window was placed to Goldsmith's memory in Forgney Church, Longford,—the church of which, at the time of his birth, his father was curate.

P. x, l. 33. *his academic career was not a success.* 'Oliver Goldsmith is recorded on two occasions as being remarkably diligent at Morning Lecture ; again, as cautioned for bad answering at Morning and Greek Lectures ; and finally, as put down into the next class for neglect of his studies ' (Dr. Stubbs's *History of the University of Dublin*, 1889, p. 201 *n.*)

P. xi, l. 21. *a scratched signature upon a window-pane.* This, which is now at Trinity College, Dublin, is here reproduced in facsimile. When the garrets of No. 35, Parliament Square, were pulled down in 1837, it was cut out of the window by the last occupant of the rooms, who broke it in the process. (Dr. J. F. Waller in Cassell's *Works* of Goldsmith, [1864–5], pp. xiii–xiv *n.*)

P. xiii, l. 23. *a poor physician.* Where he obtained his diploma is not known. It was certainly not at Padua (*Athenaeum*, July 21, 1894). At Leyden and Louvain Prior made inquiries but, in each case, without success. The annals of the University of Louvain were, however, destroyed in the revolutionary wars. (Prior, *Life*, 1837, i, pp. 171, 178).

P. xv, l. 7. *declared it to be by Goldsmith.* Goldsmith's authorship of this version has now been placed beyond a doubt by the publication in facsimile of his signed receipt to Edward Dilly for

a third share of ' my translation,' such third share amounting to
£6 13s. 4d. The receipt, which belongs to Mr. J. W. Ford of
Enfield Old Park, is dated ' January 11th, 1758.' (*Memoirs of
a Protestant*, &c., Dent's edition, 1895, i, pp. xii–xviii.)

P. xvi, l. 9. 12, *Green Arbour Court, Old Bailey.* This was a tiny
square occupying a site now absorbed by the Holborn Viaduct
and Railway Station. No. 12, where Goldsmith lived, was later
occupied by Messrs. Smith, Elder & Co. as a printing office.
An engraving of the Court forms the frontispiece to the *European
Magazine* for January, 1803.

P. xvii, l. 29. *or some of his imitators.* The proximate cause of the
Citizen of the World, as the present writer has suggested elsewhere, *may* have been Horace Walpole's *Letter from Xo Ho* [Soho ?],
a Chinese Philosopher at London, to his friend Lien Chi, at Peking.
This was noticed as ' in Montesquieu's manner ' in the May issue
of the *Monthly Review* for 1757, to which Goldsmith was a con-
tributor (*Eighteenth Century Vignettes*, first series, second edition,
1897, pp. 108–9).

P. xix, l. 23. *demonstrable from internal evidence.* e. g.—The
references to the musical glasses (ch. ix), which were the rage in
1761–2 ; and to the *Auditor* (ch. xix) established by Arthur
Murphy in June of the latter year. The sale of the *Vicar* is
discussed at length in chapter vii of the editor's *Life of Oliver
Goldsmith* (' Great Writers ' series), 1888, pp. 110–21.

P. xxii, l. 13. *started with a loss.* This, which to some critics has
seemed unintelligible, rests upon the following : ' The first three
editions, . . . resulted in a loss, and the fourth, which was not issued
until eight [four ?] years after the first, started with a balance
against it of £2 16s. 6d., and it was not until that fourth edition had
been sold that the balance came out on the right side' (*A Bookseller
of the Last Century* [John Newbery] by Charles Welsh, 1885, p. 61).
The writer based his statement upon Collins's ' Publishing book,
account of books printed and shares therein, No. 3, 1770 to 1785.'

P. xxvii, l. 7. *James's Powder.* This was a famous patent panacea,
invented by Johnson's Lichfield townsman, Dr. Robert James of
the *Medicinal Dictionary.* It was sold by John Newbery, and
had an extraordinary vogue. The King dosed Princess Elizabeth
with it ; Fielding, Gray, and Cowper all swore by it, and Horace
Walpole, who wished to try it upon Mme. du Deffand *in extremis*,

GREEN ARBOUR COURT, LITTLE OLD BAILEY

(AS IT APPEARED IN 1803)

said he should use it if the house were on fire. William Hawes, the Strand apothecary who attended Goldsmith, wrote an interesting *Account of the late Dr. Goldsmith's Illness, so far as relates to the Exhibition of Dr. James's Powders*, &c., 1774, which he dedicated to Reynolds and Burke. To Hawes once belonged the poet's worn old wooden writing-desk, now in the South Kensington Museum, where are also his favourite chair and cane. Another desk-chair, which had descended from his friend, Edmund Bott, was recently for sale at Sotheby's (July, 1906).

EDITIONS OF THE POEMS.

No collected edition of Goldsmith's poetical works appeared until after his death. But, in 1775, W. Griffin, who had published the *Essays* of ten years earlier, issued a volume entitled *The Miscellaneous Works of Oliver Goldsmith, M.B., containing all his Essays and Poems.* The ' poems ' however were confined to ' The Traveller,' ' The Deserted Village,' ' Edwin and Angelina,' ' The Double Transformation,' ' A New Simile,' and ' Retaliation,'—an obviously imperfect harvesting. In the following year G. Kearsly printed an eighth edition of *Retaliation*, with which he included ' The Hermit ' (' Edwin and Angelina '), ' The Gift,' ' Madam Blaize,' and the epilogues to *The Sister* and *She Stoops to Conquer* [1]; while to an edition of *The Haunch of Venison*, also put forth in 1776, he added the ' Epitaph on Parnell ' and two songs from the oratorio of *The Captivity*. The next collection appeared in a volume of *Poems and Plays* published at Dublin in 1777, where it was preceded by a ' Life,' written by W. Glover, one of Goldsmith's ' Irish clients.' Then, in 1780, came vol. i of T. Evans's *Poetical and Dramatic Works*, &c., *now first collected*, also having a ' Memoir,' and certainly fuller than anything which had gone before. Next followed the long-deferred *Miscellaneous Works*, &c., of 1801, in four volumes, vol. ii of which comprised the plays and poems. Prefixed to this edition is the important biographical sketch, compiled under the direction of Bishop Percy, and usually described as the *Percy Memoir*, by which title it is referred to in the ensuing

---

[1] Some copies of this are dated 1777, and contain *The Haunch of Venison* and a few minor pieces.

notes. The next memorable edition was that edited for the
Aldine Series in 1831, by the Rev. John Mitford. Prior and
Wright's edition in vol. iv of the *Miscellaneous Works*, &c., of
1837, comes after this ; then Bolton Corney's excellent *Poetical
Works* of 1845 ; and vol. i of Peter Cunningham's *Works*, &c.
of 1854. There are other issues of the poems, the latest of
which is to be found in vol. ii (1885) of the complete *Works*,
in five volumes, edited for Messrs. George Bell & Sons by
J. W. M. Gibbs.

Most of the foregoing editions have been consulted for the
following notes ; but chiefly those of Mitford, Prior, Bolton
Corney, and Cunningham. Many of the illustrations and ex-
planations now supplied will not, however, be found in any of
the sources indicated. When an elucidatory or parallel passage
is cited, an attempt has been made, as far as possible, to give
the credit of it to the first discoverer. Thus, some of the illustrations in Cunningham's notes are here transferred to Prior, some
of Prior's to Mitford, and so forth. As regards the notes themselves, care has been taken to make them full enough to obviate
the necessity, except in rare instances, of further investigation.
It is the editor's experience that references to external authorities are, as a general rule, sign-posts to routes which are seldom
travelled[1].

THE TRAVELLER.

It was on those continental wanderings which occupied
Goldsmith between February, 1755 and February, 1756 that
he conceived his first idea of this, the earliest of his poems to
which he prefixed his name ; and he probably had in mind
Addison's *Letter from Italy to Lord Halifax*, a work in which he
found 'a strain of political thinking that was, at that time [1701].
new in our poetry.' (*Beauties of English Poesy*, 1767, i. 111).
From the dedicatory letter to his brother—which says expressly,
' as a part of this Poem was formerly written to you from
Switzerland, the whole can now, with propriety, be only inscribed

---

[1] In this connexion may be recalled the dictum of Hume quoted
by Dr. Birkbeck Hill :—' Every book should be as complete as
possible within itself, and should never refer for anything material
to other books ' (*History of England*, 1802, ii. 101).

to you '—it is plain that some portion of it must have been actually composed abroad. It was not, however, actually published until the 19th of December, 1764, and the title-page bore the date of 1765 [1]. The publisher was John Newbery, of St. Paul's Churchyard, and the price of the book, a quarto of 30 pages, was 1s. 6d. A second, third, and fourth edition quickly followed, and a ninth, from which it is here reprinted, was issued in 1774, the year of the author's death. Between the first and the sixth edition of 1770 there were numerous alterations, the more important of which are indicated in the ensuing notes.

The didactic purpose of *The Traveller* is defined in the concluding paragraph of the *Dedication* ; and, like many of the thoughts which it contains, had been anticipated in a passage

---

[1] This is the generally recognized first edition. But the late Mr. Frederick Locker Lampson, the poet and collector, possessed a quarto copy, dated 1764, which had no author's name, and in which the dedication ran as follows:—'This poem is inscribed to the Rev. Henry Goldsmith, M.A. By his most affectionate Brother Oliver Goldsmith.' It was, in all probability, unique, though it is alleged that there are octavo copies which present similar characteristics. It has now gone to America with the Rowfant Library.

In 1902 an interesting discovery was made by Mr. Bertram Dobell, to whom the public are indebted for so many important literary 'finds.' In a parcel of pamphlets he came upon a number of loose printed leaves entitled *A Prospect of Society*. They obviously belonged to *The Traveller* ; but seemed to be its 'formless, unarranged material,' and contained many variations from the text of the first edition. Mr. Dobell's impression was that 'the author's manuscript, written on loose leaves, had fallen into confusion, and was then printed without any attempt at re-arrangement.' This was near the mark ; but the complete solution of the riddle was furnished by Mr. Quiller Couch in an article in the *Daily News* for March 31, 1902, since recast in his charming volume *From a Cornish Window*, 1906, pp. 86–92. He showed conclusively that *The Prospect* was 'merely an early draft of *The Traveller* printed backwards in fairly regular sections.' What had manifestly happened was this. Goldsmith, turning over each page as written, had laid it on the top of the preceding page of MS. and forgotten to rearrange them when done. Thus the series of pages were reversed ; and, so reversed, were set up in type by a matter-of-fact compositor. Mr. Dobell at once accepted this happy explanation ; which—as Mr. Quiller Couch points out—has the advantage of being a 'blunder just so natural to Goldsmith as to be almost postulable.' One or two of the variations of Mr. Dobell's 'find'—variations, it should be added, antecedent to the first edition —are noted in their places.

of *The Citizen of the World*, 1762, i. 185 :—' Every mind seems capable of entertaining a certain quantity of happiness, which no institutions can encrease, no circumstances alter, and entirely independent on fortune.' But the best short description of the poem is Macaulay's :—' In the *Traveller* the execution, though deserving of much praise, is far inferior to the design. No philosophical poem, ancient or modern, has a plan so noble, and at the same time so simple. An English wanderer, seated on a crag among the Alps, near the point where three great countries meet, looks down on the boundless prospect, reviews his long pilgrimage, recalls the varieties of scenery, of climate, of government, of religion, of national character, which he has observed, and comes to the conclusion, just or unjust, that our happiness depends little on political institutions, and much on the temper and regulation of our own minds.' (*Encyclop. Britannica*, Goldsmith, February, 1856.)

The only definite record of payment for *The Traveller* is ' Copy of the Traveller, a Poem, 21*l*,' in Newbery's MSS. ; but as the same sum occurs in Memoranda of much later date than 1764, it is possible that the success of the book may have prompted some supplementary fee.

A Prospect, i. e. 'a view.' ' I went to Putney, and other places on the Thames, to take *prospects* in crayon, to carry into France, where I thought to have them engraved ' (Evelyn, *Diary*, 20th June, 1649). And Reynolds uses the word of Claude in his Fourth Discourse :—' His pictures are a composition of the various draughts which he had previously made from various beautiful scenes and *prospects* ' (*Works*, by Malone, 1798, i. 105). The word is common on old prints, e. g. *An Exact Prospect of the Magnificent Stone Bridge at Westminster*, &c., 1751.

Dedication. The Rev. Henry Goldsmith, says the Percy *Memoir*, 1801, p. 3, ' had distinguished himself both at school and at college, but he unfortunately married at the early age of nineteen ; which confined him to a Curacy, and prevented his rising to preferment in the church.'

1. 14. *with an income of forty pounds a year*. Cf. *The Deserted Village*, ll. 141-2 :—

> A man he was, to all the country dear,
> And passing rich with *forty pounds a year*.

Cf. also Parson Adams in ch. iii of *Joseph Andrews*, who has twenty-three ; and Mr. Rivers, in the *Spiritual Quixote*, 1772 :— 'I do not choose to go into orders to be a curate all my life-time, and work for about fifteen-pence a day, or twenty-five pounds a year' (bk. vi, ch. xvii). Dr. Primrose's stipend is thirty-five in the first instance, fifteen in the second (*Vicar of Wakefield*, chapters ii and iii). But Professor Hales (*Longer English Poems*, 1885, p. 351) supplies an exact parallel in the case of Churchill, who, he says, when a curate at Rainham, 'prayed and starved on *forty pounds a year*.' The latter words are Churchill's own, and sound like a quotation ; but he was dead long before *The Deserted Village* appeared in 1770. There is an interesting paper in the *Gentleman's Magazine* for November, 1763, on the miseries and hardships of the 'inferior clergy.'

l. 20. *But of all kinds of ambition*, &c. In the first edition of 1765, p. ii, this passage was as follows :—' But of all kinds of ambition, as things are now circumstanced, perhaps that which pursues poetical fame, is the wildest. What from the encreased refinement of the times, from the diversity of judgments produced by opposing systems of criticism, and from the more prevalent divisions of opinion influenced by party, the strongest and happiest efforts can expect to please but in a very narrow circle. Though the poet were as sure of his aim as the imperial archer of antiquity, who boasted that he never missed the heart ; yet would many of his shafts now fly at random, for the heart is too often in the wrong place.' In the second edition it was curtailed ; in the sixth it took its final form.

l. 29. *they engross all that favour once shown to her*. First version—' They engross all favour to themselves.'

l. 30. *the elder's birthright*. Cunningham here aptly compares Dryden's epistle *To Sir Godfrey Kneller*, ll. 89-92 :—

> Our arts are sisters, though not twins in birth ;
> For hymns were sung in Eden's happy earth :
> But oh, the painter muse, though last in place,
> Has seized the blessing first, like Jacob's race.

l. 42. *Party*=faction. Cf. lines 31-2 on Edmund Burke in *Retaliation* :—

> Who, born for the Universe, narrow'd his mind,
> And to *party* gave up what was meant for mankind.

l. 50. *Such readers generally admire*, &c. 'I suppose this paragraph to be directed against Paul Whitehead, or Churchill,' writes Mitford. It was clearly aimed at Churchill, since Prior (*Life*, 1837, ii. 54) quotes a portion of a contemporary article in the *St. James's Chronicle* for February 7-9, 1765, attributed to Bonnell Thornton, which leaves little room for doubt upon the question. 'The latter part of this paragraph,' says the writer, referring to the passage now annotated, 'we cannot help considering as a reflection on the memory of the late Mr. Churchill, whose talents as a poet were so greatly and so deservedly admired, that during his short reign, his merit in great measure eclipsed that of others ; and we think it no mean acknowledgment of the excellencies of this poem [*The Traveller*] to say that, like the stars, they appear the more brilliant now that the sun of our poetry is gone down.' Churchill died on the 4th of November, 1764, some weeks before the publication of *The Traveller*. His powers, it may be, were misdirected and misapplied ; but his rough vigour and his manly verse deserved a better fate at Goldsmith's hands.

l. 53. *tawdry* was added in the sixth edition of 1770.

l. 56. *blank verse.* Cf. *The Present State of Polite Learning*, 1759, p. 150—'From a desire in the critic of grafting the spirit of ancient languages upon the English, has proceeded of late several disagreeable instances of pedantry. Among the number, I think we may reckon *blank verse.* Nothing but the greatest sublimity of subject can render such a measure pleasing ; however, we now see it used on the most trivial occasions'—by which last remark Goldsmith probably, as Cunningham thinks, intended to refer to the efforts of Akenside, Dyer, and Armstrong. His views upon blank verse were shared by Johnson and Gray. At the date of the present dedication, the latest offender in this way had been Goldsmith's old colleague on *The Monthly Review*, Dr. James Grainger, author of *The Sugar Cane*, which was published in June, 1764. (Cf. also *The Bee* for 24th November, 1759, 'An Account of the Augustan Age of England.')

l. 62. *and that this principle*, &c. In the first edition this read—'and that this principle in each state, and in our own in particular, may be carried to a mischievous excess.'

l. 1. *Remote, unfriended, melancholy, slow.* Mitford (Aldine edition, 1831, p. 7) compares the following lines from Ovid :—

Solus, inops, exspes, leto poenaeque relictus.

Metamorphoses, xiv. 217.

Exsul, inops erres, alienaque limina lustres, &c.

Ibis, 113.

slow. A well-known passage from Boswell must here be reproduced :—' Chamier once asked him [Goldsmith], what he meant by *slow*, the last word in the first line of *The Traveller*,

Remote, unfriended, melancholy, slow.

Did he mean tardiness of locomotion ? Goldsmith, who would say something without consideration, answered " Yes." I [Johnson] was sitting by, and said, " No, Sir, you do not mean tardiness of locomotion ; you mean, that sluggishness of mind which comes upon a man in solitude." Chamier believed then that I had written the line as much as if he had seen me write it.' (Birkbeck Hill's *Boswell*, 1887, iii. 252-3.) It is quite possible, however, that Goldsmith meant no more than he said.

l. 3. *the rude Carinthian boor.* ' Carinthia,' says Cunningham, ' was visited by Goldsmith in 1755, and still (1853) retains its character for inhospitality.'

l. 5. *Campania.* ' Intended,' says Bolton Corney, ' to denote *La campagna di Roma.* The portion of it which extends from Rome to Terracina is scarcely habitable.'

l. 10. *a lengthening chain.* Prior compares Letter iii of *The Citizen of the World*, 1762, i. 5 :—' The farther I travel I feel the pain of separation with stronger force, those ties that bind me to my native country, and you, are still unbroken. By every remove, I only drag a greater length of chain.' But, as Mitford points out, Cibber has a similar thought in his *Comical Lovers*, 1707, Act v :—' When I am with Florimel, it [my heart] is still your prisoner, *it only draws a longer chain after it.*' And earlier still in Dryden's *All for Love*, 1678, Act ii, Sc. 1 :—

My life on 't, he still drags a chain along,
That needs must clog his flight.

l. 17. *with simple plenty crown'd.* In the first edition this read ' where mirth and peace abound.'

l. 22. *the luxury of doing good.* Prior compares Garth's *Clare-mont*, 1715, where he speaks of the Druids :—

> Hard was their Lodging, homely was their Food,
> For all their *Luxury was doing Good.*

l. 24. *my prime of life.* He was seven-and-twenty when he landed at Dover in February, 1756.

l. 27. *That, like the circle bounding,* &c. Cf. *Vicar of Wakefield,* 1766, ii. 160–1 (ch. x) :—' Death, the only friend of the wretched, for a little while mocks the weary traveller with the view, and like his horizon, still flies before him.' [Prior.]

l. 30. *And find no spot of all the world my own.* Prior compares his namesake's lines *In the Beginning of* [Jacques] *Robbe's Geography,* 1700 :—

> My destin'd Miles I shall have gone,
> By THAMES or MAESE, by Po or RHONE,
> And *found no Foot of Earth my own.*

l. 33. *above the storm's career.* Cf. l. 190 of *The Deserted Village.*

l. 38. *should thankless pride repine?* First edition, ' 'twere thankless to repine.'

l. 39. *Say, should the philosophic mind,* &c. First edition :—

> 'Twere affectation all, and school-taught pride,
> To spurn the splendid things by heaven supply'd.

l. 58. *hoard.* ' Sum ' in the first edition.

l. 66. *Boldly proclaims that happiest spot his own.* In the first version this was—

> Boldly asserts that country for his own.

l. 75. *And yet, perhaps,* &c. In the first edition, for this and the following five lines appeared these eight :—

> And yet, perhaps, if states with states we scan,
> Or estimate their bliss on Reason's plan,
> Though patriots flatter, and though fools contend,
> We still shall find uncertainty suspend ;
> Find that each good, by Art or Nature given,
> To these or those, but makes the balance even :
> Find that the bliss of all is much the same,
> And patriotic boasting reason's shame !

l. 84. *On Idra's cliffs.* Bolton Corney conjectures that Gold-smith meant ' Idria, a town in Carniola, noted for its mines.' ' Goldsmith in his " History of Animated Nature " makes mention of the mines, and spells the name in the same way as here ' (Mr . J. H. Lobban's *Select Poems of Goldsmith,* 1900, p. 87). Lines 84–5, it may be added, are not in the first edition.

l. 85. *And though the rocky-crested summits frown.* In the first edition :—

And though rough rocks or gloomy summits frown.

ll. 91–2 are not in the first editions.

l. 98. *peculiar,* i. e. ' proper,' ' appropriate.'

l. 122. *winnow,* i. e. ' waft,' ' disperse.' John Evelyn refers to these ' sea-born gales ' in the ' Dedication ' of his *Fumi-fugium,* 1661 :—'Those who take notice of the scent of the orange-flowers from the rivage of Genöa, and St. Pietro dell' Arena; the blossomes of the rosemary from the Coasts of Spain, many leagues off at sea; or the manifest, and odoriferous wafts which flow from Fontenay and Vaugirard, even to Paris in the season of roses, with the contrary effect of those less pleasing smells from other accidents, will easily consent to what I suggest [i.e. the planting of sweet-smelling trees].' (*Miscellaneous Writings,* 1825, p. 208.)

l. 139. *Till, more unsteady,* &c. In the first edition :—

But, more unsteady than the southern gale,
Soon Commerce turn'd on other shores her sail.

There is a certain resemblance between this passage and one of the later paradoxes of Smollett's Lismahago;—'He affirmed, the nature of commerce was such, that it could not be fixed or perpetuated, but, having flowed to a certain height, would immediately begin to ebb, and so continue till the channels should be left almost dry; but there was no instance of the tide's rising a second time to any considerable influx in the same nation ' (*Humphry Clinker,* 1771, ii. 192. Letter of Mr. Bramble to Dr. Lewis).

ll. 141–2 are not in the first edition.

l. 144. *Its former strength was but plethoric ill.* Cf. *The Citizen of the World,* 1762, i. 98 :—' In short, the state resembled one of those bodies bloated with disease, whose bulk is only a symptom of its wretchedness.' [Mitford.]

l. 145. *Yet still the loss*, &c. In the first edition :—

> Yet, though to fortune lost, here still abide
> Some splendid arts, the wrecks of former pride.

l. 150. *The paste-board triumph and the cavalcade.* 'Happy Country [he is speaking of Italy], where the pastoral age begins to revive ! Where the wits even of Rome are united into a rural groupe of nymphs and swains, under the appellation of modern Arcadians [i. e. the Bolognese Academy of the *Arcadi*]. Where in the midst of porticos, processions, and cavalcades, abbés turn'd into shepherds, and shepherdesses without sheep, indulge their innocent *divertimenti.*' (*Present State of Polite Learning*, 1759, pp. 50–1.) Some of the ' paste-board triumphs ' may be studied in the plates of Jacques Callot.

l. 153. *By sports like these*, &c. A pretty and well-known story is told with regard to this couplet. Calling once on Goldsmith, Reynolds, having vainly tried to attract attention, entered unannounced. 'His friend was at his desk, but with hand uplifted, and a look directed to another part of the room ; where a little dog sat with difficulty on his haunches, looking imploringly at his teacher, whose rebuke for toppling over he had evidently just received. Reynolds advanced, and looked past Goldsmith's shoulder at the writing on his desk. It seemed to be some portions of a poem ; and looking more closely, he was able to read a couplet which had been that instant written. The ink of the second line was wet :—

> By sports like these are all their cares beguil'd ;
> The sports of children satisfy the child.

(Forster's *Life*, 1871, i. pp. 347–8).

l. 154. *The sports of children.* This line, in the first edition, was followed by :—

> At sports like these, while foreign arms advance,
> In passive ease they leave the world to chance.

l. 155. *Each nobler aim*, &c. The first edition reads :—

> When struggling Virtue sinks by long controul,
> She leaves at last, or feebly mans the soul.

This was changed in the second, third, fourth, and fifth editions to :—

> When noble aims have suffer'd long controul,
> They sink at last, or feebly man the soul.

l. 169. *No product here*, &c. The Swiss mercenaries, here referred to, were long famous in European warfare.

> They parted with a thousand kisses,
> And fight e'er since for pay, like Swisses.
>
> Gay's *Aye and No, a Fable.*

l. 185. This fine use of ' breasts '—as Cunningham points out —is given by Johnson as an example in his Dictionary.

l. 187. *With patient angle trolls the finny deep.* ' Troll,' i. e. as for pike. Goldsmith uses ' finny prey ' in *The Citizen of the World*, 1762, ii. 99 :—' The best manner to draw up the *finny prey*.' Cf. also ' warbling grove,' *Deserted Village*, l. 361, as a parallel to ' finny deep.'

l. 190. *the struggling savage*, i. e. wolf or bear. Mitford compares the following :—' He is a beast of prey, and the laws should make use of as many stratagems and as much force to drive the *reluctant savage* into the toils, as the Indians when they hunt the hyena or the rhinoceros.' (*Citizen of the World*, 1762, i. 112.) See also Pope's *Iliad*, Bk. xvii :—

> But if the *savage* turns his glaring eye,
> They howl aloof, and round the forest fly.

ll. 201-2 are not in the first edition.

l. 213. *For every want*, &c. Mitford quotes a parallel passage in *Animated Nature*, 1774, ii. 123 :—' Every want thus becomes a means of pleasure, in the redressing.'

l. 228. *Their morals, like their pleasures, are but low.* Probably Goldsmith only uses ' low ' here in its primitive sense, and not in that which, in his own day, gave so much umbrage to so many eighteenth-century students of humanity in the rough. Cf. Fielding, *Tom Jones*, 1749, iii. 6 :—' Some of the Author's Friends cry'd—" Look'e, Gentlemen, the Man is a Villain ; but it is Nature for all that." And all the young Critics of the Age, the Clerks, Apprentices, &c., called it *Low* and fell a Groaning.' See also *Tom Jones*, iv. 94, and 226-30. ' There's nothing comes out but the *most lowest* stuff in nature '—says Lady Blarney in ch. xi of the *Vicar*, whose author is eloquent on this topic in *The Present State of Polite Learning*, 1759, pp. 154-6, and in

She Stoops to Conquer, 1773 (Act i); while Graves (*Spiritual Quixote*, 1772, bk. i, ch. vi) gives the fashion the scientific appellation of '*tapino-phoby*,' which he defines as 'a dread of everything that is *low*, either in writing or in conversation.' To Goldsmith, if we may trust George Colman's *Prologue* to Miss Lee's *Chapter of Accidents*, 1780, belongs the credit of exorcising this particular form of depreciation :—

> When Fielding, Humour's fav'rite child, appear'd,
> *Low* was the word—a word each author fear'd !
> Till chas'd at length, by pleasantry's bright ray,
> Nature and mirth resum'd their legal sway ;
> And Goldsmith's genius bask'd in open day.

According to Borrow's *Lavengro*, ch. xli, Lord Chesterfield considered that the speeches of Homer's heroes were frequently 'exceedingly low.'

l. 243. *How often*, &c. This and the lines which immediately follow are autobiographical. Cf. George Primrose's story in *The Vicar of Wakefield*, 1766, ii. 24–5 (ch. i) :—' I passed among the harmless peasants of Flanders, and among such of the French as were poor enough to be very merry ; for I ever found them sprightly in proportion to their wants. Whenever I approached a peasant's house towards night-fall, I played one of my most merry tunes, and that procured me not only a lodging, but subsistence for the next day.'

l. 253. *gestic lore*, i. e. traditional gestures or motions. Scott uses the word 'gestic' in *Peveril of the Peak*, ch. xxx, where King Charles the Second witnesses the dancing of Fenella :— 'He bore time to her motions with the movement of his foot —applauded with head and with hand—and seemed, like herself, carried away by the enthusiasm of the *gestic* art.' [Hales.]

l. 256. *Thus idly busy rolls their world away.* Pope has ' Life's *idle business* ' (*Unfortunate Lady*, l. 81), and—

> The *busy*, *idle* blockheads of the ball.
>
> Donne's *Satires*, iv. l. 203.

l. 264. *And all are taught an avarice of praise.* Professor Hales (*Longer English Poems*) compares Horace of the Greeks :—

> Praeter laudem, nullius avaris.
>
> *Ars Poetica*, l. 324.

l. 275. *copper lace.* ' St. Martin's lace,' for which, in Strype's day, Blowbladder St. was famous. Cf. the actress's 'copper tail ' in *Citizen of the World*, 1762, ii. 60.

l. 281. *To men of other minds*, &c. Prior compares with the description that follows a passage in vol. i. p. 276 of *Animated Nature*, 1774 :—'But we need scarce mention these, when we find that the whole kingdom of Holland seems to be a conquest upon the sea, and in a manner rescued from its bosom. The surface of the earth, in this country, is below the level of the bed of the sea ; and I remember, upon approaching the coast, to have looked down upon it from the sea, as into a valley.'

l. 284. *Where the broad ocean leans against the land.* Cf. Dryden in *Annus Mirabilis*, 1666, st. clxiv. l. 654 :—

> And view the ocean leaning on the sky.

l. 286. *the tall rampire's,* i. e. rampart's (Old French, *rempart, rempar*). Cf. *Timon of Athens*, Act v. Sc. 4 :—' Our rampir'd gates.'

l. 299. *bosom reign* in the first edition was ' breast obtain.'

l. 306. *Even liberty itself is barter'd here.* ' Slavery,' says Mitford, ' was permitted in Holland ; children were sold by their parents for a certain number of years.'

l. 309. *A land of tyrants, and a den of slaves.* Goldsmith uses this very line as prose in Letter xxxiv of *The Citizen of the World,* 1762, i. 147.

l. 310. *dishonourable graves.* *Julius Caesar*, Act i. Sc. 2.

l. 313. *Heavens ! how unlike*, &c. Prior compares a passage from a manuscript *Introduction to the History of the Seven Years' War* :—' How unlike the brave peasants their ancestors, who spread terror into either India, and always declared themselves the allies of those who drew the sword in defence of freedom [1].'

l. 320. *famed Hydaspes*, i. e. the *fabulosus Hydaspes* of Horace, Bk. i. Ode xxii, and the *Medus Hydaspes* of Virgil, *Georg.* iv. 211, of which so many stories were told. It is now known as the Jhilum, one of the five rivers which give the Punjaub its name.

l. 327. *Pride in their port*, &c. In the first edition these two lines were inverted.

---

[1] J. W. M. Gibbs (*Works*, v. 9) discovered that parts of this *History*, hitherto supposed to have been written in 1761, were published in the *Literary Magazine*, 1757-8.

l. 343. *Here by the bonds of nature feebly held.* In the first edition—

> See, though by circling deeps together held.

l. 349. *Nature's ties* was *social bonds* in the first edition.

l. 358. *Where kings have toil'd, and poets wrote for fame.* In the first edition this line read :—

> And monarchs toil, and poets pant for fame.

l. 361. *Yet think not*, &c. ' In the things I have hitherto written I have neither allured the vanity of the great by flattery, nor satisfied the malignity of the vulgar by scandal, but I have endeavoured to get an honest reputation by liberal pursuits.' (Preface to *English History*.) [Mitford.]

l. 363. *Ye powers of truth*, &c. The first version has :—

> Perish the wish ; for, inly satisfy'd,
> Above their pomps I hold my ragged pride.

Mr. Forster thinks (*Life*, 1871, i. 375) that Goldsmith altered this (i. e. ' ragged pride ') because, like the omitted ' *Haud inexpertus loquor* ' of the *Enquiry*, it involved an undignified admission.

ll. 365–80 are not in the first edition.

l. 382. *Contracting regal power to stretch their own.* ' It is the interest of the great, therefore, to diminish kingly power as much as possible ; because whatever they take from it is naturally restored to themselves ; and all they have to do in a state, is to undermine the single tyrant, by which they resume their primaeval authority.' (*Vicar of Wakefield*, 1766, i. 202, ch. xix.)

l. 383. *When I behold*, &c. Prior compares a passage in Letter xlix of *The Citizen of the World*, 1762, i. 218, where the Roman senators are spoken of as still flattering the people ' with a shew of freedom, while themselves only were free.'

l. 386. *Laws grind the poor, and rich men rule the law.* Prior notes a corresponding utterance in *The Vicar of Wakefield*, 1766, i. 206, ch. xix :—' What they may then expect, may be seen by turning our eyes to Holland, Genoa, or Venice, where the laws govern the poor, and the rich govern the law.'

l. 392. *I fly from petty tyrants to the throne.* Cf. Dr. Primrose, *ut supra*, p. 201 :—' The generality of mankind also are of my way of thinking, and have unanimously created one king, whose election at once diminishes the number of tyrants, and puts tyranny at the greatest distance from the greatest number of people.' Cf. also Churchill, *The Farewell*, ll. 363-4 and 369-70 :—

> Let not a Mob of Tyrants seize the helm,
> Nor titled upstarts league to rob the realm . . .
> Let us, some comfort in our griefs to bring,
> Be slaves to one, and be that one a King.

ll. 393-4. Goldsmith's first thought was—

> Yes, my lov'd brother, cursed be that hour
> When first ambition toil'd for foreign power,—

an entirely different couplet to that in the text, and certainly more logical. (Dobell's *Prospect of Society*, 1902, pp. xi, 2, and Notes, v, vi). Mr. Dobell plausibly suggests that this Tory substitution is due to Johnson.

l. 397. *Have we not seen*, &c. These lines contain the first idea of the subsequent poem of *The Deserted Village* (*q. v.*).

l. 411. *Where wild Oswego spreads her swamps around.* The Oswego is a river which runs between Lakes Oneida and Ontario. In the *Threnodia Augustalis*, 1772, Goldsmith writes :—

> Oswego's dreary shores shall be my grave.

The 'desarts of Oswego' were familiar to the eighteenth-century reader in connexion with General Braddock's ill-fated expedition of 1755, an account of which Goldsmith had just given in *An History of England, in a Series of Letters from a Nobleman to his Son*, 1764, ii. 202-4.

l. 416. *marks with murderous aim.* In the first edition ' takes a deadly aim.'

l. 419. *pensive exile.* This, in the version mentioned in the next note, was ' famish'd exile.'

l. 420. *To stop too fearful, and too faint to go.* This line, upon Boswell's authority, is claimed for Johnson (Birkbeck Hill's *Boswell*, 1887, ii. 6). Goldsmith's original ran :—

> And faintly fainter, fainter seems to go.

(Dobell's *Prospect of Society*, 1902, p. 3).

l. 429. *How small, of all*, &c. Johnson wrote these concluding ten lines with the exception of the penultimate couplet. They and line 420 were all—he told Boswell—of which he could be sure (Birkbeck Hill's *Boswell*, *ut supra*). Like Goldsmith, he sometimes worked his prose ideas into his verse. The first couplet is apparently a reminiscence of a passage in his own *Rasselas*, 1759, ii. 112, where the astronomer speaks of 'the task of a king . . . who has the care only of a few millions, to whom he cannot do much good or harm.' (Grant's *Johnson*, 1887, p. 89.) 'I would not give half a guinea to live under one form of government rather than another,' he told that 'vile Whig,' Sir Adam Fergusson, in 1772. 'It is of no moment to the happiness of an individual' (Birkbeck Hill's *Boswell*, 1887, ii. 170).

l. 435. *The lifted axe.* Mitford here recalls Blackmore's

> Some the sharp axe, and some the painful wheel.

The 'lifted axe' he also traces to Young and Blackmore, with both of whom Goldsmith seems to have been familiar; but it is surely not necessary to assume that he borrowed from either in this instance.

l. 436. *Luke's iron crown.* George and Luke Dosa, or Doscha, headed a rebellion in Hungary in 1513. The former was proclaimed king by the peasants; and, in consequence suffered, among other things, the torture of the red-hot iron crown. Such a punishment took place at Bordeaux when Montaigne was seventeen (Morley's Florio's *Montaigne*, 1886, p. xvi). Much ink has been shed over Goldsmith's lapse of 'Luke' for George. In the book which he cited as his authority, the family name of the brothers was given as Zeck,—hence Bolton Corney, in his edition of the *Poetical Works*, 1845, p. 36, corrected the line to—

> Zeck's iron crown, &c.,

an alteration which has been adopted by other editors. (See also Forster's *Life*, 1871, i. 370.)

Damiens' bed of steel. Robert-François Damiens, 1714-57. Goldsmith writes 'Damien's.' In the *Gentleman's Magazine* for 1757, vol. xxvii. pp. 87 and 151, where there is an account of this poor half-witted wretch's torture and execution for attempting to assassinate Louis XV, the name is thus spelled, as also in other contemporary records and caricatures. The following passage explains the 'bed of steel':—'Being con-

ducted to the Conciergerie, an *iron bed*, which likewise served
for a chair, was prepared for him, and to this he was fastened
with chains. The torture was again applied, and a physician
ordered to attend to see what degree of pain he could support,'
&c. (Smollett's *History of England*, 1823, bk. iii, ch. 7, § xxv.)
Goldsmith's own explanation—according to Tom Davies, the
bookseller—was that he meant the rack. But Davies may have
misunderstood him, or Goldsmith himself may have forgotten
the facts. (See Forster's *Life*, 1871, i. 370.) At pp. 57–78 of
the *Monthly Review* for July, 1757 (upon which Goldsmith was
at this date employed), is a summary, 'from our Correspondent
at Paris,' of the official record of the Damiens' Trial, 4 vols.
12mo.; and his deed and tragedy make a graphic chapter in the
remarkable *Strange Adventures of Captain Dangerous*, by George
Augustus Sala, 1863, iii. pp. 154–180.

l. 438. In the first edition of *The Traveller* there are only 416
lines.

THE DESERTED VILLAGE.

After having been for some time announced as in preparation, *The Deserted Village* made its first appearance on May 26,
1770 [1]. It was received with great enthusiasm. In June a
second, third, and fourth edition followed, and in August a fifth
was published. The text here given is that of the fourth edition,
which was considerably revised. Johnson, we are told, thought
The Deserted Village inferior to *The Traveller* ; but ' time,' to
use Mr. Forster's words, ' has not confirmed *that* judgment.' Its
germ is perhaps to be found in ll. 397–402 of the earlier poem.

---

[1] In the American *Bookman* for February, 1901, pp. 563-7, Mr.
Luther S. Livingston gives an account (with facsimile title-pages) of
three *octavo* (or rather duodecimo) editions all dated 1770; and
ostensibly printed for 'W. Griffin, at Garrick's Head, in Catherine-
street, Strand.' He rightly describes their existence as ' a biblio-
graphical puzzle.' They afford no important variations; are not
mentioned by the early editors; and are certainly not in the form in
which the poem was first advertised and reviewed, as this was
a quarto. But they are naturally of interest to the collector; and
the late Colonel Francis Grant, a good Goldsmith scholar, described
one of them in the *Athenaeum* for June 20, 1896 (No. 3582).

Much research has been expended in the endeavour to identify
the scene with Lissoy, the home of the poet's youth (see *Introduction*, p. ix); but the result has only been partially successful.
The truth seems that Goldsmith, living in England, recalled in
a poem that was English in its conception many of the memories
and accessories of his early life in Ireland, without intending or
even caring to draw an exact picture. Hence, as Lord Macaulay
has observed, in a much criticized and characteristic passage,
'it is made up of incongruous parts. The village in its happy
days is a true English village. The village in its decay is an
Irish village. The felicity and the misery which Goldsmith
has brought close together belong to two different countries,
and to two different stages in the progress of society. He
had assuredly never seen in his native island such a rural
paradise, such a seat of plenty, content, and tranquillity, as his
" Auburn." He had assuredly never seen in England all the
inhabitants of such a paradise turned out of their homes in one
day and forced to emigrate in a body to America. The hamlet
he had probably seen in Kent ; the ejectment he had probably
seen in Munster ; but, by joining the two, he has produced
something which never was and never will be seen in any part
of the world.' (*Encyclop. Britannica*, 1856.) It is obvious also
that in some of his theories—the depopulation of the kingdom,
for example—Goldsmith was mistaken. But it was not for its
didactic qualities then, nor is it for them now, that *The Deserted
Village* delighted and delights. It maintains its popularity by
its charming *genre*-pictures, its sweet and tender passages, its
simplicity, its sympathetic hold upon the enduring in human
nature. To test it solely with a view to establish its topo-
graphical accuracy, or to insist too much upon the value of its
ethical teaching, is to mistake its real mission as a work of art.

Dedication, l. 6. *I am ignorant of that art in which you are
said to excel.* This modest confession did not prevent Goldsmith from making fun of the contemporary connoisseur. See the
letter from the young virtuoso in *The Citizen of the World*, 1762,
i. 145, announcing that a famous ' torse ' has been discovered
to be not ' a Cleopatra bathing ' but ' a Hercules spinning ' ;
and Charles Primrose's experiences at Paris (*Vicar of Wakefield*,
1766, ii. 27-8).

KILKENNY WEST CHURCH

l. 14. *He is since dead.* Henry Goldsmith died in May, 1768, at the age of forty-five, being then curate of Kilkenny West. (See note, p. 164.)

l. 33. *a long poem.* ' I might dwell upon such thoughts . . . were I not afraid of making this preface too tedious ; especially since I shall want all the patience of the reader, for having enlarged it with the following verses.' (Tickell's Preface to Addison's *Works*, at end.)

l. 35. *the increase of our luxuries.* The evil of luxury was a ' common topick ' with Goldsmith. (Birkbeck Hill's *Boswell*, 1887, ii. 217-8.) Smollett also, speaking with the voice of Lismahago, and continuing the quotation on p. 169, was of opinion that 'the sudden affluence occasioned by trade, forced open all the sluices of luxury, and overflowed the land with every species of profligacy and corruption.' (*Humphry Clinker*, 1771, ii. 192.—Letter of Mr. Bramble to Dr. Lewis.)

l. 1. *Sweet* AUBURN. Forster, *Life*, 1871, ii. 206, says that Goldsmith obtained this name from Bennet Langton. There is an Aldbourn or Auburn in Wiltshire, not far from Marlborough, which Prior thinks may have furnished the suggestion.

l. 6. *Seats of my youth.* This alone would imply that Goldsmith had in mind the environment of his Irish home.

l. 12. *The decent church that topp'd the neighbouring hill.* This corresponds with the church of Kilkenny West as seen from the house at Lissoy.

l. 13. *The hawthorn bush.* The Rev. Annesley Strean, Henry Goldsmith's successor at Kilkenny West, well remembered the hawthorn bush in front of the village ale-house. It had originally three trunks ; but when he wrote in 1807 only one remained, ' the other two having been cut, from time to time, by persons carrying pieces of it away to be made into toys, &c., in honour of the bard, and of the celebrity of his poem.' (*Essay on Light Reading*, by the Rev. Edward Mangin, M.A., 1808, 142-3.) Its remains were enclosed by a Captain Hogan previously to 1819 ; but nevertheless when Prior visited the place in 1830, nothing was apparent but ' a very tender shoot [which] had again forced its way to the surface.' (Prior, *Life*, 1837, ii. 264.) An engraving of the tree by S. Alken, from a sketch made in 1806-9, is to be found at p. 41 of Goldsmith's *Poetical Works,* R. H. Newell's edition, 1811, and is reproduced in the present volume.

l. 15. *How often have I bless'd the coming day.* Prior, *Life,* 1837, ii. 261, finds in this an allusion ' to the Sundays or numerous holidays, usually kept in Roman Catholic countries.'

l. 37. *Amidst thy bowers the tyrant's hand is seen.* Strean's explanation (Mangin, *ut supra,* pp. 140-1) of this is as follows :—
' The poem of *The Deserted Village,* took its origin from the circumstance of general Robert Napper [Napier or Naper], (the grandfather of the gentleman who now [1807] lives in the house, within half a mile of Lissoy, and built by the general) having purchased an extensive tract of the country surrounding Lissoy, or *Auburn* ; in consequence of which many families, here called *cottiers,* were removed, to make room for the intended improvements of what was now to become the wide domain of a rich man, warm with the idea of changing the face of his new acquisition ; and were forced, " *with fainting steps,*" to go in search of " *torrid tracts* " and " *distant climes.*" '

Prior (*Life,* 1837, i. 40-3) points out that Goldsmith was not the first to give poetical expression to the wrongs of the dispossessed Irish peasantry ; and he quotes a long extract from the *Works* (1741) of a Westmeath poet, Lawrence Whyte, which contains such passages as these :—

> Their native soil were forced to quit,
> So Irish landlords thought it fit ;
> Who without ceremony or rout,
> For their improvements turn'd them out . . .
>
> How many villages they razed,
> How many parishes laid waste . . .
>
> Whole colonies, to shun the fate
> Of being oppress'd at such a rate,
> By tyrants who still raise their rent,
> Sail'd to the Western Continent.

l. 44. *The hollow-sounding bittern guards its nest.* ' Of all those sounds,' says Goldsmith, speaking of the cries of waterfowl, ' there is none so dismally hollow as the booming of the bittern.' . . . ' I remember in the place where I was a boy with what terror this bird's note affected the whole village ; they con-

HAWTHORN TREE

(R. H. NEWELL)

sidered it as the presage of some sad event; and generally
found or made one to succeed it.' (*Animated Nature*, 1774, vi.
1-2, 4.)

Bewick, who may be trusted to speak of a bird which he has
drawn with such exquisite fidelity, refers (*Water Birds*, 1847,
p. 49) to 'the hollow booming noise which the bittern makes
during the night, in the breeding season, from its swampy
retreats.' Cf. also that close observer Crabbe (*The Borough*,
Letter xxii, ll. 197-8):—

> And the loud bittern, from the bull-rush home,
> Gave from the salt-ditch side the bellowing boom.

l. 53. *Princes and lords may flourish, or may fade ;*
A breath can make them, as a breath has made.

Mitford compares *Confessio Amantis*, fol. 152 :—

> A kynge may make a lorde a knave,
> And of a knave a lord also ;

and Professor Hales recalls Burns's later line in the *Cotter's
Saturday Night*, 1785 :—

> Princes and lords are but the breath of kings.

But Prior finds the exact equivalent of the second line in
the verses of an old French poet, De Caux, upon an hour-glass :—

> C'est un verre qui luit,
> Qu'un souffle peut détruire, et qu'un souffle a produit.

l. 57. *A time there was, ere England's griefs began.* Here,
wherever the locality of Auburn, the author had clearly England
in mind. A caustic commentator has observed that the ' time '
indicated must have been a long while ago.

l. 67. *opulence.* In the first edition the word is ' luxury.'

l. 79. *And, many a year elapsed, return to view.* ' It is strongly
contended at Lishoy, that " *the Poet*," as he is usually called
there, after his pedestrian tour upon the Continent of Europe,
returned to and resided in the village some time. . . . It is moreover believed, that the havock which had been made in his
absence among those favourite scenes of his youth, affected his
mind so deeply, that he actually composed great part of the
Deserted Village *at* Lishoy.' (*Poetical Works, with Remarks*, &c.,
by the Rev. R. H. Newell, 1811, p. 74.)

Notwithstanding the above, there is no evidence that Goldsmith ever returned to his native island. In a letter to his brother-in-law, Daniel Hodson, written in 1758, he spoke of hoping to do so ' in five or six years.' (*Percy Memoir*, 1801, i. 49). But in another letter, written towards the close of his life, it is still a thing to come. ' I am again,' he says, 'just setting out for Bath, and I honestly say I had much rather it had been for Ireland with my nephew, but that pleasure I hope to have before I die.' (Letter to Daniel Hodson, no date, in possession of the late Frederick Locker Lampson.)

l. 80. *Where once the cottage stood, the hawthorn grew.* Here followed, in the first edition :—

> Here, as with doubtful, pensive steps I range,
> Trace every scene, and wonder at the change,
> Remembrance, &c.

l. 84. *In all my griefs—and God has given my share.* Prior notes a slight similarity here to a line of Collins :—

> Ye mute companions of my toils, that bear,
> *In all my griefs*, a more than equal share !
> > *Hassan ; or, The Camel Driver.*

In *The Present State of Polite Learning*, 1759, p. 143, Goldsmith refers feelingly to ' the neglected author of the Persian eclogues, which, however inaccurate, excel any in our language.' He included four of them in *The Beauties of English Poesy*, 1767, i. pp. 239-53.

l. 87. *To husband out*, &c. In the first edition this ran :—

> My anxious day to husband near the close,
> And keep life's flame from wasting by repose.

l. 96. *Here to return—and die at home at last.* Forster compares a passage in *The Citizen of the World*, 1762, ii. 153 :—' There is something so seducing in that spot in which we first had existence, that nothing but it can please ; whatever vicissitudes we experience in life, however we toil, or wheresoever we wander, our fatigued wishes still recur to home for tranquillity, we long to die in that spot which gave us birth, and in that pleasing expectation opiate every calamity.' The poet Waller too—he adds—wished to die ' like the stag where he was roused.' (*Life*, 1871, ii. 202.)

SOUTH VIEW FROM GOLDSMITH'S MOUNT

l. 99. *How happy he.* ' How blest is he ' in the first edition.

l. 102. *And, since 'tis hard to combat, learns to fly.* Mitford compares *The Bee* for October 13, 1759, p. 56 :—' By struggling with misfortunes, we are sure to receive some wounds in the conflict.   The only method to come off victorious, is by running away.'

l. 105. *surly porter.* Mr. J. M. Lobban compares the *Citizen of the World*, 1762, i. 123 :—' I never see a nobleman's door half opened that some surly porter or footman does not stand full in the breach.'   (*Select Poems of Goldsmith*, 1900, p. 98.)

l. 109. *Bends.* ' Sinks ' in the first edition.

unperceived decay. Cf. Johnson, *Vanity of Human Wishes*, 1749, l. 292 :—

> An age that melts with unperceiv'd decay,
> And glides in modest innocence away ;

and *Irene*, Act ii, Sc. 7 :—

> And varied life steal unperceiv'd away.

l. 110. *While Resignation,* &c. In 1771 Sir Joshua exhibited a picture of ' An Old Man,' studied from the beggar who was his model for Ugolino.   When it was engraved by Thomas Watson in 1772, he called it ' Resignation,' and inscribed the print to Goldsmith in the following words :—' This attempt to express a Character in *The Deserted Village*, is dedicated to Dr. Goldsmith, by his sincere Friend and admirer, JOSHUA REYNOLDS.'

l. 114. *Up yonder hill.* It has been suggested that Goldsmith was here thinking of the little hill of Knockaruadh (Red Hill) in front of Lissoy parsonage, of which there is a sketch in Newell's *Poetical Works*, 1811.   When Newell wrote, it was already known as ' Goldsmith's mount ' ; and the poet himself refers to it in a letter to his brother-in-law Hodson, dated Dec. 27, 1757:—'I had rather be placed on the little mount before Lishoy gate, and there take in, to me, the most pleasing horizon in nature.'   (*Percy Memoir*, 1801, p. 43.)

l. 124. *And fill'd each pause the nightingale had made.* In *Animated Nature*, 1774, v. 328, Goldsmith says :—' The nightingale's pausing song would be the proper epithet for this bird's music.' [Mitford.]

l. 126. *No cheerful murmurs fluctuate in the gale.* Cf. Goldsmith's Essay on *Metaphors* (*British Magazine*):—' Armstrong has used the word *fluctuate* with admirable efficacy, in his philosophical poem entitled *The Art of Preserving Health*.'

> Oh ! when the growling winds contend, and all
> The sounding forest *fluctuates* in the storm,
> To sink in warm repose, and hear the din
> Howl o'er the steady battlements.

l. 136. *The sad historian of the pensive plain.* Strean (see note to l. 13) identified the old watercress gatherer as a certain Catherine Giraghty (or Geraghty). Her children (he said) were still living in the neighbourhood of Lissoy in 1807. (Mangin's *Essay on Light Reading*, 1808, p. 142.)

l. 140. *The village preacher's modest mansion rose.* ' The Rev. Charles Goldsmith is allowed by all that knew him, to have been faithfully represented by his son in the character of the Village Preacher.' So writes his daughter, Catharine Hodson (*Percy Memoir*, 1801, p. 3). Others, relying perhaps upon the ' forty pounds a year ' of the Dedication to *The Traveller*, make the poet's brother Henry the original ; others, again, incline to kindly Uncle Contarine (*vide Introduction*). But, as Prior justly says (*Life*, 1837, ii. 249), ' the fact perhaps is that he fixed upon no one individual, but borrowing like all good poets and painters a little from each, drew the character by their combination.'

l. 142. *with forty pounds a year.* Cf. Dedication to *The Traveller*, p. 3, l. 14.

l. 145. *Unpractis'd.* ' Unskilful ' in the first edition.

l. 148. *More skilled.* ' More bent ' in the first edition.

l. 151. *The long remember'd beggar.* ' The same persons,' says Prior, commenting upon this passage, ' are seen for a series of years to traverse the same tract of country at certain intervals, intrude into every house which is not defended by the usual outworks of wealth, a gate and a porter's lodge, exact their portion of the food of the family, and even find an occasional resting-place for the night, or from severe weather, in the chimney-corner of respectable farmers.' (*Life*, 1837, ii. 269.) Cf. Scott on the Scottish mendicants in the ' Advertisement ' to *The Antiquary*, 1816, and Leland's *Hist. of Ireland*, 1773, i. 35.

l. 155. *The broken soldier.* The disbanded soldier let loose upon the country at the conclusion of the 'Seven Years' War' was a familiar figure at this period. Bewick, in his *Memoir* ('Memorial Edition'), 1887, pp. 44-5, describes some of these ancient campaigners with their battered old uniforms and their endless stories of Minden and Quebec; and a picture of two of them by T. S. Good of Berwick belonged to the late Mr. Locker Lampson. Edie Ochiltree (*Antiquary*)—it may be remembered—had fought at Fontenoy.

l. 170. *Allur'd to brighter worlds.* Cf. Tickell on Addison— 'Saints who taught and led the way to Heaven.'

l. 180. *And fools, who came to scoff, remained to pray.* Prior compares the opening lines of Dryden's *Britannia Rediviva* :—

> Our vows are heard betimes, and heaven takes care
> To grant, before we can conclude the prayer ;
> Preventing angels met it half the way,
> And sent us back to praise, who came to pray.

l. 189. *As some tall cliff*, &c. Lucan, Statius, and Claudian have been supposed to have helped Goldsmith to this fine and deservedly popular simile. But, considering his obvious familiarity with French literature, and the rarity of his 'obligations to the ancients,' it is not unlikely that, as suggested by a writer in the *Academy* for Oct. 30, 1886, his source of suggestion is to be found in the following passage of an Ode addressed by Chapelain (1595-1674) to Richelieu :—

> Dans un paisible mouvement
> Tu t'élèves au firmament,
> Et laisses contre toi murmurer cette terre ;
> Ainsi le haut Olympe, à son pied sablonneux,
> Laisse fumer la foudre et gronder le tonnerre,
> Et garde son sommet tranquille et lumineux.

Or another French model—indicated to Mr. Forster (*Life*, 1871, ii. 115-16) by the late Lord Lytton—may have been these lines from a poem by the Abbé de Chaulieu (1639-1720) :—

> Au milieu cependant de ces peines cruelles
> De notre triste hiver, compagnes trop fidèles,
> Je suis tranquille et gai. Quel bien plus précieux
> Puis-je espérer jamais de la bonté des dieux !

> Tel qu'un rocher dont la tête,
> Égalant le Mont Athos,
> Voit à ses pieds la tempête
> Troubler le calme des flots,
> La mer autour bruit et gronde ;
> Malgré ses émotions,
> Sur son front élevé règne une paix profonde,
> Que tant d'agitations
> Et que ses fureurs de l'onde
> Respectent à l'égal du nid des alcyons.

On the other hand, Goldsmith may have gone no further than Young's *Complaint*: *Night the Second*, 1742, p. 42, where, as Mitford points out, occur these lines :—

> As some tall Tow'r, or lofty Mountain's Brow,
> Detains the Sun, Illustrious from its Height,
> While rising Vapours, and descending Shades,
> With Damps, and Darkness drown the Spatious Vale :
> Undampt by Doubt, Undarken'd by Despair,
> *Philander*, thus, augustly rears his Head.

Prior also (*Life*, 1837, ii. 252) prints a passage from *Animated Nature*, 1774, i. 145, derived from Ulloa, which perhaps served as the raw material of the simile.

l. 201. *Full well they laugh'd*, &c. Steele, in *Spectator*, No. 49 (for April 26, 1711), has a somewhat similar thought :—' *Eubulus* has so great an Authority in his little Diurnal Audience, that when he shakes his Head at any Piece of publick News, they all of them appear dejected ; and, on the contrary, go home to their Dinners with a good Stomach and chearful Aspect, when *Eubulus* seems to intimate that Things go well.'

l. 205. *Yet he was kind*, &c. For the rhyme of ' fault ' and ' aught ' in this couplet Prior cites the precedent of Pope :—

> Before his sacred name flies ev'ry fault,
> And each exalted stanza teems with thought !

(*Essay on Criticism*, l. 422). He might also have cited Waller, who elides the ' l ' :—

> Were we but less indulgent to our fau'ts,
> And patience had to cultivate our thoughts.

THE SCHOOL HOUSE

(R. H. NEWELL)

Goldsmith uses a like rhyme in *Edwin and Angelina*, Stanza xxxv :—

> But mine the sorrow, mine the fault,
> And well my life shall pay ;
> I'll seek the solitude he sought,
> And stretch me where he lay.

Cf. also *Retaliation*, ll. 73-4. Perhaps—as indeed Prior suggests —he pronounced ' fault ' in this fashion.

l. 216. *That one small head could carry all he knew.* Some of the traits of this portrait are said to be borrowed from Goldsmith's own master at Lissoy :—' He was instructed in reading, writing, and arithmetic '—says his sister Catherine, Mrs. Hodson— ' by a schoolmaster in his father's village, who had been a quartermaster in the army in Queen Anne's wars, in that detachment which was sent to Spain : having travelled over a considerable part of Europe and being of a very romantic turn, he used to entertain Oliver with his adventures ; and the impressions these made on his scholar were believed by the family to have given him that wandering and unsettled turn which so much appeared in his future life.' (*Percy Memoir*, 1801, pp. 3-4.) The name of this worthy, according to Strean, was Burn (Byrne). (Mangin's *Essay on Light Reading*, 1808, p. 142.)

l. 219. *Near yonder thorn.* See note to l. 13.

l. 229. *The chest contriv'd a double debt to pay.* Cf. the *Description of an Author's Bedchamber*, p. 48, l. ult. :—

> A cap by night—a stocking all the day !

l. 232. *The twelve good rules.* ' A constant one ' (i. e. picture) ' in every house was "King Charles' Twelve Good Rules." ' (Bewick's *Memoir*, ' Memorial Edition,' 1887, p. 262.) This old broadside, surmounted by a rude woodcut of the King's execution, is still prized by collectors. The rules, as ' found in the study of King Charles the First, of Blessed Memory,' are as follow :—' 1. Urge no healths ; 2. Profane no divine ordinances ; 3. Touch no state matters ; 4. Reveal no secrets ; 5. Pick no quarrels ; 6. Make no comparisons ; 7. Maintain no ill opinions ; 8. Keep no bad company ; 9. Encourage no vice ; 10. Make no long meals ; 11. Repeat no grievances ; 12. Lay no Wagers. Prior, *Misc. Works*, 1837, iv. 63, points out that Crabbe also makes the 'Twelve Good Rules' conspicuous in the *Parish Register* (ll. 51-2) :—

> There is King Charles, and all his Golden Rules,
> Who proved Misfortune's was the best of schools.

Her late Majesty, Queen Victoria, kept a copy of these rules in the servants' hall at Windsor Castle.

the royal game of goose. The 'Royal and Entertaining Game of the Goose' is described at length in Strutt's *Sports and Pastimes*, bk. iv, ch. 2 (xxv). It may be briefly defined as a game of compartments with different titles through which the player progresses according to the numbers he throws with the dice. At every fourth or fifth compartment is depicted a goose, and if the player's cast falls upon one of these, he moves forward double the number of his throw.

l. 235. *While broken tea-cups.* Cf. the *Description of an Author's Bedchamber*, p. 48, l. 18 :—

> And five crack'd teacups dress'd the chimney board.

Mr. Hogan, who repaired or rebuilt the ale-house at Lissoy, did not forget, besides restoring the 'Royal Game of Goose' and the 'Twelve Good Rules,' to add the broken teacups, 'which for better security in the frail tenure of an Irish publican, or the doubtful decorum of his guests, were embedded in the mortar.' (Prior, *Life*, 1837, ii. 265.)

l. 250. *Shall kiss the cup.* Cf. Scott's *Lochinvar* :—

> The bride kissed the goblet : the knight took it up,
> He quaff'd off the wine and he threw down the cup.

Cf. also *The History of Miss Stanton* (*British Magazine*, July, 1760).—' The earthen mug went round. *Miss touched the cup,* the stranger pledged the parson,' &c.

l. 268. *Between a splendid and a happy land.* Prior compares *The Citizen of the World*, 1762, i. 98 :—' Too much commerce may injure a nation as well as too little ; and . . . there is a wide difference between a conquering and a flourishing empire.'

l. 310. *To see profusion that he must not share.* Cf. *Animated Nature*, iv. p. 43 :—' He only guards those luxuries he is not fated to share.' [Mitford.]

l. 313. *To see those joys.* Up to the third edition the words were *each joy*.

l. 318. *There the black gibbet glooms beside the way.* The gallows, under the savage penal laws of the eighteenth century, by which horse-stealing, forgery, shop-lifting, and even the cutting of a hop-bind in a plantation were punishable with death, was a common object in the landscape. Cf. *Vicar of Wakefield*, 1766, ii. 122 :—' Our possessions are paled up with new edicts every day, and hung round with gibbets to scare every invader'; and *Citizen of the World*, 1762, ii. 63–7. Johnson, who wrote eloquently on capital punishment in *The Rambler* for April 20, 1751, No. 114, also refers to the ceaseless executions in his *London*, 1738, ll. 238–43 :—

> Scarce can our fields, such crowds at Tyburn die,
> With hemp the gallows and the fleet supply.
> Propose your schemes, ye senatorian band,
> Whose ways and means support the sinking land :
> Lest ropes be wanting in the tempting spring,
> To rig another convoy for the king.

l. 326. *Where the poor houseless shivering female lies.* Mitford compares Letter cxiv of *The Citizen of the World*, 1762, ii. 211 :— ' These *poor shivering females* have once seen happier days, and been flattered into beauty. They have been prostituted to the gay luxurious villain, and are now turned out to meet the severity of winter. Perhaps now lying at the doors of their betrayers, they sue to wretches whose hearts are insensible, or debauchees who may curse, but will not relieve them.' The same passage occurs in *The Bee*, 1759, p. 126 (*A City Night-Piece*).

l. 332. *Near her betrayer's door*, &c. Cf. the foregoing quotation.

l. 344. *wild Altama*, i.e. the Alatamaha, a river in Georgia, North America. Goldsmith may have been familiar with this name in connexion with his friend Oglethorpe's expedition of 1733.

l. 355. *crouching tigers*, a poetical licence, as there are no tigers in the locality named. But Mr. J. M. Lobban calls attention to a passage from *Animated Nature* [1774, iii. 244], in which Goldsmith seems to defend himself :—' There is an animal of

America, which is usually called the Red Tiger, but Mr. Buffon calls it the Cougar, which, no doubt, is very different from the tiger of the east. Some, however, have thought proper to rank both together, and I will take leave to follow their example.'

l. 371. *The good old sire.* Cf. *Threnodia Augustalis*, ll. 16–17:—

> The good old sire, unconscious of decay,
> The modest matron, clad in homespun gray.

l. 378. *a father's.* ' Her father's ' in the first edition.

l. 384. *silent.* ' Decent ' in the first edition.

l. 418. *On Torno's cliffs, or Pambamarca's side.* ' Torno ' = Tornea, a river which falls into the Gulf of Bothnia ; Pambamarca is a mountain near Quito, South America. ' The author '— says Bolton Corney—' bears in memory the operations of the French philosophers in the arctic and equatorial regions, as described in the celebrated narratives of M. Maupertuis and Don Antonio de Ulloa.'

ll. 427–30. *That trade's proud empire*, &c. These last four lines are attributed to Johnson on Boswell's authority :—' Dr. Johnson . . . favoured me by marking the lines which he furnished to Goldsmith's *Deserted Village*, which are only the *last four*.' (Birkbeck Hill's *Boswell*, 1887, ii. 7.)

PROLOGUE OF LABERIUS.

This translation, or rather imitation, was first published at pp. 176–7 of *An Enquiry into the Present State of Polite Learning in Europe*, 1759 (Chap. xii, ' Of the Stage '), where it is prefaced as follows :—' MACROBIUS has preserved a prologue, spoken and written by the poet [Decimus] Laberius, a Roman knight, whom Cæsar forced upon the stage, written with great elegance and spirit, which shews what opinion the Romans in general entertained of the profession of an actor.' In the second edition of 1774 the prologue was omitted. The original lines, one of which Goldsmith quotes, are to be found in the *Saturnalia* of Macrobius, lib. ii, cap. vii (*Opera*, London, 1694). He seems to have confined himself to imitating the first fifteen :—

> Necessitas, cujus cursus transversi impetum
> Voluerunt multi effugere, pauci potuerunt,

Quo me detrusit paene extremis sensibus ?
Quem nulla ambitio, nulla umquam largitio,
Nullus timor, vis nulla, nulla auctoritas
Movere potuit in juventa de statu ;
Ecce in senecta ut facile labefecit loco
Viri Excellentis mente clemente edita
Submissa placide blandiloquens oratio !
Etenim ipsi di negare cui nihil potuerunt,
Hominem me denegare quis posset pati ?
Ergo bis tricenis annis actis sine tota
Eques Romanus Lare egressus meo
Domum revertar mimus. nimirum hoc die
Uno plus vixi mihi quam vivendum fuit.

Rollin gives a French translation of this prologue in his *Traité
des Études*. It is quoted by Bolton Corney in his *Poetical
Works of Oliver Goldsmith*, 1845, pp. 203-4. In his Aldine
edition of 1831, p. 114, Mitford completed Goldsmith's version
as follows :—

Too lavish still in good, or evil hour,
To show to man the empire of thy power,
If fortune, at thy wild impetuous sway,
The blossoms of my fame must drop away,
Then was the time the obedient plant to strain
When life was warm in every vigorous vein,
To mould young nature to thy plastic skill,
And bend my pliant boyhood to thy will.
So might I hope applauding crowds to hear,
Catch the quick smile, and HIS attentive ear.
But ah ! for what hast thou reserv'd my age ?
Say, how can I expect the approving stage ;
Fled is the bloom of youth—the manly air—
The vigorous mind that spurn'd at toil and care ;
Gone is the voice, whose clear and silver tone
The enraptur'd theatre would love to own.
As clasping ivy chokes the encumber'd tree,
So age with foul embrace has ruined me.
Thou, and the tomb, Laberius, art the same,
Empty within, what hast thou but a name ?

Macrobius, it may be remembered, was the author, with a quotation from whom Johnson, after a long silence, electrified the company upon his first arrival at Pembroke College, thus giving (says Boswell) ' the first impression of that more extensive reading in which he had indulged himself' (Birkbeck Hill's *Boswell*, 1887, i. 59). If the study of Macrobius is to be regarded as a test of ' more extensive reading,' that praise must therefore be accorded to Goldsmith, who cites him in his first book.

ON A BEAUTIFUL YOUTH STRUCK BLIND WITH LIGHTNING.

This quatrain, the original of which does not appear to have been traced, was first published in *The Bee* for Saturday, the 6th of October, 1759, p. 8. It is there succeeded by the following Latin epigram, ' in the same spirit' :—

> Lumine Acon dextro capta est Leonida sinistro
>> Et poterat forma vincere uterque Deos.
> Parve puer lumen quod habes concede puellae
>> Sic tu caecus amor sic erit illa Venus.

There are several variations of this in the *Gentleman's Magazine* for 1745, pp. 104, 159, 213, 327, one of which is said to be ' By a monk of Winchester,' with a reference to ' Cambden's *Remains*, p. 413.' None of these corresponds exactly with Goldsmith's text ; and the lady's name is uniformly given as 'Leonilla.' A writer in the *Quarterly Review*, vol. 171, p. 296, prints the ' original ' thus—

> Lumine Acon dextro, capta est Leonilla sinistro,
>> Et potis est forma vincere uterque Deos.
> Blande puer, lumen quod habes concede sorori ;
>> Sic tu caecus Amor, sic erit illa Venus ;

and says ' it was written by Girolamo Amalteo, and will be found in any of the editions of the *Trium Fratrum Amaltheorum Carmina*, under the title of ' De gemellis, fratre et sorore, luscis.' According to Byron on Bowles (*Works*, 1836, vi. p. 390), the persons referred to are the Princess of Eboli, mistress of Philip II of Spain, and Maugiron, minion of Henry III of France, who had each of them lost an eye. But for this the reviewer above quoted had found no authority.

THE GIFT.

This little trifle, in which a French levity is wedded to the language of Prior, was first printed in *The Bee*, for Saturday, the 13th of October, 1759. Its original, which is as follows, is to be found where Goldsmith found it, namely in Part iii of the *Ménagiana*, (ed. 1729, iii, 397), and not far from the ditty of *le fameux la Galisse*. (See *An Elegy on Mrs. Mary Blaize, infra*, p. 198):—

ÉTRENE A IRIS.

Pour témoigner de ma flame,
Iris, du meilleur de mon ame
Je vous donne à ce nouvel an
Non pas dentelle ni ruban,
Non pas essence, ni pommade,
Quelques boites de marmelade,
Un manchon, des gans, un bouquet,
Non pas heures, ni chapelet.
Quoi donc ? Attendez, je vous donne
O fille plus belle que bonne . . .
Je vous donne : Ah ! le puis-je dire ?
Oui, c'est trop souffrir le martyre,
Il est tems de s'émanciper,
Patience va m'échaper,
Fussiez-vous cent fois plus aimable,
Belle Iris, je vous donne . . . au Diable.

In Bolton Corney's edition of Goldsmith's *Poetical Works*, 1845, p. 77, note, these lines are attributed to Bernard de la Monnoye (1641–1728), who is said to have included them in a collection of *Étrennes en vers*, published in 1715.

l. 20. *I'll give thee.* See an anecdote *à propos* of this anti-climax in Trevelyan's *Life and Letters of Lord Macaulay*, ed. 1889, p. 600 :—' There was much laughing about Mrs. Beecher Stowe [then (16th March, 1853) expected in England], and what we were to give her. I referred the ladies to Goldsmith's poems for what I should give. Nobody but Hannah understood me ; but some of them have since been thumbing Goldsmith to make out the riddle.'

THE LOGICIANS REFUTED.

These lines, which have often, and even of late years, been
included among Swift's works, were first printed as Goldsmith's
by T. Evans at vol. i. pp. 115–17 of *The Poetical and Dramatic
Works of Oliver Goldsmith, M.B.*, 1780. They originally appeared
in *The Busy Body* for Thursday, October the 18th, 1759 (No. v),
having this notification above the title : ' The following Poem
written by DR. SWIFT, is communicated to the Public by the
BUSY BODY, to whom it was presented by a Nobleman of distinguished Learning and Taste.' In No. ii they had already
been advertised as forthcoming. The sub-title, ' In imitation
of Dean Swift,' seems to have been added by Evans. The text
here followed is that of the first issue.

l. 5. *Wise Aristotle and Smiglecius.* Cf. *The Life of Parnell*,
1770, p. 3 :—' His imagination might have been too warm to
relish the cold logic of Burgersdicius, or the dreary subtleties of
Smiglesius ; but it is certain, that as a classical scholar, few
could equal him.' Martin Smiglesius or Smigletius, a Polish Jesuit,
theologian and logician, who died in 1618, appears to have been
a special *bête noire* to Goldsmith ; and the reference to him here
would support the ascription of the poem to Goldsmith's pen,
were it not that Swift seems also to have cherished a like antipathy :—' He told me that he had made many efforts, upon his
entering the College [i. e. Trinity College, Dublin], to read some
of the old treatises on logic writ by *Smeglesius*, Keckermannus,
Burgersdicius, &c., and that he never had patience to go through
three pages of any of them, he was so disgusted at the stupidity
of the work.' (Sheridan's *Life of Swift*, 2nd ed., 1787, p. 4.)

l. 16. *Than reason-boasting mortal's pride.* So in *The Busy
Body.* Some editors—Mitford, for example—print the line :—

Than reason,—boasting mortals' pride.

l. 18. *Deus est anima brutorum.* Cf. Addison in *Spectator*,
No. 121 (July 19, 1711) : ' A modern Philosopher, quoted by
Monsieur *Bale* in his Learned Dissertation on the Souls of Brutes
delivers the same Opinion [i. e.—That Instinct is the immediate
direction of Providence], tho' in a bolder form of words, where
he says *Deus est Anima Brutorum*, God himself is the Soul of

Brutes.' There is much in 'Monsieur Bayle' on this theme. Probably Addison had in mind the following passage of the *Dict. Hist. et Critique* (3rd ed., 1720, 2481*b*.) which Bayle cites from M. Bernard:—' Il me semble d'avoir lu quelque part cette Thèse, *Deus est anima brutorum* : l'expression est un peu dure ; mais elle peut recevoir un fort bon sens.'

l. 32. *B–b* = Bob, i. e. Sir Robert Walpole, the Prime Minister, for whom many venal ' quills were drawn ' *circa* 1715–42. Cf. Pope's *Epilogue to the Satires*, 1738, Dialogue i, ll. 27–32 :—

> Go see Sir ROBERT—
> P. See Sir ROBERT !—hum—
> And never laugh—for all my life to come ?
> Seen him I have, but in his happier hour
> Of Social Pleasure, ill-exchang'd for Pow'r ;
> Seen him, uncumber'd with the Venal tribe,
> Smile without Art, and win without a Bribe.

l. 46. *A courtier any ape surpasses.* Cf. Gay's *Fables, passim.* Indeed there is more of Gay than Swift in this and the lines that follow. Gay's life was wasted in fruitless expectations of court patronage, and his disappointment often betrays itself in his writings.

l. 56. *And footmen, lords and dukes can act.* Cf. *Gil Blas,* 1715–35, liv. iii, chap. iv :—' Il falloit voir comme nous nous portions des santés à tous moments, en nous donnant les uns aux autres les surnoms de nos maîtres. Le valet de don Antonio appeloit Gamboa celui de don Fernand, et le valet de don Fernand appeloit Centellès celui de don Antonio. Ils me nommoient de même Silva ; et nous nous enivrions peu à peu sous ces noms empruntés, tout aussi bien que les seigneurs qui les portoient véritablement.' But Steele had already touched this subject in *Spectator*, No. 88, for June 11, 1711, ' On the Misbehaviour of Servants,' a paper supposed to have afforded the hint for Townley's farce of *High Life below Stairs*, which, about a fortnight after *The Logicians Refuted* appeared, was played for the first time at Drury Lane, not much to the gratification of the gentlemen's gentlemen in the upper gallery. Goldsmith himself wrote ' A Word or two on the late Farce, called *High Life below Stairs*,' in *The Bee* for November 3, 1759, pp. 154–7.

A SONNET.

This little piece first appears in *The Bee* for October 20, 1759 (No. iii). It is there called ' A Sonnet,' a title which is only accurate in so far as it is ' a little song.' Bolton Corney affirms that it is imitated from the French of Saint-Pavin (i.e. Denis Sanguin de Saint-Pavin, d. 1670), whose works were edited in 1759, the year in which Goldsmith published the collection of essays and verses in which it is to be found. The text here followed is that of the ' new edition ' of *The Bee*, published by W. Lane, Leadenhall Street, no date, p. 94. Neither by its motive nor its literary merits—it should be added—did the original call urgently for translation ; and the poem is here included solely because, being Goldsmith's, it cannot be omitted from his complete works.

l. 5. This and the following line in the first version run :—

Yet, why this killing soft dejection ?
Why dim thy beauty with a tear ?

STANZAS ON THE TAKING OF QUEBEC.

Quebec was taken on the 13th September, 1759. Wolfe was wounded pretty early in the action, while leading the advance of the Louisbourg grenadiers. ' A shot shattered his wrist. He wrapped his handkerchief about it and kept on. Another shot struck him, and he still advanced, when a third lodged in his breast. He staggered, and sat on the ground. Lieutenant Brown, of the grenadiers, one Henderson, a volunteer in the same company, and a private soldier, aided by an officer of artillery who ran to join them, carried him in their arms to the rear. He begged them to lay him down. They did so, and asked if he would have a surgeon. " There 's no need," he answered ; " it 's all over with me." A moment after, one of them cried out, " They run ; see how they run ! " " Who run ? " Wolfe demanded, like a man roused from sleep. " The enemy, sir. They give way everywhere ! " " Go, one of you, to Colonel Burton," returned the dying man ; " tell him to march Webb's regiment down to Charles River, to cut off their retreat from the bridge." Then, turning on his side, he mur-

mured, " Now, God be praised, I will die in peace ! " and in a few moments his gallant soul had fled.' (Parkman's *Montcalm and Wolfe*, 1885, ii. 296-7.) In his *History of England in a Series of Letters*, 1764, ii. 241, Goldsmith says of this event :—' Perhaps the loss of such a man was greater to the nation than the conquering of all Canada was advantageous ; but it is the misfortune of humanity, that we can never know true greatness till the moment when we are going to lose it [1].' The present stanzas were first published in *The Busy Body* (No. vii) for Tuesday, the 22nd October, 1759, a week after the news of Wolfe's death had reached this country (Tuesday the 16th). According to Prior (*Life*, 1837, i. 6), Goldsmith claimed to be related to Wolfe by the father's side, the maiden name of the General's mother being Henrietta Goldsmith. It may be noted that Benjamin West's popular rendering of Wolfe's death (1771)—a rendering which Nelson never passed in a print shop without being stopped by it—was said to be based upon the descriptions of an eye-witness. It was engraved by Woollett and Ryland in 1776. A key to the names of those appearing in the picture was published in the *Army and Navy Gazette* of January 20, 1893.

AN ELEGY ON MRS. MARY BLAIZE.

The publication in February, 1751, of Gray's *Elegy Wrote in a Country Church Yard* had set a fashion in poetry which long continued. Goldsmith, who considered that work ' a very fine poem, but overloaded with epithet ' (*Beauties of English Poesy*, 1767, i. 53), and once proposed to amend it ' by leaving out an idle word in every line ' [!] (Cradock's *Memoirs*, 1826, i. 230), resented these endless imitations, and his antipathy to them frequently reveals itself. Only a few months before the appearance of Mrs. Blaize in *The Bee* for October 27, 1759, he had written in the *Critical Review*, vii. 263, when noticing Langhorne's *Death of Adonis*, as follows :—' It is not thus that many of our moderns have composed what they call elegies ; they seem scarcely to have known its real character. If an hero or a poet

---

[1] He repeats this sentiment, in different words, in the later *History of England* of 1771, iv. 400.

happens to die with us, the whole band of elegiac poets raise
the dismal chorus, adorn his herse with all the paltry escutcheons
of flattery, rise into bombast, paint him at the head of his thunder-
ing legions, or reining Pegasus in his most rapid career ; they are
sure to strew cypress enough upon the bier, dress up all the muses
in mourning, and look themselves every whit as dismal and
sorrowful as an undertaker's shop.'   He returned to the subject
in a *Chinese Letter* of March 4, 1761, in the *Public Ledger*
(afterwards Letter ciii of *The Citizen of the World*, 1762, ii.
162–5), which contains the lines *On the Death of the Right Honour-
able * * *; and again, in *The Vicar of Wakefield*, 1766, i. 174,
à propos of the *Elegy on the Death of a Mad Dog*, he makes Dr.
Primrose say, ' I have wept so much at all sorts of elegies of
late, that without an enlivening glass I am sure this will over-
come me.'

The model for *An Elegy on Mrs. Mary Blaize* is to be found
in the old French popular song of Monsieur de la Palisse or
Palice, about fifty verses of which are printed in Larousse's
Grand Dictionnaire Universel du XIX me Siècle, x. p. 179.   It is
there stated to have originated in some dozen stanzas suggested
to la Monnoye (*v. supra*, p. 193) by the extreme artlessness of
a military quatrain dating from the battle of Pavia, and the
death upon that occasion of the famous French captain, Jacques
de Chabannes, seigneur de la Palice :—

> Monsieur d'La Palice est mort,
> Mort devant Pavie ;
> Un quart d'heure avant sa mort,
> *Il était encore en vie.*

The remaining verses, i. e. in addition to those of la Monnoye,
are the contributions of successive generations.   Goldsmith
probably had in mind the version in Part iii of the *Ménagiana*,
(ed. 1729, iii, 384–391) where, apparently by a typographical error,
the hero is called ' *le fameux la Galisse, homme imaginaire.*'   The
verses he imitated most closely are reproduced below.   It may be
added that this poem supplied one of its last inspirations to the
pencil of Randolph Caldecott, who published it as a picture-
book in October, 1885.   (See also *An Elegy on the Death of a
Mad Dog*, p. 212.)

l. 8. *Who left a pledge behind.* Caldecott cleverly converted this line into the keynote of the poem, by making the heroine a pawnbroker.

l. 20. *When she has walk'd before.* Cf. the French :—

> On dit que dans ses amours
> Il fut caressé des belles,
> Qui le suivirent toujours,
> *Tant qu'il marcha devant elles.*

l. 24. *Her last disorder mortal.* Cf. the French :—

> Il fut par un triste sort
> Blessé d'une main cruelle.
> On croit, puis qu'il en est mort,
> *Que la plaie étoit mortelle.*

l. 26. *Kent Street,* Southwark, 'chiefly inhabited,' said Strype, 'by Broom Men and Mumpers'; and Evelyn tells us (*Diary* 5th December, 1683) that he assisted at the marriage, to her fifth husband, of a Mrs. Castle, who was 'the daughter of one Burton, a broom-man . . . in Kent Street' who had become not only rich, but Sheriff of Surrey. It was a poor neighbourhood corresponding to the present 'old Kent-road, from Kent to Southwark and old London Bridge' (Cunningham's *London* [1]). Goldsmith himself refers to it in *The Bee* for October 20, 1759, being the number immediately preceding that in which *Madam Blaize* first appeared :—' You then, O ye beggars of my acquaintance, whether in rags or lace ; whether in *Kent-street* or the Mall ; whether at the Smyrna or St. Giles's, might I advise as a friend, never seem in want of the favour which you solicit' (p. 72). Three years earlier he had practised as 'a physician, in a humble way' in Bankside, Southwark, and was probably well acquainted with the humours of Kent Street.

DESCRIPTION OF AN AUTHOR'S BEDCHAMBER.

In a letter written to the Rev. Henry Goldsmith in 1759 (*Percy Memoir*, 1801, pp. 53–9), Goldsmith thus refers to the first form of these verses :—' Your last letter, I repeat it, was

---

[1] In contemporary maps Kent (now Tabard) Street is shown extending between the present New Kent Road and Blackman Street.

too short ; you should have given me your opinion of the design of the heroicomical poem which I sent you : you remember I intended to introduce the hero of the poem, as lying in a paltry alehouse. You may take the following specimen of the manner, which I flatter myself is quite original. The room in which he lies, may be described somewhat this way :—

> The window, patch'd with paper, lent a ray,
> That feebly shew'd the state in which he lay.
> The sanded floor, that grits beneath the tread :
> The humid wall with paltry pictures spread ;
> The game of goose was there expos'd to view
> And the twelve rules the royal martyr drew :
> The seasons, fram'd with listing, found a place,
> And Prussia's monarch shew'd his lamp-black face
> The morn was cold ; he views with keen desire,
> A rusty grate unconscious of a fire.
> An unpaid reck'ning on the frieze was scor'd,
> And five crack'd tea-cups dress'd the chimney board.

And now imagine after his soliloquy, the landlord to make his appearance, in order to dun him for the reckoning :—

> Not with that face, so servile and so gay,
> That welcomes every stranger that can pay,
> With sulky eye he smoak'd the patient man,
> Then pull'd his breeches tight, and thus began, &c.

All this is taken, you see, from nature. It is a good remark of Montaign[e]'s, that the wisest men often have friends, with whom they do not care how much they play the fool. Take my present follies as instances of regard. Poetry is a much easier, and more agreeable species of composition than prose, and could a man live by it, it were no unpleasant employment to be a poet.'

In Letter xxix of *The Citizen of the World*, 1762, i. 119-22, which first appeared in *The Public Ledger* for May 2, 1760, they have a different setting. They are read at a club of authors by a ' poet, in shabby finery,' who asserts that he has composed them the day before. After some preliminary difficulties, arising from the fact that the laws of the club do not permit any author to inflict his own works upon the assembly without a money payment, he introduces them as follows :—

' Gentlemen, says he, the present piece is not one of your common epic poems, which come from the press like paper kites in summer; there are none of your Turnuses or Dido's in it ; it is an heroical description of nature. I only beg you'll endeavour to make your souls unison [1] with mine, and hear with the same enthusiasm with which I have written. The poem begins with the description of an author's bedchamber : the picture was sketched in my own apartment ; for you must know, gentlemen, that I am myself the heroe. Then putting himself into the attitude of an orator, with all the emphasis of voice and action, he proceeded.

> Where the Red Lion, &c.'

The verses then follow as they are printed at p. 48 of this volume ; but he is unable to induce his audience to submit to a further sample. In a slightly different form, some of them were afterwards worked into *The Deserted Village*, 1770. (See ll. 227–36.)

l. 3. *Where Calvert's butt, and Parsons' black champagne.* The Calverts and Humphrey Parsons were noted brewers of ' entire butt beer ' or porter, also known familiarly as ' British Burgundy ' and ' black Champagne.' Calvert's ' Best Butt Beer ' figures on the sign in Hogarth's *Beer Street*, 1751.

l. 10. *The humid wall with paltry pictures spread.* Bewick gives the names of some of these popular, if paltry, decorations :—' In cottages everywhere were to be seen the " Sailor's Farewell " and his " Happy Return," " Youthful Sports," and the " Feats of Manhood," " The Bold Archers Shooting at a Mark," " The Four Seasons," &c.' (*Memoir*, ' Memorial Edition,' 1887, p. 263.)

l. 11. *The royal game of goose was there in view.* (See note, p. 188, l. 232.)

l. 12. *And the twelve rules the royal martyr drew.* (See note, p. 187, l. 232.)

l. 13. *The Seasons, fram'd with listing.* See note to l. 10 above, as to ' The Seasons.' Listing, ribbon, braid, or tape is still used as a primitive *encadrement*. In a letter dated August 15, 1758, to his cousin, Mrs. Lawder (Jane Contarine), Goldsmith again refers to this device. Speaking of some ' maxims of frugality ' with which he intends to adorn his room, he adds—

[1] i. e. accord, conform.

' my landlady's daughter shall frame them with the parings of my black waistcoat.' (Prior, *Life*, 1837, i. 271.)

l. 14. *And brave Prince William.* William Augustus, Duke of Cumberland, 1721–65. The 'lamp-black face' would seem to imply that the portrait was a silhouette. In the letter quoted on p. 200 it is 'Prussia's monarch' (i. e. Frederick the Great).

l. 17. *With beer and milk arrears.* See the lines relative to the landlord in Goldsmith's above-quoted letter to his brother. In another letter of August 14, 1758, to Robert Bryanton, he describes himself as ' in a garret writing for bread, and expecting to be dunned for a milk score.' Hogarth's *Distrest Poet*, 1736, it will be remembered, has already realized this expectation.

l. 20. *A cap by night—a stocking all the day.* ' With this last line,' says *The Citizen of the World*, 1762, i. 121, ' he [the author] seemed so much elated, that he was unable to proceed : " There gentlemen, cries he, there is a description for you ; Rab[e]lais's bed-chamber is but a fool to it :

A cap by night—a stocking all the day !

There is sound and sense, and truth, and nature in the trifling compass of ten little syllables." ' (Letter xxix.) Cf. also *The Deserted Village*, l. 230 :—

A bed by night, a chest of drawers by day.

If Goldsmith's lines did not belong to 1759, one might suppose he had in mind the later *Pauvre Diable* of his favourite Voltaire. (See also APPENDIX B.)

ON SEEING MRS. ** PERFORM IN THE CHARACTER OF ****.

These verses, intended for a specimen of the newspaper Muse, are from Letter lxxxii of *The Citizen of the World*, 1762, ii. 87, first printed in *The Public Ledger*, October 21, 1760.

ON THE DEATH OF THE RIGHT HON. ***

From Letter ciii of *The Citizen of the World*, 1762, ii. 164, first printed in *The Public Ledger*, March 4, 1761. The verses are

given as a 'specimen of a poem on the decease of a great man.'
Goldsmith had already used the trick of the final line of the
quatrain in *An Elegy on Mrs. Mary Blaize*, ante, p. 198.

AN EPIGRAM.

From Letter cx of *The Citizen of the World*, 1762, ii. 193, first
printed in *The Public Ledger*, April 14, 1761.   It had, however,
already been printed in the *Ledger*, ten days before.   Goldsmith's
animosity to Churchill (cf. note to l. 41 of the dedication to *The
Traveller*) was notorious ; but this is one of his doubtful pieces.

l. 3. *virtue.* ' Charity' (*Author's note*).

l. 4. *bounty.* ' Settled at One Shilling—the Price of the Poem '
(*Author's note*).

TO G. C. AND R. L.

From the same letter as the preceding.   George Colman and
Robert Lloyd of the *St. James's Magazine* were supposed to have
helped Churchill in *The Rosciad*, the ' it ' of the epigram.

TRANSLATION OF A SOUTH AMERICAN ODE.

From Letter cxiii of *The Citizen of the World*, 1762, ii. 209, first
printed in *The Public Ledger*, May 13, 1761.

THE DOUBLE TRANSFORMATION.

The Double Transformation first appeared in *Essays : By
Mr. Goldsmith*, 1765, where it figures as Essay xxvi, occupying
pp. 229–33.   It was revised for the second edition of 1766,
becoming Essay xxviii, pp. 241–45.   This is the text here followed.
The poem is an obvious imitation of what its author calls (*Letters
from a Nobleman to his Son*, 1764, ii. 140) that ' French elegant
easy manner of telling a story,' which Prior had caught from La
Fontaine.   But the inherent simplicity of Goldsmith's style is

curiously evidenced by the absence of those illustrations and ingenious allusions which are Prior's chief characteristic. And although Goldsmith included *The Ladle* and *Hans Carvel* in his *Beauties of English Poesy*, 1767, he refrained wisely from copying the licence of his model.

l. 2. *Jack Book-worm led a college life.* The version of 1765 reads 'liv'd' for 'led.'

l. 6. *And freshmen wonder'd as he spoke.* The earlier version adds here—

> Without politeness aim'd at breeding,
> And laugh'd at pedantry and reading.

l. 18. *Her presence banish'd all his peace.* Here in the first version the paragraph closes, and a fresh one is commenced as follows :—

> Our alter'd Parson now began
> To be a perfect ladies' man ;
> Made sonnets, lisp'd his sermons o'er,
> And told the tales he told before,
> Of bailiffs pump'd, and proctors bit,
> At college how he shew'd his wit ;
> And, as the fair one still approv'd,
> He fell in love—or thought he lov'd.
> So with decorum, &c.

The fifth line was probably a reminiscence of the college riot in which Goldsmith was involved in May, 1747, and for his part in which he was publicly admonished. (See *Introduction*, p. xi, l. 3.)

l. 27. *usage.* This word, perhaps by a printer's error, is 'visage' in the first version

l. 39. *Skill'd in no other arts was she.* Cf. Prior :—

> For in all Visits who but She,
> To Argue, or to Repartée.

l. 46. *Five greasy nightcaps wrapp'd her head.* Cf. *Spectator*, No. 494—'At length the Head of the Colledge came out to him, from an inner Room, with half a Dozen Night-Caps upon his Head.' See also Goldsmith's essay on the Coronation (*Essays*, 1766, p. 238), where Mr. Grogan speaks of his wife as habitually

' mobbed up in flannel night caps, and trembling at a breath of air.'

l. 52. *By day, 'twas gadding or coquetting.* The first version after ' coquetting ' begins a fresh paragraph with—

> Now tawdry madam kept, &c.

l. 58. *A sigh in suffocating smoke.* Here in the first version follows :—

> She, in her turn, became perplexing,
> And found substantial bliss in vexing.
> Thus every hour was pass'd, &c.

l. 61. *Thus as her faults each day were known.* First version : ' Each day, the more her faults,' &c.

l. 71. *Now, to perplex.* The first version has ' Thus.' But the alteration in line 61 made a change necessary.

l. 85. *paste.* First version ' pastes.'

l. 91. *condemn'd to hack,* i. e. to hackney, to plod.

A NEW SIMILE.

The *New Simile* first appears in *Essays : By Mr. Goldsmith,* 1765, pp. 234–6, where it forms Essay xxvii. In the second edition of 1766 it occupies pp. 246–8 and forms Essay xix. The text here followed is that of the second edition, which varies slightly from the first. In both cases the poem is followed by the enigmatical initials ' *J. B.,' which, however, as suggested by Gibbs, may simply stand for ' Jack Bookworm' of *The Double Transformation.* (See p. 204.)

l. 1. *Long had I sought in vain to find.* The text of 1765 reads—' I long had rack'd my brains to find.'

l. 6. *Tooke's Pantheon.* Andrew Tooke (1673–1732) was first usher and then Master at the Charterhouse. In the latter capacity he succeeded Thomas Walker, the master of Addison and Steele. His *Pantheon,* a revised translation from the Latin of the Jesuit, Francis Pomey, was a popular school-book of mythology, with copper-plates.

l. 16. *Wings upon either side—mark that.* The petasus of Mercury, like his sandals (l. 24), is winged.

l. 36. *No poppy-water half so good.* Poppy-water, made by

boiling the heads of the white, black, or red poppy, was a favourite eighteenth-century soporific :—' Juno shall give her peacock *poppy-water*, that he may fold his ogling tail.' (Congreve's *Love for Love*, 1695, iv. 3.)

l. 42. *With this he drives men's souls to hell.*

> Tu . . . .
> . . . . virgaque levem coerces
> Aurea turbam.—Hor. *Od.* i. 10.

l. 57. *Moreover, Merc'ry had a failing.*

> Te canam . . . .
> Callidum, quidquid placuit, iocoso
> Condere furto.—Hor. *Od.* i. 10.

Goldsmith, it will be observed, rhymes ' failing ' and ' stealing.' But Pope does much the same :—

> That Jelly's rich, this Malmsey healing,
> Pray dip your Whiskers and your tail in.
> > (*Imitation of Horace*, Bk. ii, Sat. vi.)

Unless this is to be explained by poetical licence, one of these words must have been pronounced in the eighteenth century as it is not pronounced now.

l. 59. *In which all modern bards agree.* The text of 1765 reads ' our scribling bards.'

EDWIN AND ANGELINA.

This ballad, usually known as *The Hermit*, was written in or before 1765, and printed privately in that year 'for the amusement of the Countess of Northumberland,' whose acquaintance Goldsmith had recently made through Mr. Nugent. (See the prefatory note to *The Haunch of Venison*.) Its title was ' *Edwin and Angelina. A Ballad.* By Mr. Goldsmith.' It was first published in *The Vicar of Wakefield*, 1766, where it appears at pp. 70–7, vol. i. In July, 1767, Goldsmith was accused [by Dr. Kenrick] in the *St. James's Chronicle* of having taken it from Percy's *Friar of Orders Gray*. Thereupon he addressed a letter to the paper, of which the following is the material portion :—' Another Correspondent of yours accuses me of having taken a Ballad, I published some Time ago, from one by the ingenious Mr. Percy. I do not think there is any great Resemblance between the two Pieces in Question. If there be any, his Ballad is taken from mine. I read it to Mr. Percy some Years ago, and he (as we both considered these Things as Trifles at best) told me, with his usual Good Humour, the next Time I saw him, that he had taken my Plan to form the fragments of Shakespeare into a Ballad of his own. He then read me his little Cento, if I may so call it, and I highly approved it. Such petty Anecdotes as these are scarce worth printing, and were it not for the busy Disposition of some of your Correspondents, the Publick should never have known that he owes me the Hint of his Ballad, or that I am obliged to his Friendship and Learning for Communications of a much more important Nature.—I am, Sir, your's, &c. OLIVER GOLDSMITH.' (*St. James's Chronicle,* July 23–5, 1767.) No contradiction of this statement appears to have been offered by Percy; but in re-editing his *Reliques of Ancient English Poetry* in 1775, shortly after Goldsmith's death, he affixed this note to *The Friar of Orders Gray* :—' As the foregoing song has been thought to have suggested to our late excellent poet, Dr. Goldsmith, the plan of his beautiful ballad of *Edwin and Emma* [*Angelina*], first printed [published?] in his *Vicar of Wakefield*, it is but justice to his memory to declare, that his poem was written first, and that if there is any imitation in the case, they will be found both to be indebted to the beautiful old ballad, *Gentle Herdsman, &c.*, printed in the second volume of this work, which the doctor had much admired in manuscript, and has finely improved ' (vol. i. p. 250). The same story is told, in slightly different terms, at pp. 74–5 of the *Memoir* of Goldsmith drawn up under Percy's superintendence for the *Miscellaneous Works* of 1801, and a few stanzas of *Gentle Herdsman*, which Goldsmith is supposed to have had specially in mind, are there reproduced. References to them will be found in the ensuing notes. The text here adopted (with exception of ll. 117–20) is that of the fifth edition of *The Vicar of Wakefield*, 1773[4], i. pp. 78–85 ; but the variations of the earlier version of 1765 are duly chronicled, together with certain hitherto neglected differences between the first and later editions of the novel. The poem was also printed in the *Poems for Young*

Ladies, 1767, pp. 91–8 [1]. The author himself, it may be added, thought highly of it. ' As to my " Hermit," that poem,' he is reported to have said, ' cannot be amended.' (Cradock's *Memoirs*, 1828, iv. 286.)

l. 1. *Turn*, &c. The first version has—

> Deign saint-like tenant of the dale,
> To guide my nightly way,
> To yonder fire, that cheers the vale
> With hospitable ray.

l. 11. *For yonder faithless phantom flies. The Vicar of Wakefield*, first edition, has—' For yonder phantom only flies.'

l. 30. *All. Vicar of Wakefield*, first edition, ' For.'

l. 31. *Man wants but little here below.* Cf. Young's *Complaint*, 1743, *Night* iv. 9, of which this and the next line are a recollection. According to Prior (*Life*, 1837, ii. 83), they were printed as a quotation in the version of 1765. Young's line is—

> Man wants but Little ; nor thât Little, long.

l. 35. *modest. Vicar of Wakefield*, first edition, 'grateful.'

l. 37. *Far in a wilderness obscure.* First version, and *Vicar of Wakefield*, first edition :—

> Far shelter'd in a glade obscure
> The modest mansion lay.

l. 43. *The wicket, opening with a latch.* First version, and *Vicar of Wakefield*, first edition :—

> The door just opening with a latch.

l. 45. *And now, when busy crowds retire.* First version, and *Vicar of Wakefield*, first edition :—

> And now, when worldly crowds retire
> To revels or to rest.

l. 57. *But nothing*, &c. In the first version this stanza runs as follows :—

> But nothing mirthful could assuage
> The pensive stranger's woe ;
> For grief had seized his early age,
> And tears would often flow.

---

[1] This version differs considerably from the others, often following that of 1765 ; but it has not been considered necessary to record the variations here. That Goldsmith unceasingly revised the piece is sufficiently established.

l. 78. *modern.* *Vicar of Wakefield*, first edition, reads 'haughty.'

l. 84. *His love-lorn guest betray'd.* First version, and *Vicar of Wakefield*, first edition :—

> The bashful guest betray'd.

l. 85. *Surpris'd, he sees,* &c. First version, and *Vicar of Wakefield*, first edition :—

> He sees unnumber'd beauties rise,
> Expanding to the view;
> Like clouds that deck the morning skies,
> As bright, as transient too.

l. 89. *The bashful look, the rising breast.* First version, and *Vicar of Wakefield*, first edition :—

> Her looks, her lips, her panting breast.

l. 97. *But let a maid,* &c. For this, and the next two stanzas, the first version substitutes :—

> Forgive, and let thy pious care
> A heart's distress allay;
> That seeks repose, but finds despair
> Companion of the way.

> My father liv'd, of high degree,
> Remote beside the Tyne;
> And as he had but only me,
> Whate'er he had was mine.

> To win me from his tender arms,
> Unnumber'd suitors came;
> Their chief pretence my flatter'd charms,
> My wealth perhaps their aim.

l. 109. *a mercenary crowd.* *Vicar of Wakefield*, first edition, has :—' the gay phantastic crowd.'

l. 111. *Amongst the rest young Edwin bow'd.* First version :—

> Among the rest young Edwin bow'd,
> Who offer'd only love.

l. 115. *Wisdom and worth,* &c. First version, and *Vicar of Wakefield*, first edition :—

> A constant heart was all he had,
> But that was all to me.

l. 117. *And when beside me,* &c.   For this ' additional stanza,'
says the *Percy Memoir*, p. 76, ' the reader is indebted to Richard
Archdal, Esq., late a member of the Irish Parliament, to whom
it was presented by the author himself.'   It was first printed in
the *Miscellaneous Works*, 1801, ii. 25.   In Prior's edition of the
Miscellaneous Works, 1837, iv. 41, it is said to have been ' written
some years after the rest of the poem.'

l. 121. *The blossom opening to the day,* &c.   For this and the
next two stanzas the first version substitutes :—

> Whene'er he spoke amidst the train,
>   How would my heart attend !
> And till delighted even to pain,
>   How sigh for such a friend !
> And when a little rest I sought
>   In Sleep's refreshing arms,
> How have I mended what he taught,
>   And lent him fancied charms !
> Yet still (and woe betide the hour !)
>   I spurn'd him from my side,
> And still with ill-dissembled power
>   Repaid his love with pride.

l. 129. *For still I tried each fickle art,* &c.   Percy finds the
prototype of this in the following stanza of *Gentle Herdsman* :—

> And grew soe coy and nice to please,
>   As women's lookes are often soe,
> He might not kisse, nor hand forsoothe,
>   Unlesse I willed him soe to doe.

l. 133. *Till quite dejected with my scorn,* &c.   The first edition
reads this stanza and the first two lines of the next thus :—

> Till quite dejected by my scorn,
>   He left me to deplore ;
> And sought a solitude forlorn,
>   And ne'er was heard of more.
> Then since he perish'd by my fault,
>   This pilgrimage I pay, &c.

l. 135. *And sought a solitude forlorn.*   Cf. *Gentle Herdsman* :—

> He gott him to a secrett place,
>   And there he dyed without releeffe.

l. 141. *And there forlorn, despairing, hid,* &c.   The first edition
for this and the next two stanzas substitutes the following :—

> And there in shelt'ring thickets hid,
>   I'll linger till I die ;
> 'Twas thus for me my lover did,
>   And so for him will I.
>
> ' Thou shalt not thus,' the Hermit cried,
>   And clasp'd her to his breast ;
> The astonish'd fair one turned to chide,—
>   'Twas Edwin's self that prest.
>
> For now no longer could he hide,
>   What first to hide he strove ;
> His looks resume their youthful pride,
>   And flush with honest love.

l. 143. *'Twas so for me,* &c.   Cf. *Gentle Herdsman* :—

> Thus every day I fast and pray,
>   And ever will doe till I dye ;
> And gett me to some secret place,
>   For soe did hee, and soe will I.

l. 145. *Forbid it, Heaven. Vicar of Wakefield,* first edition,
like the version of 1765, has ' Thou shalt not thus.'

l. 156. *My life. Vicar of Wakefield,* first edition, has ' O
thou.'

l. 157. *No, never from this hour,* &c.   The first edition reads :—

> No, never, from this hour to part,
>   Our love shall still be new ;
> And the last sigh that rends thy heart,
>   Shall break thy Edwin's too.

The poem then concluded thus :—

> Here amidst sylvan bowers we'll rove,
>   From lawn to woodland stray ;
> Blest as the songsters of the grove,
>   And innocent as they.
>
> To all that want, and all that wail,
>   Our pity shall be given,
> And when this life of love shall fail,
>   We'll love again in heaven.

These couplets, with certain alterations in the first and last lines, are to be found in the version printed in *Poems for Young Ladies*, 1767, p. 98.

AN ELEGY ON THE DEATH OF A MAD DOG.

This poem was first published in *The Vicar of Wakefield*, 1766, i. 175–6, where it is sung by one of the little boys. In common with the *Elegy on Mrs. Mary Blaize* (p. 47) it owes something of its origin to Goldsmith's antipathy to fashionable elegiacs, something also to the story of M. de la Palisse. As regards mad dogs, its author seems to have been more reasonable than many of his contemporaries, since he ridiculed, with much common sense, their exaggerated fears on this subject (*v. Chinese Letter* in *The Public Ledger* for August 29, 1760, afterwards Letter lxvi of *The Citizen of the World*, 1762, ii. 15). But it is ill jesting with hydrophobia. Like *Madam Blaize*, these verses have been illustrated by Randolph Caldecott.

l. 5. *In Islington there was a man.* Goldsmith had lodgings at Mrs. Elizabeth Fleming's in Islington (or 'Isling town' as the earlier editions have it) in 1763–4 ; and the choice of the locality may have been determined by this circumstance. But the date of the composition of the poem is involved in the general obscurity which hangs over the *Vicar* in its unprinted state. (See *Introduction*, pp. xviii–xix.)

l. 19. *The dog, to gain some private ends.* The first edition reads 'his private ends.'

l. 32. *The dog it was that died.* This catastrophe suggests the couplet from the *Greek Anthology*, ed. Jacobs, 1813–7, ii. 387 :—

> Καππαδόκην ποτ' ἔχιδνα κακὴ δάκεν· ἀλλὰ καὶ αὐτὴ
> κάτθανε, γευσαμένη αἵματος ἰοβόλου.

Goldsmith, however, probably went no farther back than Voltaire on Fréron :—

> L'autre jour, au fond d'un vallon,
> Un serpent mordit Jean Fréron.
> Devinez ce qu'il arriva ?
> Ce fut le serpent qui creva.

This again, according to M. Edouard Fournier (*L'Esprit des Autres*, sixth edition, 1881, p. 288), is simply the readjustment of an earlier quatrain, based upon a Latin distich in the *Epigrammatum delectus*, 1659 :—

> Un gros serpent mordit Aurelle.
> Que croyez-vous qu'il arriva ?
> Qu'Aurelle en mourût ?—Bagatelle !
> Ce fut le serpent qui creva.

SONG

FROM 'THE VICAR OF WAKEFIELD.'

First published in *The Vicar of Wakefield*, 1766, ii. 78 (chap. v). It is there sung by Olivia Primrose, after her return home with her father. 'Do, my pretty Olivia,' says Mrs. Primrose, 'let us have that little melancholy air your pappa was so fond of, your sister Sophy has already obliged us. Do child, it will please your old father.' 'She complied in a manner so exquisitely pathetic,' continues Dr. Primrose, 'as moved me.' The charm of the words, and the graceful way in which they are introduced, seem to have blinded criticism to the impropriety, and even inhumanity, of requiring poor Olivia to sing a song so completely applicable to her own case. No source has been named for this piece ; and its perfect conformity with the text would appear to indicate that Goldsmith was not indebted to any earlier writer for his idea.

His well-known obligations to French sources seem, however, to have suggested that, if a French original could not be discovered for the foregoing lyric, it might be desirable to invent one. A clever paragraphist in the *St. James's Gazette* for January 28th, 1889, accordingly reproduced the following stanzas, which, he alleged, were to be found in the poems of Ségur, 'printed in Paris in 1719' :—

> Lorsqu'une femme, après trop de tendresse,
>   D'un homme sent la trahison,
> Comment, pour cette si douce foiblesse
>   Peut-elle trouver une guérison ?

Le seul remède qu'elle peut ressentir,
    La seul revanche pour son tort,
Pour faire trop tard l'amant repentir,
    Hélas ! trop tard—est la mort.

As a correspondent was not slow to point out, Goldsmith, if a copyist, at all events considerably improved his model (see in particular lines 7 and 8 of the French). On the 30th of the month the late Sir William Fraser gave it as his opinion, that, until the volume of 1719 should be produced, the ' very inferior verses quoted ' must be classed with the fabrications of ' Father Prout,' and he instanced that very version of the *Burial of Sir John Moore* (*Les Funérailles de Beaumanoir*) which has recently (August 1906) been going the round of the papers once again.   No Ségur volume of 1719 was, of course, forthcoming.

Kenrick, as we have already seen, had in 1767 accused Goldsmith of taking *Edwin and Angelina* from Percy (p. 206).   Thirty years later, the charge of plagiarism was revived in a different way when *Raimond and Angéline*, a French translation of the same poem, appeared, as Goldsmith's original, in a collection of Essays called *The Quiz*, 1797.   It was eventually discovered to be a translation *from* Goldsmith by a French poet named Léonard, who had included it in a volume dated 1792, entitled *Lettres de deux Amans, Habitans de Lyon* (Prior's *Life*, 1837, ii. 89-94). It may be added that, according to the *Biographie Universelle*, 1847, vol. 18 (Art. ' Goldsmith '), there were then no fewer than at least three French imitations of *The Hermit* besides Léonard's.

EPILOGUE TO ' THE GOOD NATUR'D MAN.'

Goldsmith's comedy of *The Good Natur'd Man* was produced by Colman, at Covent Garden, on Friday, January 29, 1768. The following note was appended to the Epilogue when printed : —' The Author, in expectation of an Epilogue from a friend at Oxford, deferred writing one himself till the very last hour. What is here offered, owes all its success to the graceful manner of the Actress who spoke it.'   It was spoken by Mrs. Bulkley, the ' Miss Richland ' of the piece.   In its first form it is to be found in *The Public Advertiser* for February 3. Two days later the play was published, with the version here followed.

l. 1. *As puffing quacks.* Goldsmith had devoted a Chinese letter to this subject. See *Citizen of the World*, 1762, ii. 10 (Letter lxv).

l. 17. *No, no ; I've other contests*, &c. This couplet is not in the first version. The old building of the College of Physicians was in Warwick Lane ; and the reference is to the long-pending dispute, occasionally enlivened by personal collision, between the Fellows and Licentiates respecting the exclusion of certain of the latter from Fellowships. On this theme Bonnell Thornton, himself an M.B. like Goldsmith, wrote a satiric additional canto to Garth's *Dispensary*, entitled *The Battle of the Wigs*, long extracts from which are printed in *The Gentleman's Magazine* for March, 1768, p. 132. The same number also reviews *The Siege of the Castle of Æsculapius, an heroic Comedy, as it is acted in War-wick-Lane.* Goldsmith's couplet is, however, best illustrated by the title of one of Sayer's caricatures, *The March of the Medical Militants to the Siege of Warwick-Lane-Castle in the Year* 1767. The quarrel was finally settled in favour of the college in June, 1771.

l. 19. *Go, ask your manager.* Colman, the manager of Covent Garden, was not a prolific, although he was a happy writer of prologues and epilogues.

l. 32. The quotation is from *King Lear*, Act iii, Sc. 4.

l. 34. In the first version the last line runs :—

And view with favour, the ' Good-natur'd Man.'

EPILOGUE TO ' THE SISTER.'

The Sister, produced at Covent Garden February 18, 1769, was a comedy by Mrs. Charlotte Lenox or Lennox, ' an ingenious lady,' says *The Gentleman's Magazine* for April in the same year, ' well known in the literary world by her excellent writings, particularly the Female Quixote, and Shakespeare illustrated. . . . The audience expressed their disapprobation of it with so much clamour and appearance of prejudice, that she would not suffer an attempt to exhibit it a second time (p. 199).' According to the same authority it was based upon one of the writer's own novels, *Henrietta*, published in 1758. Though tainted with the prevailing sentimentalism, *The Sister* is described by Forster as 'both amusing and interesting'; and it is probable that it was not fairly treated when it was acted. Mrs. Lenox (1720–1804), daughter of Colonel Ramsay, Lieut.-Governor of New York, was a favourite with the literary magnates of her day. Johnson was half suspected of having helped her in her book on Shakespeare; Richardson admitted her to his readings at Parson's Green; Fielding, who knew her, calls her, in the *Journal of a Voyage to Lisbon*, 1755, p. 35 (first version), 'the inimitable author of the Female Quixote'; and Goldsmith, though he had no kindness for genteel comedy (see *post*, p. 228), wrote her this lively epilogue, which was spoken by Mrs. Bulkley, who personated the 'Miss Autumn' of the piece. Mrs. Lenox died in extremely reduced circumstances, and was buried by the Right Hon. George Ross, who had befriended her later years. There are several references to her in Boswell's *Life of Johnson*. (See also Hawkins' *Life*, 2nd ed. 1787, pp. 285–7.)

PROLOGUE TO 'ZOBEIDE.'

Zobeide, a play by Joseph Cradock (1742–1826), of Gumley, in Leicestershire, was produced by Colman at Covent Garden on Dec. 11, 1771. It was a translation from three acts of *Les Scythes*, an unfinished tragedy by Voltaire. Goldsmith was applied to, through the Yates's, for a prologue, and sent that here printed to the author of the play with the following note:—
'Mr. Goldsmith presents his best respects to Mr. Cradock, has sent him the Prologue, such as it is. He cannot take time to make it better. He begs he will give Mr. Yates the proper instructions; and so, even so, commits him to fortune and the publick.' (Cradock's *Memoirs*, 1826, i. 224.) Yates, to the acting of whose wife in the character of the heroine the success of the piece, which ran for thirteen nights, was mainly attributable, was to have spoken the prologue, but it ultimately fell to Quick, later the 'Tony Lumpkin' of *She Stoops to Conquer*, who delivered it in the character of a sailor. Cradock seems sub-

sequently to have sent a copy of *Zobeide* to Voltaire, who replied in English as follows :—

9ᵉ. 8ᵇʳᵉ. 1773. à ferney.

Sʳ.

Thanks to yʳ muse a foreign copper shines
Turn'd in to gold, and coin'd in sterling lines.
You have done to much honour to an old
sick man of eighty.

I am vith the most sincere esteem and
gratitude

Sʳ.

Yʳ. obdᵗ. Servᵗ. Voltaire.

A Monsieur Monsieur J. Cradock.

The text of the prologue is here given as printed in Cradock's *Memoirs*, 1828, iii. 8-9. It is unnecessary to specify the variations between this and the earlier issue of 1771.

l. 1. *In these bold times*, &c. The reference is to Cook, who, on June 12, 1771, had returned to England in the *Endeavour*, after three years' absence, having gone to Otaheite to observe the transit of Venus (l. 4).

l. 5. *Botanists.* Mr. (afterward Sir Joseph) Banks and Dr. Solander, of the British Museum, accompanied Cook.

l. 6. *go simpling*, i. e. gathering simples, or herbs. Cf. *Merry Wives of Windsor*, Act iii, Sc. 3 :—

' —These lisping hawthorn buds that . . . smell like Bucklersbury in *simple*-time.'

In the caricatures of the day Solander figured as ' The *simpling* Macaroni.' (See note, p. 247, l. 31.)

l. 11. *With Scythian stores.* The scene of the play was laid in Scythia (*v. supra*).

l. 28. *to make palaver*, to hold a parley, generally with the intention of cajoling. Two of Goldsmith's notes to Garrick in 1773 are endorsed by the actor—'Goldsmith's parlaver.' (Forster's *Life*, 1871, ii. 397.)

l. 32. *mercenary.* Cradock gave the profits of *Zobeide* to Mrs. Yates. ' I mentioned the disappointment it would be to you '—she says in a letter to him dated April 26, 1771—' as you had generously given the emoluments of the piece to me.' (*Memoirs*, 1828, iv. 211.)

THRENODIA AUGUSTALIS.

Augusta, widow of Frederick, Prince of Wales, and mother of George the Third, died at Carlton House, February 8, 1772. This piece was spoken and sung in Mrs. Teresa Cornelys's Great Room in Soho Square, on the Thursday following (the 20th), being sold at the door as a small quarto pamphlet, printed by William Woodfall. The author's name was not given ; but it was prefaced by this 'advertisement,' &c. :—

'The following may more properly be termed a compilation than a poem. It was prepared for the composer in little more than two days : and may be considered therefore rather as an industrious effort of gratitude than of genius. In justice to the composer it may likewise be right to inform the public, that the music was adapted in a period of time equally short.

SPEAKERS.

Mr. Lee and Mrs. Bellamy.

SINGERS.

Mr. Champnes, Mr. Dine, and Miss Jameson ; with twelve chorus singers. The music prepared and adapted by Signor Vento.'

It is—as Cunningham calls it—a 'hurried and unworthy off-spring of the muse of Goldsmith.'

l. 122 (Part I). *Celestial-like her bounty fell.* The Princess's benefactions are not exaggerated. 'She had paid off the whole of her husband's debts, and she had given munificent sums in charity. More than 10,000*l.* a year were given away by her in pensions to individuals whom she judged deserving, very few of whom were aware, until her death, whence the bounty came. The whole of her income she spent in England, and very little on herself' (*Augusta : Princess of Wales,* by W. H. Wilkins, *Nineteenth Century,* October, 1903, p. 675).

l. 132. *There faith shall come.* This, and the three lines that follow, are borrowed from Collins's *Ode written in the beginning of the year* 1746.

l. 22 (Part II). *The towers of Kew.* 'The embellishments of Kew palace and gardens, under the direction of [Sir William]

Chambers, and others, was the favourite object of her [Royal Highness's] widowhood' (Bolton Corney).

l. 77. *Along the billow'd main.* Cf. *The Captivity*, Act ii, l. 18.

l. 83. *Oswego's dreary shores.* Cf. *The Traveller*, l. 411.

l. 91. *And with the avenging fight.* Varied from Collins's *Ode on the Death of Colonel Charles Ross at Fontenoy.*

l. 117. *Its earliest bloom.* Cf. Collins's *Dirge in Cymbeline.*

SONG

FROM ' SHE STOOPS TO CONQUER.'

This thoroughly characteristic song, for a parallel to which one must go to Congreve, or to the 'Here's to the maiden of bashful fifteen' of *The School for Scandal*, has one grave defect, —it is too good to have been composed by Tony Lumpkin, who, despite his inability to read anything but ' print-hand,' declares, in Act i. Sc. 2 of *She Stoops to Conquer*, 1773, that he himself made it upon the ale-house (' The Three Pigeons') in which he sings it, and where it is followed by the annexed comments, directed by the author against the sentimentalists, who, in *The Good Natur'd Man* of five years before, had insisted upon the omission of the Bailiff scene :—

' OMNES.

Bravo, bravo !

First FELLOW.

The 'Squire has got spunk in him.

Second FELLOW.

I loves to hear him sing, bekeays he never gives us nothing that's *low* . . .

Fourth FELLOW.

The genteel thing is the genteel thing at any time. If so be that a gentleman bees in a concatenation accordingly.

Third FELLOW.

I like the maxum of it, Master Muggins. What, tho' I am obligated to dance a bear, a man may be a gentleman for all that. May this be my poison if my bear ever dances but to the very genteelest of tunes. *Water Parted* [1], or the minuet in *Ariadne.*'

l. 9. *When Methodist preachers,* &c. Tony Lumpkin's utterance accurately represents the view of this sect taken by some of his contemporaries. While moderate and just spectators of the Johnson type could recognize the sincerity of men, who, like Wesley, travelled ' nine hundred miles in a month, and preached twelve times a week ' for no ostensibly-adequate reward, there were others who saw in Methodism, and especially in the extravagancies of its camp followers, nothing but cant and duplicity. It was this which prompted on the stage Foote's *Minor* (1760) and Bickerstaffe's *Hypocrite* (1768) ; in art the *Credulity, Superstition, and Fanaticism* of Hogarth (1762); and in literature the *New Bath Guide* of Anstey (1766), the *Spiritual Quixote* of Graves, 1772, and the sarcasms of Sterne, Smollett and Walpole.

It is notable that the most generous contemporary portrait of these much satirised sectaries came from one of the originals of the *Retaliation* gallery. Scott highly praises the character of Ezekiel Daw in Cumberland's *Henry,* 1795, adding, in his large impartial fashion, with reference to the general practice of representing Methodists either as idiots or hypocrites, ' A very different feeling is due to many, perhaps to most, of this enthusiastic sect ; nor is it rashly to be inferred, that he who makes religion the general object of his life, is for that sole reason to be held either a fool or an impostor.' (Scott's *Miscellaneous Prose Works,* 1834, iii. 222.)

l. 23. *But of all the birds in the air.* Hypercriticism may object that ' the hare ' is not a bird. But exigence of rhyme has to answer for many things. Some editors needlessly read ' the *gay* birds ' to lengthen the line. There is no sanction for this in the earlier editions.

EPILOGUE TO 'SHE STOOPS TO CONQUER.'

This epilogue was spoken by Mrs. Bulkley in the character of Miss Hardcastle. It is probably the epilogue described by

---

[1] i.e. Arne's *Water Parted from the Sea,*—the song of Arbaces in the opera of *Artaxerxes,* 1762. The minuet in *Ariadne* was by Handel. It came at the end of the overture, and is said to have been the best thing in the opera.

Goldsmith to Cradock, in the letter quoted at p. 246, as ' a very mawkish thing,' a phrase not so incontestable as Bolton Corney's remark that it is ' an obvious imitation of Shakespere.'

l. 6. *That pretty Bar-maids have done execution.* Cf. *The Vicar of Wakefield*, 1766, i. 7 :—' Sophia's features were not so striking at first ; but often did more certain execution.'

l. 16. *coquets the guests.* Johnson explains this word ' to entertain with compliments and amorous tattle,' and quotes the following illustration from Swift, ' You are *coquetting* a maid of honour, my lord looking on to see how the gamesters play, and I railing at you both.'

l. 26. *Nancy Dawson.* Nancy Dawson was a famous ' toast ' and horn-pipe dancer, who died at Haverstock Hill, May 27, 1767, and was buried behind the Foundling, in the burial-ground of St. George the Martyr. She first appeared at Sadler's Wells, and speedily passed to the stage of Covent Garden, where she danced in the *Beggar's Opera.* There is a portrait of her in the Garrick Club, and there are several contemporary prints. She was the heroine of a popular song, here referred to, beginning :—

> Of all the girls in our town,
> The black, the fair, the red, the brown,
> Who dance and prance it up and down,
>   There 's none like Nancy Dawson :
> Her easy mien, her shape so neat,
> She foots, she trips, she looks so sweet,
> Her ev'ry motion is complete ;
>   I die for Nancy Dawson.

Its tune—says J. T. Smith (*Book for a Rainy Day*, Whitten's ed., 1905, p. 10) was ' as lively as that of " Sir Roger de Coverley." '

Che farò, i. e. *Che farò senza Euridice*, the lovely lament from Glück's *Orfeo*, 1764.

l. 28. *the Heinel of Cheapside.* The reference is to Mademoiselle Anna-Frederica Heinel, 1752–1808, a beautiful Prussian, subsequently the wife of Gaetano Apollino Balthazar Vestris, called ' Vestris the First.' After extraordinary success as a *danseuse* at Stuttgard and Paris, where Walpole saw her in 1771

(Letter to the Earl of Strafford 25th August), she had come to London; and, at this date, was the darling of the Macaronies (cf. the note on p. 247, l. 31), who, from their club, added a *regallo* (present) of six hundred pounds to the salary allowed her at the Haymarket.   On April 1, 1773, Metastasio's *Artaserse* was performed for her benefit, when she was announced to dance a minuet with Monsieur Fierville, and ' Tickets were to be had, at her house in Piccadilly, two doors from Air Street.'

l. 31.   *spadille,* i. e. the ace of spades, the first trump in the game of Ombre.   Cf. Swift's *Journal of a Modern Lady in a Letter to a Person of Quality,* 1728 :—

> She draws up card by card, to find
> Good fortune peeping from behind ;
> With panting heart, and earnest eyes,
> In hope to see *spadillo* rise ;
> In vain, alas ! her hope is fed ;
> She draws an ace, and sees it red.

l. 35.   *Bayes.*   The chief character in Buckingham's *Rehearsal,* 1672, and intended for John Dryden.   Here the name is put for the ' poet ' or ' dramatist.'   Cf. Murphy's Epilogue to Cradock's *Zobeide,* 1771 :—

> Not e'en poor *Bayes* within must hope to be
> Free from the lash :—His Play he writ for me
> 'Tis true—and now my gratitude you'll see ;

and Colman's Epilogue to *The School for Scandal,* 1777 :—

> So wills our virtuous bard—the motley *Bayes*
> Of crying epilogues and laughing plays !

RETALIATION.

Retaliation : A Poem.   By Doctor Goldsmith.   Including Epitaphs on the Most Distinguished Wits of this Metropolis, was first published by G. Kearsly in April, 1774, as a 4to pamphlet of 24 pp. On the title-page is a vignette head of the author, etched by James Basire, after Reynolds's portrait ; and the verses are prefaced by an anonymous letter to the publisher, concluding as follows :—' Dr. Goldsmith *belonged to a Club of* Beaux Esprits, *where* Wit *sparkled sometimes at the Expence of Good-nature.*

*It was proposed to write Epitaphs on the Doctor ; his Country,
Dialect and Person, furnished Subjects of Witticism.—The
Doctor was called on for* Retaliation, *and at their next Meeting
produced the following Poem, which I think adds one Leaf to his
immortal Wreath.'* This account seems to have sufficed for
Evans, Percy, and the earlier editors.   But in vol. i. p. 78 of
his edition of Goldsmith's *Works,* 1854, Mr. Peter Cunningham
published for the first time a fuller version of the circumstances,
derived from a manuscript lent to him by Mr. George Daniel
of Islington ; and (says Mr. Cunningham) ' evidently designed
as a preface to a collected edition of the poems which grew out
of Goldsmith's trying his epigrammatic powers with Garrick.'
It is signed ' D. Garrick.' ' At a meeting '—says the writer—
' of a company of gentlemen, who were well known to each other,
and diverting themselves, among many other things, with the
peculiar oddities of Dr. Goldsmith, who would never allow a
superior in any art, from writing poetry down to dancing a horn-
pipe, the Dr. with great eagerness insisted upon trying his
epigrammatic powers with Mr. Garrick, and each of them was
to write the other's epitaph. Mr. Garrick immediately said
that his epitaph was finished, and spoke the following distich
extempore :—

Here lies NOLLY Goldsmith, for shortness call'd Noll,
Who wrote like an angel, but talk'd like poor Poll.

Goldsmith, upon the company's laughing very heartily, grew
very thoughtful, and either would not, or could not, write anything at that time : however, he went to work, and some weeks
after produced the following printed poem called *Retaliation,*
which has been much admired, and gone through several editions.'
This account, though obviously from Garrick's point of view, is
now accepted as canonical, and has superseded those of Davies,
Cradock, Cumberland, and others, to which some reference is
made in the ensuing notes.

A few days after the publication of the first edition, which
appeared on the 18th or 19th of April, a ' new ' or second edition
was issued, with four pages of ' Explanatory Notes, Observa-
tions, &c.'   At the end came the following announcement :—
' G. Kearsly, the Publisher, thinks it his duty to declare, that

Dr. Goldsmith wrote the Poem as it is here printed, a few errors of the press excepted, which are taken notice of at the bottom of this page.' From this version *Retaliation* is here reproduced. In the third edition, probably in deference to some wounded susceptibilities, the too comprehensive ' most Distinguished Wits of the Metropolis ' was qualified into ' *some of the* most Distinguished Wits,' &c., but no further material alteration was made in the text until the suspicious lines on Caleb Whitefoord were added to the fifth edition.

With the exception of Garrick's couplet, and the fragment of Whitefoord referred to at p. 234, none of the original epitaphs upon which Goldsmith was invited to ' retaliate ' have survived. But the unexpected ability of the retort seems to have prompted a number of *ex post facto* performances, some of which the writers would probably have been glad to pass off as their first essays. Garrick, for example, produced three short pieces, one of which (' Here, Hermes ! says Jove, who with nectar was mellow ') hits off many of Goldsmith's contradictions and foibles with considerable skill (*v.* Davies's *Garrick*, 2nd ed., 1780, ii. 157). Cumberland (*v. Gent. Mag.*, Aug. 1778, p. 384) parodied the poorest part of *Retaliation*, the comparison of the guests to dishes, by likening them to liquors, and Dean Barnard in return rhymed upon Cumberland. He wrote also an apology for his first attack, which is said to have been very severe, and conjured the poet to set his wit at Garrick, who, having fired his first shot, was keeping out of the way :—

On him let all thy vengeance fall ;
On me you but misplace it :
Remember how he called thee *Poll*—
But, ah ! he dares not face it.

For these, and other forgotten pieces arising out of *Retaliation*, Garrick had apparently prepared the above-mentioned introduction. It may be added that the statement, prefixed to the first edition, that *Retaliation*, as we now have it, was produced at the ' next meeting ' of the Club, is manifestly incorrect. It was composed and circulated in detached fragments, and Goldsmith was still working at it when he was seized with his last illness.

l. 1. *Of old, when Scarron,* &c. Paul Scarron (1610-60), the author *inter alia* of the *Roman Comique*, 1651-7, upon a translation

of which Goldsmith was occupied during the last months of his
life.   It was published by Griffin in 1776.

l. 2. *Each guest brought his dish.*   ' Chez Scarron,'—says his
editor, M. Charles Baumet, when speaking of the poet's enter-
tainments,—' venait d'ailleurs l'élite des dames, des courtisans
& des hommes de lettres.   On y dînait joyeusement.   *Chacun
apportait son plat.*'   (*Œuvres de Scarron,* 1877, i. viii.)   Scarron's
company must have been as brilliant as Goldsmith's.   Villar-
ceaux, Vivonne, the Maréchal d'Albret, figured in his list of
courtiers ; while for ladies he had Mesdames Deshoulières, de
Scudéry, de la Sablière, and de Sévigné, to say nothing of Ninon
de Lenclos and Marion Delorme.   (Cf. also Guizot, *Corneille et
son Temps,* 1862, 429–30.)

l. 3. *If our landlord.*   The ' explanatory note ' to the second
edition says—' The master of the St. James's coffee-house,
where the Doctor, and the friends he has characterized in this
Poem, held an occasional club.'   This, it should be stated, was
not the famous ' Literary Club,' which met at the Turk's Head
Tavern in Gerrard Street.   The St. James's Coffee-house, as
familiar to Swift and Addison at the beginning, as it was to
Goldsmith and his friends at the end of the eighteenth century,
was the last house but one on the south-west corner of St. James's
Street.   It now no longer exists.   Cradock (*Memoirs,* 1826, i. 228–
30) speaks of dining *at the bottom of St. James's Street* with Goldsmith, Percy, the two Burkes (*v. infra*), Johnson, Garrick, Dean
Barnard, and others.   ' We sat very late ;' he adds in conclusion,
' and the conversation that at last ensued, was the direct cause
of my friend Goldsmith's poem, called " *Retaliation.*" '

l. 5. *Our Dean.*   Dr. Thomas Barnard, an Irishman, at this
time Dean of Derry.   He died at Wimbledon in 1806.   It was
Dr. Barnard who, in reply to a rude sally of Johnson, wrote the
charming verses on improvement after the age of forty-five,
which end—

> If I have thoughts, and can't express them,
> Gibbon shall teach me how to dress them,
>   In terms select and terse ;
> Jones teach me modesty and Greek,
> Smith how to think, Burke how to speak,
>   And Beauclerk to converse.

> Let Johnson teach me how to place
> In fairest light, each borrow'd grace,
> From him I'll learn to write ;
> Copy his clear, familiar style,
> And from the roughness of his file
> Grow like himself—polite.

(Northcote's *Life of Reynolds*, 2nd ed., 1819, i. 221.) According to Cumberland (*Memoirs*, 1807, i. 370), ' The dean also gave him [Goldsmith] an epitaph, and Sir Joshua illuminated the dean's verses with a sketch of his bust in pen and ink inimitably caricatured.' What would collectors give for that sketch and epitaph ! Unfortunately in Cumberland's septuagenarian recollections the ' truth severe ' is mingled with an unusual amount of ' fairy fiction.' However Sir Joshua *did* draw caricatures, for a number of them were exhibited at the Grosvenor Gallery (by the Duke of Devonshire) in the winter of 1883–4.

l. 6. *Our Burke.* The Right Hon. Edmund Burke, 1729–97.

l. 7. *Our Will.* ' Mr. William Burke, late Secretary to General Conway, and member for Bedwin, Wiltshire ' (Note to second edition). He was a kinsman of Edmund Burke, and one of the supposed authors of Junius's *Letters.* He died in 1798. ' It is said that the notices Goldsmith first wrote of the Burkes were so severe that Hugh Boyd persuaded the poet to alter them, and entirely rewrite the character of William, for he was sure that if the Burkes saw what was originally written of them the peace of the Club would be disturbed.' (Rev. W. Hunt in *Dict. Nat. Biography*, Art. ' William Burke.')

l. 8. *And Dick.* Richard Burke, Edmund Burke's younger brother. He was for some years Collector to the Customs at Grenada, being on a visit to London when *Retaliation* was written (Forster's *Life*, 1871, ii. 404). He died in 1794, Recorder of Bristol.

l. 9. *Our Cumberland's sweetbread.* Richard Cumberland, the poet, novelist, and dramatist, 1732–1811, author of *The West Indian*, 1771, *The Fashionable Lover*, 1772, and many other more or less sentimental plays. In his *Memoirs*, 1807, i. 369–71, he gives an account of the origin of *Retaliation*, which adds a few dubious particulars to that of Garrick. But it was written from memory long after the events it records.

l. 10. *Douglas.* ' Dr. Douglas, since Bishop of Salisbury,' says Cumberland. He died in 1807 (*v. infra*).

l. 14. *Ridge.* ' Counsellor John Ridge, a gentleman belonging to the Irish Bar' (Note to second edition). 'Burke,' says Bolton Corney, ' in 1771, described him as " one of the honestest and best-natured men living, and inferior to none of his profession in ability." ' (See also note to line 125.)

l. 15. *Hickey.* The commentator of the second edition of *Retaliation* calls this gentleman ' honest Tom Hickey '. His Christian name, however, was *Joseph* (Letter of Burke, November 8, 1774). He was a jovial, good-natured, over-blunt Irishman, the legal adviser of both Burke and Reynolds. Indeed it was Hickey who drew the conveyance of the land on which Reynolds's house ' next to the Star and Garter ' at Richmond (Wick House) was built by Chambers the architect. Hickey died in 1794. Reynolds painted his portrait for Burke, and it was exhibited at the Royal Academy in 1772 (No. 208). In 1833, it belonged to Mr. T. H. Burke. Sir Joshua also painted Miss Hickey in 1769–73. Her father, not much to Goldsmith's satisfaction, was one of the Paris party in 1770. See also note to l. 125.

l. 16. *Magnanimous Goldsmith.* According to Malone (Reynolds's *Works*, second edition, 1801, i. xc), Goldsmith intended to have concluded with his own character.

l. 34. *Tommy Townshend*, M.P. for Whitchurch, Hampshire, afterwards first Viscount Sydney. He died in 1800. Junius, says Bolton Corney, gives a portrait of him as *still life*. His presence in *Retaliation* is accounted for by the fact that he had commented in Parliament upon Johnson's pension. ' I am well assured,' says Boswell, ' that Mr. Townshend's attack upon Johnson was the occasion of his " hitching in a rhyme " ; for, that in the original copy of Goldsmith's character of Mr. Burke, in his *Retaliation*, another person's name stood in the couplet where Mr. Townshend is now introduced.' (Birkbeck Hill's *Boswell*, 1887, iv. 318.)

l. 35. *too deep for his hearers.* ' The emotion to which he commonly appealed was that too rare one, the love of wisdom, and he combined his thoughts and knowledge in propositions of wisdom so weighty and strong, that the minds of ordinary hearers were not on the instant prepared for them.' (Morley's *Burke*, 1882, 209-10.)

l. 36. *And thought of convincing, while they thought of dining.* For the reason given in the previous note, many of Burke's hearers often took the opportunity of his rising to speak, to retire to dinner. Thus he acquired the nickname of the ' Dinner Bell.'

l. 42. *To eat mutton cold.* There is a certain resemblance between this character and Gray's lines on himself written in 1761, beginning ' Too poor for a bribe, and too proud to importune.' (See Gosse's *Gray's Works*, 1884, i. 127.) But both Gray and Goldsmith may have been thinking of a line in the once popular song of *Ally Croaker* :—

Too dull for a wit, too grave for a joker.

l. 43. *honest William*, i. e. William Burke (*v. supra*).

l. 54. *Now breaking a jest, and now breaking a limb.* A note to the second edition says—' The above Gentleman [Richard Burke, *v. supra*] having slightly fractured one of his arms and legs, at different times, the Doctor [i. e. Goldsmith] has rallied him on those accidents, as a kind of *retributive* justice for breaking his jests on other people.'

l. 61. *Here Cumberland lies.* According to Boaden's *Life of Kemble*, 1825, i. 438, Mrs. Piozzi rightly regarded this portrait as wholly ironical ; and Bolton Corney, without much expenditure of acumen, discovers it to have been written in a spirit of *persiflage*. Nevertheless, Cumberland himself (*Memoirs*, 1807, i. 369) seems to have accepted it in good faith. Speaking of Goldsmith he says—' I conclude my account of him with gratitude for the epitaph he bestowed on me in his poem called *Retaliation*.' From the further details which he gives of the circumstances, it would appear that his own performance, of which he could recall but one line—

All mourn the poet, I lament the man—

was conceived in a less malicious spirit than those of the others, and had predisposed the sensitive bard in his favour. But no very genuine cordiality could be expected to exist between the rival authors of *The West Indian* and *She Stoops to Conquer*.

l. 66. *And Comedy wonders at being so fine.* It is instructive here to transcribe Goldsmith's serious opinion of the kind of work which Cumberland essayed :—' A new species of Dramatic Composition has been introduced, under the name of *Sentimental* Comedy, in which the virtues of Private Life are exhibited, rather than the Vices exposed ; and the Distresses rather than the Faults of Mankind, make our interest in the piece. . . . In these Plays almost all the Characters are good, and exceedingly generous ; they are lavish enough of their *Tin* Money on the Stage, and though they want Humour, have abundance of Sentiment and Feeling. If they happen to have Faults or Foibles, the Spectator is taught not only to pardon, but to applaud them, in consideration of the goodness of their hearts ; so that Folly, instead of being ridiculed, is commended, and the Comedy aims at touching our Passions without the power of being truly pathetic.' (*Westminster Magazine*, 1772, i. 5.) Cf. also the *Preface* to *The Good Natur'd Man*, where he ' hopes that too much refinement will not banish humour and character from our's, as it has already done from the French theatre. Indeed the French comedy is now become so very elevated and sentimental, that it has not only banished humour and *Moliere* from the stage, but it has banished all spectators too.'

l. 80. *The scourge of impostors, the terror of quacks.* Dr. John Douglas (*v. supra*) distinguished himself by his exposure of two of his countrymen, Archibald Bower, 1686–1766, who, being secretly a member of the Catholic Church, wrote a *History of the Popes*; and William Lauder 1710–1771, who attempted to prove Milton a plagiarist. Cf. Churchill's *Ghost*, Bk. ii :—

> By TRUTH inspir'd, when *Lauder's* spight
> O'er MILTON cast the Veil of Night,
> DOUGLAS arose, and thro' the maze
> Of intricate and winding ways,
> Came where the subtle Traitor lay,
> And dragg'd him trembling to the day.

' Lauder on Milton ' is one of the books bound to the trunk-maker's in Hogarth's *Beer Street*, 1751. He imposed on Johnson, who wrote him a ' Preface ' and was consequently trounced by Churchill (*ut supra*) as ' *our Letter'd* POLYPHEME.'

l. 86. *Our Dodds shall be pious.* The reference is to the Rev.

Dr. William Dodd, who three years after the publication of *Retaliation* (i.e. June 27, 1777) was hanged at Tyburn for forging the signature of the fifth Earl of Chesterfield, to whom he had been tutor. His life previously had long been scandalous enough to justify Goldsmith's words. Johnson made strenuous and humane exertions to save Dodd's life, but without avail. (See Birkbeck Hill's *Boswell*, 1887, iii. 139-48.) There is an account of Dodd's execution at the end of vol. i of Angelo's *Reminiscences*, 1830.

our Kenricks. Dr. William Kenrick—say the earlier annotators—who 'read lectures at the Devil Tavern, under the Title of " The School of Shakespeare." ' The lectures began January 19, 1774, and help to fix the date of the poem. Goldsmith had little reason for liking this versatile and unprincipled Ishmaelite of letters, who, only a year before, had penned a scurrilous attack upon him in *The London Packet*. Kenrick died in 1779.

l. 87. *Macpherson.* ' David [James] Macpherson, Esq. ; who lately, from the mere *force of his style*, wrote down the first poet of all antiquity.' (Note to second edition.) This was ' Ossian ' Macpherson, 1738-96, who, in 1773, had followed up his Erse epics by a prose translation of Homer, which brought him little but opprobrium. ' Your abilities, since your Homer, are not so formidable,' says Johnson in the knockdown letter which he addressed to him in 1775. (Birkbeck Hill's *Boswell*, 1887, ii. 298.)

l. 88. *Our Townshend.* See note to line 34.

l. 89. *New Lauders and Bowers.* See note to l. 80.

l. 92. *And Scotchman meet Scotchman, and cheat in the dark.* Mitford compares Farquhar's *Love and a Bottle*, 1699, Act iii—

But gods meet gods and jostle in the dark.

But Farquhar was quoting from Dryden and Lee's *Oedipus*, 1679, Act iv (at end).

l. 93. *Here lies David Garrick.* ' The sum of all that can be said for and against Mr. Garrick, some people think, may be found in these lines of Goldsmith,' writes Davies in his *Life of Garrick*, 2nd ed., 1780, ii. 159. Posterity has been less hesitating in its verdict. ' The lines on Garrick,' says Forster, *Life of Goldsmith*, 1871, ii. 409, ' are quite perfect writing. Without anger, the satire is finished, keen, and uncompromising ; the wit is adorned by most discriminating praise ; and the truth is only the more unsparing for its exquisite good manners and good taste.'

l. 115. *Ye Kenricks.* See note to line 86.

ye Kellys. Hugh Kelly (1739–1777), an Irishman, the author of *False Delicacy*, 1768 ; *A Word to the Wise*, 1770 ; *The School for Wives*, 1774, and other ' sentimental dramas,' is here referred to. His first play, which is described in Garrick's prologue as a 'Sermon,' 'preach'd in Acts,' was produced at Drury Lane just six days before Goldsmith's comedy of *The Good Natur'd Man* appeared at Covent Garden, and obtained a success which it ill deserved. *False Delicacy*—said Johnson truly (Birkbeck Hill's *Boswell*, 1887, ii. 48)—' was totally void of character,'— a crushing accusation to make against a drama. But Garrick, for his private ends, had taken up Kelly as a rival to Goldsmith ; and the *comédie sérieuse* or *larmoyante* of La Chaussée, Sedaine, and Diderot had already found votaries in Engand. *False Delicacy*, weak, washy, and invertebrate as it was, completed the transformation of ' genteel' into ' sentimental' comedy, and establishing that *genre* for the next few years, effectually retarded the wholesome reaction towards humour and character which Goldsmith had tried to promote by *The Good Natur'd Man*. (See note to l. 66.)

Woodfalls. ' William Woodfall'—says Bolton Corney— ' successively editor of *The London Packet* and *The Morning Chronicle*, was matchless as a reporter of speeches, and an able theatrical critic. He made lofty pretensions to editorial impartiality—but the actor [i. e. Garrick] was not *always* satisfied.' He died in 1803. He must not be confounded with Henry Sampson Woodfall, the editor of Junius's *Letters*. (See note to l. 162.)

l. 120. *To act as an angel.* There is a sub-ironic touch in this phrase which should not be overlooked. Cf. l. 102.

l. 125. *Here Hickey reclines.* See note to l. 15. In Cumberland's *Poetical Epistle to Dr. Goldsmith ; or Supplement to his Retaliation* (*Gentleman's Magazine*, Aug. 1778, p. 384) Hickey's genial qualities are thus referred to :—

> Give RIDGE and HICKY, generous souls !
> Of WHISKEY PUNCH convivial bowls.

l. 134. *a special attorney.* A special attorney was merely an

attorney who practised in one court only. The species is now
said to be extinct.

l. 135. *burn ye.* The annotator of the second edition, apologiz-
ing for this ' forced ' rhyme to 'attorney,' informs the English
reader that the phrase of ' burn ye ' is ' a familiar method of
salutation in Ireland amongst the lower classes of the people.'

l. 137. *Here Reynolds is laid.* This shares the palm with the
admirable epitaphs on Garrick and Burke. But Goldsmith
loved Reynolds, and there are no satiric strokes in the picture.
If we are to believe Malone (Reynolds's *Works*, second edition,
1801, i. xc), ' these were the last lines the author wrote.'

l. 140. *bland.* Malone (*ut supra*, lxxxix) notes this word as
' eminently happy, and characteristick of his [Reynolds's] easy
and placid manners.' Boswell (Dedication of *Life of Johnson*)
refers to his ' equal and placid temper.' Cf. also Dean Barnard's
verses (Northcote's *Life of Reynolds*, 2nd ed., 1819. i. 220), and
Mrs. Piozzi's lines in her *Autobiography*, 2nd ed., 1861, ii. 175–6.

l. 146. *He shifted his trumpet.* While studying Raphael in
the Vatican in 1751, Reynolds caught so severe a cold ' as to
occasion a deafness which obliged him to use an ear-trumpet
for the remainder of his life.' (Taylor and Leslie's *Reynolds*,
1865, i. 50.) This instrument figures in a portrait of himself
which he painted for Thrale about 1775. See also Zoffany's
picture of the ' Academicians gathered about the model in the
Life School at Somerset House,' 1772, where he is shown employ-
ing it to catch the conversation of Wilton and Chambers.

and only took snuff. Sir Joshua was a great snuff-taker.
His snuff-box, described in the Catalogue as the one ' immor-
talized in Goldsmith's *Retaliation*,' was exhibited, with his
spectacles and other personal relics, at the Grosvenor Gallery
in 1883–4. In the early editions this epitaph breaks off abruptly
at the word ' snuff.' But Malone says that half a line more
had been written. Prior gives this half line as ' By flattery
unspoiled—,' and affirms that among several erasures in the
manuscript sketch devoted to Reynolds it ' remained unaltered.'
(*Life*, 1837, ii. 499.) See notes to ll. 53, 56, and 91 of *The Haunch
of Venison.*

l. 147. *Here Whitefoord reclines.* The circumstances which led
to the insertion of these lines in the fifth edition are detailed in

the prefatory words of the publisher given at p. 92. There is more than a suspicion that Whitefoord wrote them himself; but they have too long been accepted as an appendage to the poem to be now displaced. Caleb Whitefoord (born 1734) was a Scotchman, a wine-merchant, and an art connoisseur, to whom J. T. Smith, in his *Life of Nollekens*, 1828, i. 333–41, devotes several pages. He was one of the party at the St. James's Coffee-house. He died in 1810. There is a caricature of him in ' Connoisseurs inspecting a Collection of George Morland,' November, 16, 1807 ; and Wilkie's *Letter of Introduction*, 1814, was a reminiscence of a visit which, when he first came to London, he paid to Whitefoord. He was also painted by Reynolds and Stuart. Hewins's *Whitefoord Papers*, 1898, throw no light upon the story of the epitaph.

l. 148. *a grave man*. Cf. *Romeo and Juliet*, Act iii, Sc. 1 :— ' Ask for me to-morrow, and you shall find me *a grave man.*' This Shakespearean recollection is a little like Goldsmith's way. (See note to *The Haunch of Venison*, l. 120.)

l. 150. *and rejoic'd in a pun*. ' Mr. W. is so notorious a punster, that Doctor Goldsmith used to say, it was impossible to keep him company, without being *infected* with the *itch* of *punning.*' (Note to fifth edition.)

l. 160. ' *if the table he set on a roar.*' Cf. *Hamlet*, Act v, Sc. 1.

l. 162. *Woodfall*, i. e. Henry Sampson Woodfall, printer of *The Public Advertiser*. He died in 1805. (See note to l. 115.)

l. 170. *Cross-Readings, Ship-News, and Mistakes of the Press*. Over the *nom de guerre* of ' Papyrius Cursor,' a real Roman name, but as happy in its applicability as Thackeray's ' Manlius Pennialinus,' Whitefoord contributed many specimens of this mechanic wit to *The Public Advertiser*. The ' Cross Readings ' were obtained by taking two or three columns of a newspaper horizontally and *onwards* instead of *vertically* and downwards, thus :—

> Colds caught at this season are
> the Companion to the Playhouse.

or

> To be sold to the best Bidder,
> My seat in Parliament being vacated.

A more elaborate example is

> On Tuesday an address was presented;
> it unhappily missed fire and the villain made off,
> when the honour of knighthood was conferred on him
> to the great joy of that noble family

Goldsmith was hugely delighted with Whitefoord's 'lucky inventions' when they first became popular in 1766. 'He declared, in the heat of his admiration of them, it would have given him more pleasure to have been the author of them than of all the works he had ever published of his own' (Northcote's *Life of Reynolds*, 2nd ed., 1819, i. 217). What is perhaps more remarkable is, that Johnson spoke of Whitefoord's performances as 'ingenious and diverting' (Birkbeck Hill's *Boswell*, 1887, iv. 322); and Horace Walpole laughed over them till he cried (Letter to Montagu, December 12, 1766). To use Voltaire's witticism, he is *bien heureux* who can laugh now. It may be added that Whitefoord did not, as he claimed, originate the 'Cross Readings.' They had been anticipated in No. 49 of Harrison's spurious *Tatler*, vol. v [1720].

The fashion of the 'Ship-News' was in this wise: 'August 25 [1765]. We hear that his Majestys Ship *Newcastle* will soon have a new figurehead, the old one being almost worn out.' The 'Mistakes of the Press' explain themselves. (See also Smith's *Life of Nollekens*, 1828, i. 336–7; Debrett's *New Foundling Hospital for Wit*, 1784, vol. ii, and *Gentleman's Magazine*, 1810, p. 300.)

l. 172. *That a Scot may have humour, I had almost said wit.* Goldsmith,—if he wrote these verses,—must have forgotten that he had already credited Whitefoord with ' wit ' in l. 153.

l. 174. *Thou best humour'd man with the worst humour'd muse.* Cf. Rochester of Lord Buckhurst, afterwards Earl of Dorset:—

> The best good man, with the worst-natur'd muse.

Whitefoord's contribution to the epitaphs on Goldsmith is said to have been unusually severe,—so severe that four only of its eight lines are quoted in the *Whitefoord Papers*, 1898, the rest being ' unfit for publication' (p. xxvii). He afterwards addressed a metrical apology to Sir Joshua, which is printed at pp. 217–8 of Northcote's *Life*, 2nd ed., 1819. See also Forster's *Goldsmith*, 1871, ii. 408–9.

SONG FOR 'SHE STOOPS TO CONQUER.'

Boswell, to whom we are indebted for the preservation of this lively song, sent it to *The London Magazine* for June, 1774 (vol. xliii, p. 295), with the following :—

'To the Editor of *The London Magazine.*

SIR,—I send you a small production of the late Dr. *Goldsmith*, which has never been published, and which might perhaps have been totally lost had I not secured it. He intended it as a song in the character of Miss *Hardcastle*, in his admirable comedy, *She stoops to conquer* ; but it was left out, as Mrs. *Bulkley* who played the part did not sing. He sung it himself in private companies very agreeably. The tune is a pretty Irish air, called *The Humours of Balamagairy*, to which, he told me, he found it very difficult to adapt words ; but he has succeeded happily in these few lines. As I could sing the tune, and was fond of them, he was so good as to give me them about a year ago, just as I was leaving London, and bidding him adieu for that season, little apprehending that it was a last farewell. I preserve this little relick in his own handwriting with an affectionate care.

I am, Sir,

Your humble Servant,

JAMES BOSWELL.'

When, seventeen years later, Boswell published his *Life of Samuel Johnson, LL.D.*, he gave an account of his dining at General Oglethorpe's in April, 1773, with Johnson and Goldsmith ; and he says that the latter sang the *Three Jolly Pigeons*, and this song, to the ladies in the tea-room. Croker, in a note, adds that the younger Colman more appropriately employed the 'essentially low comic' air for Looney Mactwolter in the [*Review; or the*] *Wags of Windsor*, 1808 [i. e. in that character's song beginning—'Oh, whack ! Cupid 's a mannikin '], and that Moore tried to bring it into good company in the ninth number of the *Irish Melodies.* But Croker did not admire the tune, and thought poorly of Goldsmith's words. Yet they are certainly fresher than Colman's or Moore's :—

Sing—sing—Music was given,
    To brighten the gay, and kindle the loving ;
Souls here, like planets in Heaven,
    By harmony's laws alone are kept moving, &c.

TRANSLATION.

These lines, which appear at p. 312 of vol. v of the *History of the Earth and Animated Nature*, 1774, are freely translated from some Latin verses by Addison in No 412 of the *Spectator*, where they are introduced as follows :—' Thus we see that every different Species of sensible Creatures has its different Notions of Beauty, and that each of them is most affected with the Beauties of its own kind. This is nowhere more remarkable than in Birds of the same Shape and Proportion, where we often see the Male determined in his Courtship by the single Grain or Tincture of a Feather, and never discovering any Charms but in the Colour of its own Species.' Addison's lines, of which Goldsmith translated the first fourteen only, are printed from his corrected MS. at p. 4 of *Some Portions of Essays contributed to the Spectator by Mr. Joseph Addison* [by the late J. Dykes Campbell], 1864.

THE HAUNCH OF VENISON.

It is supposed that this poem was written early in 1771, although it was not printed until 1776, when it was published by G. Kearsly and J. Ridley under the title of *The Haunch of Venison, a Poetical Epistle to Lord Clare. By the late Dr. Goldsmith. With a Head of the Author, Drawn by Henry Bunbury, Esq ; and Etched by [James] Bretherton*. A second edition, the text of which is here followed, appeared in the same year 'With considerable Additions and Corrections, Taken from the Author's *last* Transcript.' The Lord Clare to whom the verses are addressed was Robert Nugent, of Carlanstown, Westmeath, M.P. for St. Mawes in 1741–54. In 1766 he was created Viscount Clare ; in 1776 Earl Nugent. In his youth he had himself been an easy if not very original versifier ; and there are several of his performances in the second volume of Dodsley's *Collection of Poems by Several Hands*, 4th ed., 1755. One of the Epistles, beginning 'Clarinda, dearly lov'd, attend The Counsels of a faithful friend,' seems to have betrayed Goldsmith into the blunder of confusing it, in the *Poems for Young Ladies*, 1767, p. 114, with Lyttelton's better-known *Advice to a Lady* (' The counsels of a friend, Belinda, hear '), also in Dodsley's miscellany ; while another piece, an *Ode to William Pultney, Esq.*, contains a stanza so good that Gibbon worked it into his character of Brutus :—

> What tho' the good, the brave, the wise,
> With adverse force undaunted rise,
>   To break th' eternal doom !
> Tho' CATO liv'd, tho' TULLY spoke,
> Tho' BRUTUS dealt the godlike stroke,
>   Yet perish'd fated ROME.

Detraction, however, has insinuated that Mallet, his step-son's tutor, was Nugent's penholder in this instance. 'Mr. Nugent sure did not write his own Ode,' says Gray to Walpole (Gray's *Works*, by Gosse, 1884, ii. 220). Earl Nugent died in Dublin in October, 1788, and was buried at Gosfield in Essex, a property he had acquired with his second wife. A *Memoir* of him was written in 1898 by Mr. Claud Nugent. He is described by Cunningham as ' a big, jovial, voluptuous Irishman, with a loud voice, a strong Irish accent, and a ready though coarse wit.' According to Percy (*Memoir*, 1801, p. 66), he had been attracted to Goldsmith by the publication of *The Traveller* in 1764, and he mentioned him favourably to the Earl of Northumberland, then Lord Lieutenant of Ireland. A note in Forster's *Life*, 1871, ii. 329–30, speaks of Goldsmith as a frequent visitor at Gosfield, and at Nugent's house in Great George Street, Westminster, where he had often for playmate his host's daughter, Mary, afterwards Marchioness of Buckingham.

Scott and others regarded *The Haunch of Venison* as auto-biographical. To what extent this is the case, it is difficult to say. That it represents the actual thanks of the poet to Lord Clare for an actual present of venison, part of which he promptly transferred to Reynolds, is probably the fact. But, as the following notes show, it is also clear that Goldsmith borrowed, if not his entire fable, at least some of its details from Boileau's third satire ; and that, in certain of the lines, he had in memory Swift's *Grand Question Debated*, the measure of which he adopts. This throws more than a doubt upon the truth of the whole. 'His genius' (as Hazlitt says) 'was a mixture of originality and imitation '; and fact and fiction often mingle inseparably in his work. The author of the bailiff scene in the *Good Natur'd Man* was quite capable of inventing for the nonce the tragedy of the unbaked pasty, or of selecting from the Pilkingtons and Purdons of his acquaintance such appropriate guests for his Mile End Amphitryon as the writers of the *Snarler* and the *Scourge*. It may indeed even be doubted whether, if *The Haunch of Venison* had been absolute personal history, Goldsmith would ever have retailed it to his noble patron at Gosfield, although it may include enough of real experience to serve as the basis for a *jeu d'esprit*.

l. 4. *The fat was so white*, &c. The first version reads—' The white was so white, and the red was so ruddy.'

l. 5. *Though my stomach was sharp*, &c. This couplet is not in the first version.

l. 10. *One gammon of bacon.* Prior compares a passage from Goldsmith's *Animated Nature*, 1774, iii. 9, *à propos* of a similar practice in Germany, Poland, and Switzerland. ' A piece of beef,' he says, ' hung up there, is considered as an elegant piece of furniture, which, though seldom touched, at least argues the possessor's opulence and ease.'

l. 14. *a bounce*, i. e. a braggart falsehood. Steele, in No. 16 of *The Lover*, 1715, p. 110, says of a manifest piece of brag, ' But this is supposed to be only a *Bounce*.'

l. 18. *Mr. Byrne*, spelled ' Burn ' in the earlier editions, was a relative of Lord Clare.

l. 24. *M—r—'s.* MONROE'S in the first version. ' Dorothy Monroe,' says Bolton Corney, ' whose various charms are celebrated in verse by Lord Townshend.'

l. 27. *There's H—d, and C—y, and H—rth, and H—ff.* In the first version—

' There's COLEY, and WILLIAMS, and HOWARD, and HIFF.'—Hiff was Paul Hiffernan, M.B., 1719–77, a Grub Street author and practitioner. Bolton Corney hazards some conjectures as to the others; but Cunningham wisely passes them over.

l. 29. *H—gg—ns.* Perhaps, suggests Bolton Corney, this was the Captain Higgins who assisted at Goldsmith's absurd *fracas* with Evans the bookseller, upon the occasion of Kenrick's letter in *The London Packet* for March 24, 1773. Other accounts, however, state that his companion was Captain Horneck (Prior, *Life*, 1837, ii. 411–12). This couplet is not in the first version.

l. 33. *Such dainties to them*, &c. The first version reads—

Such dainties to them ! It *would* look like a flirt,
Like sending 'em Ruffles when wanting a Shirt.

Cunningham quotes a similar idea from T. Brown's *Laconics*, *Works*, 1709, iv. 14. 'To treat a poor wretch with a bottle of Burgundy, or fill his snuff-box, is like giving a pair of lace ruffles to a man that has never a shirt on his back.' But Goldsmith, as was his wont, had already himself employed the same figure. 'Honours to one in my situation,' he says in a letter to his brother Maurice, in January, 1770, when speaking of his appointment as Professor of Ancient History to the Royal Academy, 'are something like ruffles to a man that wants a shirt' (*Percy Memoir*, 1801, 87–8). His source was probably, not Brown's *Laconics*, but those French *ana* he knew so well. According to M. J. J. Jusserand (*English Essays from a French Pen*, 1895, pp. 160–1), the originator of this conceit was M. Samuel de Sorbières, the traveller in England who was assailed by Bishop Sprat. Considering himself inadequately rewarded by his patrons, Mazarin, Louis XIV, and Pope Clement IX, he said bitterly—'They give lace cuffs to a man without a shirt'; a 'consolatory witticism' which he afterwards remodelled into, 'I wish they would send me bread for the butter they kindly provided me with.' In this form it appears in the Preface to the *Sorberiana*, Toulouse, 1691.

a flirt is a jibe or jeer. 'He would sometimes . . . cast out a jesting *flirt* at me.' (Morley's *History of Thomas Ellwood*, 1895, p. 104.) Swift also uses the word.

l. 37. *An under-bred, fine-spoken fellow*, &c. The first version reads—

A fine-spoken Custom-house Officer he,
Who smil'd as he gaz'd on the Ven'son and me.

l. 44. *but I hate ostentation*. Cf. Beau Tibbs :—' She was bred, *but that 's between ourselves*, under the inspection of the Countess of All-night.' (*Citizen of the World*, 1762, i. 238.)

l. 49. *We'll have Johnson, and Burke*. Cf. Boileau, *Sat.* iii. ll. 25–6, which Goldsmith had in mind :—

Molière avec Tartufe y doit jouer son rôle,
Et Lambert, qui plus est, m'a donné sa parole.

l. 53. *What say you—a pasty ? it shall, and it must.* The first version reads—

> I'll take no denial—you shall, and you must.

Mr. J. M. Lobban, *Goldsmith, Select Poems,* 1900, notes a hitherto undetected similarity between this and the ' It *must,* and it *shall* be a barrack, my life ' of Swift's *Grand Question Debated.* See also ll. 56 and 91.

l. 56. *No stirring, I beg—my dear friend—my dear friend.* In the first edition—

> No words, my dear GOLDSMITH ! my very good Friend !

Mr. Lobban compares :—

> ' Good morrow, good captain.' ' I'll wait on you down,'—
> ' You shan't stir a foot.' ' You'll think me a clown.'

l. 60. ' *And nobody with me at sea but myself.*' This is almost a textual quotation from one of the letters of Henry Frederick, Duke of Cumberland, to Lady Grosvenor, a correspondence which in 1770 gave great delight to contemporary caricaturists and scandal-mongers. Other poets besides Goldsmith seem to have been attracted by this particular lapse of his illiterate Royal Highness, since it is woven into a ballad printed in *The Public Advertiser* for August 2 in the above year :—

> The Miser who wakes in a Fright for his Pelf,
> And finds *no one by him except his own Self,* &c.

l. 67. *When come to the place,* &c. Cf. Boileau, *ut supra,* ll. 31–4 :—

> A peine étais-je entré, que, ravi de me voir,
> Mon homme, en m'embrassant, m'est venu recevoir ;
> Et montrant à mes yeux une allégresse entière,
> Nous n'avons, m'a-t-il dit, ni Lambert ni Molière.

Lambert the musician, it may be added, had the special reputation of accepting engagements which he never kept.

l. 72. *and t'other with Thrale.* Henry Thrale, the Southwark brewer, and the husband of Mrs. Thrale, afterwards Mrs. Piozzi. Johnson first made his acquaintance in 1765. Strahan complained to Boswell that, by this connexion, Johnson ' was in a great measure absorbed from the society of his old friends.'

(Birkbeck Hill's *Boswell*, 1887, iii. 225.) Line 72 in the first edition reads—

> The one at the House, and the other with THRALE.

l. 76. *They both of them merry and authors like you.* 'They' should apparently be 'they're.' The first version reads—

> Who dabble and write in the Papers—like you.

l. 78. *Some think he writes Cinna—he owns to Panurge.* 'Panurge' and 'Cinna' are signatures which were frequently to be found at the foot of letters addressed to the *Public Advertiser* in 1770-1 in support of Lord Sandwich and the Government. They are said to have been written by Dr. W. Scott, Vicar of Simonburn, Northumberland, and chaplain of Greenwich Hospital, both of which preferments had been given him by Sandwich. In 1765 he had attacked Lord Bute and his policy over the signature of 'Anti-Sejanus.' 'Sandwich and his parson Anti-Sejanus [are] hooted off the stage'—writes Walpole to Mann, March 21, 1766. According to Prior, it was Scott who visited Goldsmith in his Temple chambers, and invited him to 'draw a venal quill' for Lord North's administration. Goldsmith's noble answer, as reported by his reverend friend, was—'I can earn as much as will supply my wants without writing for any party; the assistance therefore you offer is unnecessary to me.' (*Life*, 1837, ii. 278.) There is a caricature portrait of Scott at p. 141 of *The London Museum* for February, 1771, entitled 'Twitcher's Advocate,' 'Jemmy Twitcher' being the nickname of Lord Sandwich.

l. 82. *Swinging*, great, huge. 'Bishop Lowth has just finished the Dramas, and sent me word, that although I have paid him the most *swinging* compliment he ever received, he likes the whole book more than he can say.' (*Memoirs of Hannah More*, 1834, i. 236.)

l. 84. *pasty.* The first version has 'Ven'son.'

l. 87. *So there I sat*, &c. This couplet is not in the first version.

l. 91. *And, 'Madam,' quoth he.* Mr. Lobban again quotes Swift's *Grand Question Debated* :—

> And 'Madam,' says he, 'if such dinners you give
> You'll ne'er want for parsons as long as you live.'

These slight resemblances, coupled with the more obvious likeness of the ' Raphaels, Correggios, and stuff ' of *Retaliation* (ll. 145-6) to the '*Noueds* and *Bluturks* and *Omurs* and stuff ' (also pointed out by Mr. Lobban) are interesting, because they show plainly that Goldsmith remembered the works of Swift far better than *The New Bath Guide*, which has sometimes been supposed to have set the tune to the *Haunch* and *Retaliation*.

l. 91. ' *may this bit be my poison.*' The gentleman in *She Stoops to Conquer*, Act i, who is ' obligated to dance a bear,' uses the same asseveration (*v.* p. 219 of this volume). Cf. also Squire Thornhill's somewhat similar formula in chap. vii of *The Vicar of Wakefield*, 1766, i. 59.

l. 95. ' *The tripe,*' *quoth the Jew*, &c. The first version reads—

' Your Tripe ! ' quoth the *Jew*, ' if the truth I may speak,
I could eat of this Tripe seven days in the week.'

l. 103. *Re-echoed*, i.e. ' returned ' in first edition.

l. 104. *thot*. This, probably by a printer's error, is altered to ' that ' in the second version. But the first reading is the more in keeping, besides being a better rhyme.

l. 110. *Wak'd Priam.* Cf. 2 *Henry IV*, Act i, Sc. 1 :—

Even such a man, so faint, so spiritless,
So dull, so dead in look, so woe-begone,
Drew Priam's curtain in the dead of night.
And would have told him half his Troy was burnt.

l. 120. *sicken'd over by learning.* Cf. *Hamlet*, Act iii, Sc. 1 :

And thus the native hue of resolution
Is *sicklied o'er* with the pale cast of thought.

Notwithstanding the condemnation of Shakespeare in the *Present State of Polite Learning*, and elsewhere, Goldsmith frequently weaves Shakespearean recollections into his work. Cf. *She Stoops to Conquer*, 1773, Act i, p. 13, ' We wanted no ghost to tell us that ' (*Hamlet*, Act i, Sc. 5) ; and Act i, p. 9, where he uses Falstaff's words (1 *Henry IV*, Act v, Sc. 1) :—

Would it were bed-time and all were well.

l. 121. *as very well known.* The first version has, ' 'tis very well known.'

EPITAPH ON THOMAS PARNELL.

This epitaph, apparently never used, was published with *The Haunch of Venison*, 1776 ; and is supposed to have been written about 1770. In that year Goldsmith wrote a *Life of Thomas Parnell, D.D.*, to accompany an edition of his poems, printed for Davies of Russell Street. Parnell was born in 1679, and died at Chester in 1718, on his way to Ireland. He was buried at Trinity Church in that town, on the 24th of October. Goldsmith says that his father and uncle both knew Parnell (*Life of Parnell*, 1770, p. v), and that he received assistance from the poet's nephew, Sir John Parnell, the singing gentleman who figures in Hogarth's *Election Entertainment*. Why Goldsmith should write an epitaph upon a man who died ten years before his own birth, is not easy to explain. But Johnson also wrote a Latin one, which he gave to Boswell. (Birkbeck Hill's *Life*, 1887, iv. 54.)

l. 1. *gentle Parnell's name*. Mitford compares Pope on Parnell [*Epistle to Harley*, l. iv] :—

> With softest manners, gentlest Arts adorn'd.

Pope published Parnell's *Poems* in 1722, and his sending them to Harley, Earl of Oxford, after the latter's disgrace and retirement, was the occasion of the foregoing epistle, from which the following lines respecting Parnell may also be cited :—

> For him, thou oft hast bid the World attend,
> Fond to forget the statesman in the friend ;
> For SWIFT and him despis'd the farce of state,
> The sober follies of the wise and great ;
> Dext'rous the craving, fawning crowd to quit,
> And pleas'd to 'scape from Flattery to Wit.

l. 3. *his sweetly-moral lay*. Cf. *The Hermit*, the *Hymn to Contentment*, the *Night Piece on Death*—which Goldsmith certainly recalled in his own *City Night-Piece*. Of the last-named Goldsmith says (*Life of Parnell*, 1770, p. xxxii), not without an obvious side-stroke at Gray's too-popular *Elegy*, that it ' deserves every praise, and I should suppose with very little amendment, might be made to surpass all those night pieces and church yard scenes that have since appeared.' This is certainly (as Longfellow sings) to

> rustling hear in every breeze
> The laurels of Miltiades.

Of Parnell, Hume wrote (*Essays*, 1770, i. 244) that ' after the fiftieth reading ; [he] is as fresh as at the first.'   But Gray (speaking—it should be explained—of a dubious volume of his posthumous works) said : ' Parnell is the dung-hill of Irish Grub Street' (Gosse's Gray's *Works*, 1884, ii. 372).   Meanwhile, it is his fate to-day to be mainly remembered by three words (not always attributed to him) in a couplet from what Johnson styled ' perhaps the meanest' of his performances, the *Elegy—to an Old Beauty* :—

> And all that's madly wild, or oddly gay,
> We call it only *pretty Fanny's way*.

THE CLOWN'S REPLY.

This, though dated ' Edinburgh, 1753,' was first printed in *Poems and Plays*, 1777, p. 79.

l. 1. *John Trott* is a name for a clown or commonplace character. Miss Burney (*Diary*, 1904, i. 222) says of Dr. Delap :—' As to his person and appearance, they are much in the *John-trot* style.' Foote, Chesterfield, and Walpole use the phrase ; Fielding Scotticizes it into ' John Trott-Plaid, Esq. ' ; and Bolingbroke employs it as a pseudonym.

l. 6. *I shall ne'er see your graces.*   ' I shall never see a Goose again without thinking on Mr. *Neverout*,'—says the 'brilliant Miss Notable ' in Swift's *Polite Conversation*, 1738, p. 156.

EPITAPH ON EDWARD PURDON.

The occasion of this quatrain, first published as Goldsmith's [1] in *Poems and Plays*, 1777, p. 79, is to be found in Forster's *Life and Times of Oliver Goldsmith*, 1871, ii. 60.   Purdon died on March 27, 1767 (*Gentleman's Magazine*, April, 1767, p. 192).   ' " Dr. Goldsmith made this epitaph," says William Ballantyne [the author of *Mackliniana*], " in his way from his chambers in the Temple to the Wednesday evening's club at the Globe. *I think he will never come back*, I believe he said.   I was

---

[1] It had previously appeared as an extempore by a correspondent in the *Weekly Magazine*, Edin., August 12, 1773 (*Notes and Queries*, February 14, 1880).

sitting by him, and he repeated it more than twice. *I think he will never come back.*" ' Purdon had been at Trinity College, Dublin, with Goldsmith; he had subsequently been a foot soldier; ultimately he became a 'bookseller's hack.' He wrote an anonymous letter to Garrick in 1759, and translated the *Henriade* of Voltaire. This translation Goldsmith is supposed to have revised, and his own life of Voltaire was to have accompanied it, though finally the Memoir and Translation seem to have appeared separately. (Cf. prefatory note to *Memoirs of M. de Voltaire* in Gibbs's *Works of Oliver Goldsmith*, 1885, iv. 2.)

Forster says further, in a note, 'The original ... is the epitaph on "La Mort du Sieur Etienne" :—

> Il est au bout de ses travaux,
>
> Il a passé, le Sieur Etienne ;
>
> En ce monde il eut tant des maux
>
> Qu'on ne croit pas qu'il revienne.

With this perhaps Goldsmith was familiar, and had therefore less scruple in laying felonious hands on the epigram in the *Miscellanies* (Swift, xiii. 372):—

> Well, then, poor G—— lies underground !
>
> So there's an end of honest Jack.
>
> So little justice here he found,
>
> 'Tis ten to one he'll ne'er come back.'

Mr. Forster's 'felonious hands' recalls a passage in Goldsmith's *Life of Parnell*, 1770, in which, although himself an habitual sinner in this way, he comments gravely upon the practice of plagiarism:—'It was the fashion with the wits of the last age, to conceal the places from whence they took their hints or their subjects. A trifling acknowledgment would have made that lawful prize, which may now be considered as plunder' (p. xxxii).

EPILOGUE FOR LEE LEWES'S BENEFIT.

This benefit took place at Covent Garden on May 7, 1773, the pieces performed being Rowe's *Lady Jane Grey*, and a popular pantomimic after-piece by Theobald, called *Harlequin Sorcerer*. Charles Lee Lewes (1740-1803) was the original 'Young Marlow' of *She Stoops to Conquer*. When that part was thrown up by

' Gentleman ' Smith, Shuter, the ' Mr. Hardcastle ' of the comedy, suggested Lewes, who was the harlequin of the theatre, as a substitute, and the choice proved an admirable one.   Goldsmith was highly pleased with his performance, and in consequence wrote for him this epilogue.   It was first printed by Evans, 1780, i. 112–4.

l. 9. *in thy black aspect*, i. e. the half-mask of harlequin, in which character the Epilogue was spoken.

l. 18. *rosined lightning*, stage-lightning, in which rosin is an ingredient.

EPILOGUE INTENDED FOR ' SHE STOOPS TO CONQUER.'

This epilogue was first printed at pp. 82–6, vol. ii, of the *Miscellaneous Works of* 1801.   Bolton Corney says it had been given to Percy by Goldsmith.   It is evidently the ' quarrelling Epilogue ' referred to in the following letter from Goldsmith to Cradock (*Miscellaneous Memoirs*, 1826, i. 225–6) :—

' My dear Sir,

        The Play [*She Stoops to Conquer*] has met with a success much beyond your expectations or mine.   I thank you sincerely for your Epilogue, which, however could not be used, but with your permission, shall be printed [1].   The story in short is this ; Murphy sent me rather the outline of an Epilogue than an Epilogue, which was to be sung by Mrs. Catley, and which she approved.   Mrs. Bulkley hearing this, insisted on throwing up her part, unless according to the custom of the theatre, she were permitted to speak the Epilogue.   In this embarrassment I thought of making a quarrelling Epilogue between Catley and her, debating who should speak the Epilogue, but then Mrs. Catley refused, after I had taken the trouble of drawing it out. I was then at a loss indeed ; an Epilogue was to be made, and for none but Mrs. Bulkley.   I made one, and Colman thought it too bad to be spoken ; I was obliged therefore to try a fourth time, and I made a very mawkish thing, as you'll shortly see. Such is the history of my Stage adventures, and which I have at last done with.   I cannot help saying that I am very sick of the

[1] It is so printed with the note—' This came too late to be Spoken.'

stage; and though I believe I shall get three tolerable benefits, yet I shall upon the whole be a loser, even in a pecuniary light; my ease and comfort I certainly lost while it was in agitation.

> I am, my dear Cradock,
>
> your obliged, and obedient servant,
>
> OLIVER GOLDSMITH.

P.S.—Present my most humble respects to Mrs. Cradock.'

According to Prior (*Miscellaneous Works*, 1837, iv. 154), Goldsmith's friend, Dr. Farr, had a copy of this epilogue which still, when Prior wrote, remained in that gentleman's family.

l. 21. *Who mump their passion*, i. e. grimace their passion.

l. 31. *ye macaroni train*. The Macaronies were the foplings, fribbles, or beaux of Goldsmith's day. Walpole refers to them as early as 1764; but their flourishing time was 1770–3, when the print-shops, and especially Matthew Darly's in the Strand, No. 39, swarmed with satirical designs of which they were the subject. Selwyn, March—many well-known names—are found in their ranks. Richard Cosway figured as 'The Macaroni Painter'; Angelica Kauffmann as 'The Paintress of Maccaroni's'; Thrale as 'The Southwark Macaroni.' Another caricature ('The Fluttering Macaroni') contains a portrait of Miss Catley, the singing actress of the present epilogue; while Charles Horneck, the brother of 'The Jessamy Bride' (see p. 251, l. 14), is twice satirized as 'The Martial Macaroni' and 'The Military Macaroni.' The name, as may be guessed, comes from the Italian dish first made fashionable by the 'Macaroni Club,' being afterwards applied by extension to 'the younger and gayer part of our nobility and gentry, who, at the same time that they gave in to the luxuries of eating, went equally into the extravagancies of dress.' (*Macaroni and Theatrical Magazine*, Oct. 1772.) Cf. Sir Benjamin Backbite's later epigram in *The School for Scandal*, 1777, Act ii, Sc. 2:—

> Sure never was seen two such beautiful ponies;
> Other horses are clowns, but these *macaronies*:
> To give them this title I'm sure can't be wrong,
> Their legs are so slim and their tails are so long.

l. 36. *Their hands are only lent to the Heinel.* See note to l. 28, p. 85.

EPILOGUE INTENDED FOR 'SHE STOOPS TO CONQUER.'

This epilogue, given by Goldsmith to Dr. Percy in MS., was first published in the *Miscellaneous Works* of 1801, ii. 87–8, as *An Epilogue intended for Mrs. Bulkley*. Percy did not remember for what play it was intended; but it is plainly (see note to l. 40) the second epilogue for *She Stoops to Conquer* referred to in the letter printed at p. 246 of this volume.

l. 1. *There is a place, so Ariosto sings.* 'The poet alludes to the thirty-fourth canto of *The Orlando furioso*. Ariosto, as translated by Mr. Stewart Rose, observes of the *lunar world*:

> There thou wilt find, if thou wilt thither post,
> Whatever thou on earth beneath hast lost.

Astolpho undertakes the journey; discovers a portion of his own sense; and, in an ample flask, the lost wits of Orlando.' (Bolton Corney.) Cf. also *Rape of the Lock*, Canto v, ll. 113–14:

> Some thought it mounted to the Lunar sphere,
> Since all things lost on earth are treasur'd there.

Lord Chesterfield also refers to the 'happy extravagancy' of Astolpho's journey in his *Letters*, 1774, i. 557.

l. 9. *at Foote's alone.* 'Foote's' was the Little Theatre in the Haymarket, where, in February, 1773, he brought out what he described as a 'Primitive Puppet Show,' based upon the Italian Fantoccini, and presenting a burlesque sentimental Comedy called *The Handsome Housemaid; or, Piety in Pattens*, which did as much as *She Stoops* to laugh false sentiment away. Foote warned his audience that they would not discover 'much wit or humour' in the piece, since 'his brother writers had all agreed that it was highly improper, and beneath the dignity of a mixed assembly, to show any signs of joyful satisfaction; and that creating a laugh was forcing the higher order of an audience to a vulgar and mean use of their muscles'—for which reason, he explained, he had, like them, given up the sensual for the sentimental style. And thereupon followed the story of a maid of low degree who, 'by the mere effects of morality and virtue, raised herself [like Richardson's *Pamela*], to riches and honours.' The public, who for some time had acquiesced in the new order of things under the belief that it tended to the reformation of the stage, and who were beginning to weary of the 'moral essay thrown into dialogue,' which had for some time supplanted humorous situation, promptly came round under the influence of Foote's Aristophanic ridicule, and the *comédie larmoyante* received an appreciable check. Goldsmith himself had prepared the way in a paper contributed to the *Westminster Magazine* for December, 1772 (vol. i. p. 4), with the title of 'An Essay on the Theatre; or, A Comparison between Laughing and Sentimental Comedy.' The specific reference in the Prologue is to the fact that Foote gave morning performances of *The Handsome House-maid*. There was one, for instance, on Saturday, March 6, 1773.

l. 27. *The Mohawk.* This particular species of the genus 'rake' belongs more to Swift's than Goldsmith's time, though the race is eternal. There is an account of the 'Mohock Club' in *Spectator*, No. 324. See also *Spectator*, No. 347; Gay's *Trivia*, 1716, Book iii. p. 74; Swift's *Journal to Stella*, March 8 and 26, 1712; and the *Wentworth Papers*, 1883, pp. 277-8.

l. 40. *Still stoops among the low to copy nature.* This line, one would think, should have helped to convince Percy that the epilogue was intended for *She Stoops to Conquer*, and for no other play

THE CAPTIVITY.

The Oratorio of the *Captivity* was written in 1764; but never set to music. It was first printed in 1820 at pp. 451-70 of vol. ii of the octavo edition of the *Miscellaneous Works* issued by the trade in that year. Prior reprinted it in 1837 (*Works*, iv. pp. 79-95) from the 'original manuscript' in Mr. Murray's possession; and Cunningham again in 1854 (*Works*, i. pp. 63-76). It is here reproduced from Prior. James Dodsley, who bought the MS. for Newbery and himself, gave Goldsmith ten guineas. Murray's copy was the one made for Dodsley, October 31, 1764; the one printed in 1820, that made for Newbery. The latter, which once belonged to the autograph collector, William Upcott, was in the market in 1887.

l. 23, Act i. This song had been published in the first edition of *The Haunch of Venison*, 1776, with the second stanza varied thus :—

> Thou, like the world, th' opprest oppressing,
> Thy smiles increase the wretch's woe ;
> And he who wants each other blessing,
> In thee must ever find a foe.

l. 33, Act ii. This song also had appeared in the first edition of *The Haunch of Venison*, 1776, in a different form :—

> The Wretch condemn'd with life to part,
> Still, still on Hope relies ;
> And ev'ry pang that rends the heart,
> Bids Expectation rise.

> Hope, like the glim'ring taper's light,
> Adorns and chears the way ;
> And still, as darker grows the night,
> Emits a brighter ray.

Mitford, who printed *The Captivity* from Newbery's version, records a number of ' first thoughts ' afterwards altered or improved by the author in his MS. Modern editors have not reproduced them, and their example has been followed here. *The Captivity* is not, in any sense, one of Goldsmith's important efforts.

VERSES IN REPLY TO AN INVITATION TO DINNER.

These were first published in the *Miscellaneous Works* of 1837, iv. 132-3, having been communicated to the editor by Major-General Sir H. E. Bunbury, Bart., the son of Henry William Bunbury, the well-known comic artist, and husband of Catherine Horneck, the ' Little Comedy ' to whom Goldsmith refers. Dr. Baker, to whose house the poet was invited, was Dr. (afterwards Sir George) Baker, 1722–1809. He was Sir Joshua's doctor ; and in 1776 became physician to George III, whom he attended during his illness of 1788-9. He is often mentioned by Fanny Burney and Hannah More.

l. 11. *Horneck*, i. e. Mrs. Hannah Horneck—the ' Plymouth Beauty '—widow of Captain Kane William Horneck, grandson of Dr. Anthony Horneck of the Savoy, mentioned in Evelyn's *Diary*, for whose *Happy Ascetick*, 1724, Hogarth designed a frontispiece. Mrs. Horneck died in 1803. Like Sir Joshua, the Hornecks came from Devonshire ; and through him, had made the acquaintance of Goldsmith.

Nesbitt. Mr. Nesbitt was the husband of one of Mr. Thrale's handsome sisters. He was a member of the Devonshire Club, and twice (1759-61) sat to Reynolds, with whom he was intimate. He died in 1779, and his widow married a Mr. Scott.

l. 13. *Kauffmann.* Angelica Kauffmann, the artist, 1741-1807. She had come to London in 1766. At the close of 1767 she had been cajoled into a marriage with an impostor, Count de Horn, and had separated from him in 1768. In 1769 she painted a ' weak and uncharacteristic ' portrait of Reynolds for Mr. Parker of Saltram (afterwards Baron Boringdon), which is now in the possession of the Earl of Morley. It was exhibited at the Royal Academy in the winter of 1876, and is the portrait referred to at l. 44 below.

l. 14. *the Jessamy Bride.* This was Goldsmith's pet-name for Mary, the younger Miss Horneck, at this time a girl of seventeen. After Goldsmith's death she married Colonel F. E. Gwyn (1779). She survived until 1840. ' Her own picture with a turban,' painted by Reynolds, was left to her in his will (*Works* by Malone, 2nd ed., 1798, p. cxviii). She was also painted by Romney and Hoppner. ' Jessamy,' or ' jessimy,' with its suggestion of jasmine flowers, seems in eighteenth-century parlance to have stood for ' dandified,' ' superfine,' ' delicate,' and the whole name was probably coined after the model of some of the titles to Darly's prints, then common in all the shops.

l. 16. *The Reynoldses two,* i. e. Sir Joshua and his sister, Miss Reynolds.

l. 17. *Little Comedy's face.* ' Little Comedy ' was Goldsmith's name for the elder Miss Horneck, Catherine, then nineteen, and already engaged to H. W. Bunbury (*v. supra*), to whom she was married in 1771. She died in 1799, and had also been painted by Reynolds.

l. 18. *the Captain in lace.* This was Charles Horneck, Mrs. Horneck's son, an officer in the Foot-guards. He afterwards became a general, and died in 1804. (See note, p. 247, l. 31.)

l. 44. *to-day's Advertiser.* The lines referred to **are** said by Prior to have been as follows :—

> While fair Angelica, with matchless grace,
> Paints Conway's lovely form and Stanhope's face ;
> Our hearts to beauty willing homage pay,
> We praise, admire, and gaze our souls away.
> But when the likeness she hath done for thee,
> O Reynolds ! with astonishment we see,
> Forced to submit, with all our pride we own,
> Such strength, such harmony, excell'd by none,
> And thou art rivall'd by thyself alone.

They probably appeared in the newspaper at some date between 1769, when the picture was painted, and August 1771, when ' Little Comedy ' was married, after which time Goldsmith would scarcely speak of her except as ' Mrs. Bunbury ' (see p. 132, l. 15).

LETTER IN PROSE AND VERSE TO MRS. BUNBURY.

This letter, which contains some of the brightest and easiest of Goldsmith's familiar verses, was addressed to Mrs. Bunbury (the ' Little Comedy ' of the *Verses in Reply to an Invitation to Dinner*, pp. 250-2), in answer to a rhymed summons on her part to spend Christmas at Great Barton in Suffolk, the family seat of the Bunburys. It was first printed by Prior in the *Miscellaneous Works* of 1837, iv. 148-51, and again in 1838 in Sir Henry Bunbury's *Correspondence of Sir Thomas Hanmer, Bart.*, pp. 379-83. The text of the latter issue is here followed. When Prior published the verses, they were assigned to the year 1772 ; in the *Hanmer Correspondence* it is stated that they were ' probably written in 1773 or 1774.'

P. 130. *your spring velvet coat.* Goldsmith's pronounced taste in dress, and his good-natured simplicity, made his costume a fertile subject for playful raillery,—sometimes, for rather discreditable practical jokes. (See next note.)

P. 131. *a wig, that is modish and gay.* ' He always wore a wig '— said the ' Jessamy Bride ' in her reminiscences to Prior—' a peculiarity which those who judge of his appearance only from the fine poetical head of Reynolds, would not suspect ; and on one occasion some person contrived to seriously injure this important adjunct to dress. It was the only one he had in the country, and the misfortune seemed irreparable until the services of Mr. Bunbury's valet were called in, who however performed his functions so indifferently that poor Goldsmith's appearance became the signal for a general smile' (Prior's *Life*, 1837, ii. 378–9).

P. 131. *Naso contemnere adunco*. Cf. Horace, *Sat.* i. 6. 5 :—

> naso suspendis adunco
> Ignotos,

and Martial, *Ep.* i. 4. 6 :—

> Et pueri nasum Rhinocerotis habent.

l. 2. *Loo*, i. e. Lanctre- or Lanterloo, a popular eighteenth-century game, in which *Pam*, l. 6, the knave of clubs, is the highest card. Cf. Pope, *Rape of the Lock*, 1714, iii. 61 :—

> Ev'n mighty *Pam*, that Kings and Queens o'erthrew,
> And mow'd down armies in the fights of Lu ;

and Colman's epilogue to *The School for Scandal*, 1777 :—

> And at backgammon mortify my soul,
> That pants for *loo*, or flutters at a vole ?

l. 17. *Miss Horneck*. Miss Mary Horneck, the 'Jessamy Bride' (*vide* note, p. 251, l. 14).

l. 36. *Fielding*. Sir John Fielding, d. 1780, Henry Fielding's blind half-brother, who succeeded him as a Justice of the Peace for the City and Liberties of Westminster. He was knighted in 1761. There are two portraits of him by Nathaniel Hone.

l. 40. *by quinto Elizabeth, Death without Clergy*. Legal authorities affirm that the Act quoted should be 8 Eliz. cap. iv, under which those who stole more than twelvepence ' privately from a man's person ' were debarred from benefit of clergy. But ' quint. Eliz.' must have offered some special attraction to poets, since Pope also refers to it in the *Satires and Epistles*, i. 147–8 :—

Consult the Statute : *quart.* I think, it is,
Edwardi sext. or prim. et quint. Eliz.

l. 44. *With bunches of fennel, and nosegays before 'em.* This
was a custom dating from the fearful jail fever of 1750, which
carried off, not only prisoners, but a judge (Mr. Justice Abney)
' and many jurymen and witnesses.' ' From that time up to
this day [i. e. 1855] it has been usual to place sweet-smelling herbs
in the prisoner's dock, to prevent infection.' (Lawrence's *Life
of Henry Fielding*, 1855, p. 296.) The close observation of
Cruikshank has not neglected this detail in the Old Bailey plate
of *The Drunkard's Children*, 1848, v.

l. 45. *mobs.* The mob was a loose undress or *déshabillé*, sometimes a hood. ' When we poor souls had presented ourselves
with a contrition suitable to our worthlessness, some pretty
young ladies in *mobs*, popped in here and there about the church.'
(*Guardian*, No. 65, May 26, 1713.) Cf. also Addison's ' Fine
Lady's Diary' (*Spectator*, No. 323); 'Went in our *Mobbs* to the
Dumb Man ' (Duncan Campbell).

l. 50. *yon solemn-faced.* Cf. *Introduction*, p. xxvii. According
to the ' Jessamy Bride,' Goldsmith sometimes aggravated his
plainness by an ' assumed frown of countenance ' (Prior, *Life*,
1837, ii. 379).

l. 55. *Sir Charles*, i. e. Sir Thomas Charles Bunbury, Bart.,
M.P., Henry Bunbury's elder brother. He succeeded to the
title in 1764, and died without issue in 1821. Goldsmith, it
may be observed, makes ' Charles ' a disyllable. Probably, like
many of his countrymen, he so pronounced it. (Cf. Thackeray's
Pendennis, 1850, vol. ii, chap. 5 [or xliii], where this is humorously
illustrated in Captain Costigan's ' Sir *Chorlus*, I saw your neem
at the Levēe.' Perhaps this accounts for ' failing ' and ' stealing,'—' day on ' and ' Pantheon,' in the *New Simile*. Cooke
(*European Magazine*, October, 1793, p. 259) says that Goldsmith
' rather cultivated (than endeavoured to get rid of) his brogue.'

l. 58. *dy'd in grain*, i. e. fixed, ineradicable. To ' dye in
grain ' means primarily to colour with the scarlet or purple
dye produced by the *kermes* insect, called *granum* in Latin,
from its similarity to small seeds. Being what is styled a
' fast ' dye, the phrase is used by extension to signify perma-
nence.

VIDA'S GAME OF CHESS.

Forster thus describes the MS. of this poem in his *Life of Goldsmith* :—' It is a small quarto manuscript of thirty-four pages, containing 679 lines, to which a fly-leaf is appended in which Goldsmith notes the differences of nomenclature between Vida's chessmen and our own. It has occasional interlineations and corrections, but such as would occur in transcription rather than in a first or original copy. Sometimes indeed choice appears to have been made (as at page 29) between two words equally suitable to the sense and verse, as " to " for " toward " ; but the insertions and erasures refer almost wholly to words or lines accidentally omitted and replaced. The triplet is always carefully marked ; and seldom as it is found in any other of Goldsmith's poems, I am disposed to regard its frequent recurrence here as even helping, in some degree, to explain the motive which had led him to the trial of an experiment in rhyme comparatively new to him. If we suppose him, half consciously, it may be, taking up the manner of the great master of translation, Dryden, who was at all times so much a favourite with him, he would at least, in so marked a peculiarity, be less apt to fall short than to err perhaps a little on the side of excess. Though I am far from thinking such to be the result in the present instance. The effect of the whole translation is pleasing to me, and the mock-heroic effect I think not a little assisted by the reiterated use of the triplet and alexandrine. As to any evidences of authorship derivable from the appearance of the manuscript, I will only add another word. The lines in the translation have been carefully counted, and the number is marked in Goldsmith's hand at the close of his transcription. Such a fact is, of course, only to be taken in aid of other proof ; but a man is not generally at the pains of counting, still less, I should say in such a case as Goldsmith's, of elaborately transcribing, lines which are not his own.' (Forster's *Goldsmith*, 1871, ii. 235–6).

When Forster wrote the above, the MS. was in the possession of Mr. Bolton Corney, who had not been aware of its existence when he edited Goldsmith's Poems in 1845. In 1854 it was, with his permission, included in vol. iv of Cunningham's *Works* of 1854, and subsequently in the Aldine *Poems* of 1866.

Mark Jerome Vida of Cremona, 1490–1566, was Bishop of Alba, and favourite of Leo the Magnificent. Several translators had tried their hand at his *Game of Chess* before Goldsmith. Lowndes mentions Rowbotham, 1562; Jeffreys, 1736; Erskine, 1736; Pullin, 1750; and *Anon.* (Eton), 1769 (who may have preceded Goldsmith). But after his (Goldsmith's) death appeared another Oxford anonymous version, 1778, and one by Arthur Murphy, 1786.

APPENDIXES

OLIVER GOLDSMITH

(H. W. BUNBURY)

APPENDIX A

PORTRAITS OF GOLDSMITH.

PORTRAITS of Goldsmith are not numerous; and the best known are those of Reynolds and H. W. Bunbury. That by Sir Joshua was painted in 1766-70, and exhibited in the Royal Academy (No. 151) from April 24th to May 28th in the latter year. It represents the poet in a plain white collar, furred mantle open at the neck, and holding a book in his right hand. Its general characteristics are given at p. xxviii of the 'Introduction.' It was scraped in mezzotint in 1770 by Reynolds's Italian pupil, Giuseppe, or Joseph Marchi; and it is dated 1st December.[1] Bunbury's portrait first appeared, after Goldsmith's death, as a frontispiece to the *Haunch of Venison*; and it was etched in facsimile by James Bretherton. The plate is dated May 24, 1776. In his loyal but despotic *Life of Goldsmith* (Bk. iv, ch. 6), Mr. John Forster reproduces these portraits side by side; in order, he professes, to show 'the distinction between truth and a caricature of it.' Bunbury, it may be, was primarily a caricaturist, and possibly looked at most things from a more or less grotesque point of view; but this sketch—it should be observed—was meant for a likeness, and we have the express testimony of one who, if she was Bunbury's sister-in-law, was also Goldsmith's friend, that it rendered Goldsmith accurately. It 'gives the head with admirable fidelity'—says the 'Jessamy Bride' (afterwards Mrs. Gwyn)—'as he actually lived among us; nothing can exceed its truth' (Prior's *Life*, 1837, ii. 380). In other words, it delineates Goldsmith as his contemporaries saw him, with bulbous

---

[1] This was the print to which Goldsmith referred in a well-known anecdote. Speaking to his old Peckham pupil, Samuel Bishop, whom, after many years, he met accidentally in London, he asked him eagerly whether he had got an engraving of the new portrait, and finding he had not, 'said, with some emotion, "if your picture had been published, I should not have suffered an hour to elapse without procuring it."' But he was speedily 'appeased by apologies.' (Prior's *Life*, 1837, i. 219-20.)

forehead, indecisive chin, and long protruding upper lip,—awkward, insignificant, ill at ease,—restlessly burning ' to get in and shine.' It enables us moreover to understand how people who knew nothing of his better and more lovable qualities, could speak of him as an ' inspired idiot,' as ' silly Dr. Goldsmith,' as ' talking like poor Poll.' It is, in short, his external, objective presentment. The picture by Sir Joshua, on the contrary, is almost wholly subjective. Draped judiciously in a popular studio costume, which is not that of the sitter's day, it reveals to us the author of *The Deserted Village* as Reynolds conceived him to be at his best, serious, dignified, introspective, with his physical defects partly extenuated by art, partly over-mastered by his intellectual power. To quote the ' Jessamy Bride ' once more—it is ' a fine poetical head for the admiration of posterity, but as it is divested of his wig and with the shirt collar open, it was not the man as seen in daily life ' (*Ib.* ii. 380). Had Goldsmith lived in our era of photography, photography would doubtless have given us something which would have been neither the one nor the other, but more like Bunbury than Reynolds. Yet we may be grateful for both. For Bunbury's sketch and Reynolds's portrait are alike indispensable to the true comprehension of Goldsmith's curiously dual personality.[1]

The portrait by Reynolds, above referred to, was painted for the Thrale Gallery at Streatham, on the dispersion of which, in May, 1816, it was bought for the Duke of Bedford for £133 7s. It is now at Woburn Abbey (Cat. No. 254). At Knole, Lord Sackville possesses another version (Cat. No. 239), which was purchased in 1773 by the Countess Delawarr, and was shown at South Kensington in 1867. Here the dress is a black coat and a brown mantle with fur. The present owner exhibited it at the Guelph Exhibition of 1891. A third version, now in the Irish National Gallery, once belonged to Goldsmith himself, and then to his brother-in-law, Daniel Hodson. Finally, there is a copy, by a pupil of Reynolds, in the National Portrait Gallery, to which

---

[1] There is in existence another undated etching by Bretherton after Bunbury on a larger scale, which comes much nearer to Reynolds ; and it is of course possible, though not in our opinion probable, that Mrs. Gwyn may have referred to this. But Forster selected the other for his comparison ; it is prefixed to the *Haunch of Venison*; it is certainly the better known ; and (as we believe) cannot ever have been intended for a caricature.

SILHOUETTE OF GOLDSMITH

(OZIAS HUMPHRY)

it was bequeathed in 1890 by Dr. Leifchild, having formerly been the property of Caleb Whitefoord. Caleb Whitefoord also had an 'admirable miniature' by Reynolds, which belongs to the Rev. Benjamin Whitefoord, Hon. Canon of Salisbury (*Whitefoord Papers*, 1898, p. xxvii). A small circular print, based upon Reynolds, and etched by James Basire, figures on the title-page of *Retaliation*. Some of the plates are dated April 18, 1774.[1] The National Portrait Gallery has also a silhouette, attributed to Ozias Humphry, R.A., which was presented in 1883 by Sir Theodore Martin, K.C.B. Then there is the portrait by Hogarth shown at South Kensington in 1867 by the late Mr. Studley Martin of Liverpool. It depicts the poet writing at a round table in a black cap, claret-coloured coat and ruffles. Of this there is a wood-cut in the later editions of Forster's *Life* (Bk. iii, ch. 14). The same exhibition of 1867 contained a portrait of Goldsmith in a brown coat and red waistcoat, 'as a young man.' It was said to be extremely like him in face, and was attributed to Gainsborough. In Evans's edition of the *Poetical and Dramatic Works* is another portrait engraved by Cook, said, on some copies, to be 'from an original drawing'; and there is in the Print Room at the British Museum yet another portrait still, engraved by William Ridley 'from a painting in the possession of the Rev. Mr. Williams,' no doubt Goldsmith's friend, the Rev. David Williams, founder of the Royal Literary Fund. One of these last may have been the work to which the poet refers in a letter to his brother Maurice in January, 1770. 'I have sent my cousin Jenny [Jane Contarine] a miniature picture of myself . . . The face you well know, is ugly enough, but it is finely painted' (*Misc. Works*, 1801, p. 88).

In front of Dublin University is a bronze statue of Goldsmith by J. H. Foley, R.A., erected in 1864.[2] Of this there is a good engraving by G. Stodart. On the memorial in Westminster Abbey erected in 1776 is a medallion by Joseph Nollekens.

---

[1] There is also a sketch by Reynolds (?) at the British Museum.

[2] Goldsmith's traditional ill-luck pursued him after death. During some public procession in front of Trinity College, a number of undergraduates climbed on the statue, with the result that the thin metal of the poet's head was flattened or crushed in, requiring for its readjustment very skilful restorative treatment. The Editor is indebted for this item of information to the kindness of Mr. Percy Fitzgerald, who was present at the subsequent operation.

APPENDIX B

DESCRIPTIONS OF NEWELL'S VIEWS OF LISSOY, ETC.

In 1811, the Rev. R. H. Newell, B.D. and Fellow of St. John's College, Cambridge, issued an edition of the *Poetical Works* of Goldsmith. The distinctive feature of this lay in the fact that it was illustrated by a number of aquatints ' by Mr. Alkin ' (i.e. Samuel Alken), after drawings made by Newell in 1806–9, and was accompanied by a series of ' Remarks, attempting to ascertain, chiefly from local observation, the actual scene of *The Deserted Village*.' Some quotations from these ' Remarks ' have already been made in the foregoing notes ; but as copies of six of the drawings are given in this volume, it may be well, in each case, to reproduce Newell's ' descriptions.'

LISHOY, OR LISSOY MILL.

The west end of it, as seen from a field near the road ; to the north the country slopes away in coarsely cultivated enclosures, and the distance eastward is bounded by the Longford hills. The stream ran from the south side of the mill (where it is still of some width though nearly choked up), and fell over the once busy wheel, into a deep channel, now overgrown with weeds. Neglect and poverty appear all around. The farm house and barn-like buildings, which fill up the sketch, seem to have no circumstances of interest attached to them (p. 83).

KILKENNY WEST CHURCH.

This south-west view was taken from the road, which passes by the church, towards Lishoy, and overlooks the adjacent country to the west. The church appears neat, its exterior having been lately repaired. The tree added to the foreground is the only liberty taken with the subject (p. 83).

HAWTHORN TREE.

An east view of the tree, as it stood in August, 1806. The Athlone road occupies the centre of the sketch, winding round

LISSOY MILL

(R. H. NEWELL.)

the stone wall to the right, into the village, and to the left leading
toward the church.   The cottage and tree opposite the hawthorn,
adjoin the present public-house ; the avenue before the parsonage
tops the distant eminence (p. 84).

SOUTH VIEW FROM GOLDSMITH'S MOUNT.

In this sketch ' the decent church,' at the top of the hill in
the distance, is an important object, from its exact correspondence with the situation given it in the poem.   Half-way up
stands the solitary ruin of Lord Dillon's castle.   The hill in
shadow, on the left, is above the village, and is supposed to be
alluded to in the line—

> Up yonder hill the distant murmur rose.

A flat of bogland extends from the narrow lake in the centre
to the mount on the right of the foreground (p. 84).

THE PARSONAGE.

A south view from the Athlone road, which runs parallel with
the stone wall, and nearly east and west : the gateway is that
mentioned in Goldsmith's letter [1], the mount being directly
opposite, in a field contiguous with the road.

The ruinous stone wall in this and three other sketches,
which is a frequent sort of fence in the neighbourhood, gives
a characteristic propriety to the line (48)

> And the long grass o'ertops the mould'ring wall.

(pp. 84-5).

THE SCHOOL-HOUSE.

This cottage is situated, as the poem describes it, by the road-
side, just where it forms a sharp angle by branching out from the
village eastward : at this point a south-west view was taken
(p. 85).

Newell's book was reissued in 1820 ; but no alterations were
made in the foregoing descriptions which, it must be borne in

---

[1] See note to l. 114 of *The Deserted Village.*

mind, refer to 1806–9. His enthusiastic identifications will no doubt be taken by the reader with the needful grain of salt. Goldsmith probably remembered the hawthorn bush, the church upon the hill, the watercress gatherer, and some other familiar objects of the 'seats of his youth.' But distance added charm to the regretful retrospect ; and in the details his fancy played freely with his memories. It would be unwise, for example, to infer—as Mr. Hogan did—the decorations of the *Three Pidgeons* at Lissoy from the account of the inn in the poem.[1] Some twelve years before its publication, when he was living miserably in Green Arbour Court, Goldsmith had submitted to his brother Henry a sample of a heroi-comic poem describing a Grub Street writer in bed in 'a paltry ale-house.' In this 'the sanded floor,' the 'twelve good rules' and the broken tea-cups all played their parts as accessories, and even the double-dealing chest had its prototype in the poet's night-cap, which was 'a cap by night—a stocking all the day.' A year or two later he expanded these lines in the *Citizen of the World*, and the scene becomes the Red Lion in Drury Lane. From this second version he adapted, or extended again, the description of the inn parlour in *The Deserted Village*. It follows therefore, either that he borrowed for London the details of a house in Ireland, or that he used for Ireland the details of a house in London. If, on the other hand, it be contended that those details were common to both places, then the identification in these particulars of Auburn with Lissoy falls hopelessly to the ground.

APPENDIX C

THE EPITHET 'SENTIMENTAL.'

Goldsmith's use of 'sentimental' in the 'Prologue' to *She Stoops to Conquer* (p. 109, l. 36)—the only occasion upon which he seems to have employed it in his *Poems*—affords an excuse for bringing together one or two dispersed illustrations of the rise and growth of this once highly-popular adjective, not as yet

---

[1] What follows is taken from the writer's 'Introduction' to Mr. Edwin Abbey's illustrated edition of *The Deserted Village*, 1902, p. ix.

THE PARSONAGE

(R. H. NEWELL)

reached in the *N. E. D.* Johnson, who must often have heard it,
ignores it altogether ; and in Todd's edition of his *Dictionary*
(1818) it is expressly marked with a star as one of the modern
words which are *not* to be found in the Doctor's collection.
According to Mr. Sidney Lee's admirable article in the *Dictionary
of National Biography* on Sterne, that author is to be regarded
as the ' only begetter ' of the epithet. Mr. Lee says that it first
occurs in a letter of 1740 written by the future author of *Tristram
Shandy* to the Miss Lumley he afterwards married. Here is the
precise and characteristic passage :—' I gave a thousand pensive,
penetrating looks at the chair thou hadst so often graced, in
those quiet and *sentimental* repasts—then laid down my knife
and fork, and took out my handkerchief, and clapped it across
my face, and wept like a child ' (Sterne's *Works* by Saintsbury,
1894, v. 25). Nine years later, however circulated, ' sentimental '
has grown ' so much in vogue ' that it has reached from London
to the provinces. ' Mrs. Belfour ' (Lady Bradshaigh) writing
from Lincolnshire to Richardson says :—' Pray, Sir, give me
leave to ask you . . . what, in your opinion, is the meaning of the
word *sentimental*, so much in vogue amongst the polite, both in
town and country ? In letters and common conversation, I have
asked several who make use of it, and have generally received
for answer, it is—it is—*sentimental*. Every thing clever and
agreeable is comprehended in that word ; but [I] am convinced
a wrong interpretation is given, because it is impossible every
thing clever and agreeable can be so common as this word. I am
frequently astonished to hear such a one is a *sentimental* man ;
we were a *sentimental* party ; I have been taking a *sentimental*
walk. And that I might be reckoned a little in the fashion, and,
as I thought, show them the proper use of the word, about six
weeks ago, I declared I had just received a *sentimental* letter.
Having often laughed at the word, and found fault with the
application of it, and this being the first time I ventured to make
use of it, I was loudly congratulated upon the occasion : but
I should be glad to know your interpretation of it ' (Richardson's
Correspondence, 1804, iv. pp. 282–3). The reply of the author
of *Clarissa*, which would have been interesting, is not given ;
but it is clear that by this date (1749) ' sentimental ' must already
have been rather overworked by ' the polite.' Eleven years
after this, we meet with it in the Prologue to Colman's ' Drama-

tick Novel' of *Polly Honeycombe.* 'And then,' he says, commenting upon the fiction of the period,—

> And then so *sentimental* is the Stile,
> So chaste, yet so bewitching all the while!
> Plot, and elopement, passion, rape, and rapture,
> The total sum of ev'ry dear—dear—Chapter.

With February, 1768, came Sterne's *Sentimental Journey* upon which Wesley has this comment :—' I casually took a volume of what is called, " A Sentimental Journey through France and Italy." *Sentimental* ! what is that ? It is not English : he might as well say, *Continental* [!]. It is not sense. It conveys no determinate idea ; yet one fool makes many. And this nonsensical word (who would believe it ?) is become a fashionable one ! ' (*Journal*, February 11, 1772). In 1773, Goldsmith puts it in the ' Dedication ' to *She Stoops* :—' The undertaking a comedy, not merely *sentimental*, was very dangerous ; ' and Garrick (forgetting Kelly and *False Delicacy*) uses it more than once in his ' Prologue ' to the same play, e.g.—' Faces are blocks in *sentimental* scenes.' Further examples might easily be multiplied, for the word, in spite of Johnson, had now come to stay. Two years subsequently we find Sheridan referring to

> The goddess of the woful countenance,
> The *sentimental* Muse !—

in an occasional ' Prologue ' to *The Rivals.* It must already have passed into the vocabulary of the learned. Todd gives examples from Shenstone and Langhorne. Warton has it more than once in his *History of English Poetry* ; and it figures in the *Essays* of Vicesimus Knox. Thus academically launched, we need no longer follow its fortunes.

APPENDIX D

FRAGMENTS OF TRANSLATIONS, ETC., BY GOLDSMITH.

To the Aldine edition of 1831, the Rev. John Mitford added several fragments of translation from Goldsmith's *Essays.* About a third of these were traced by Bolton Corney in 1845 to the *Horace* of Francis. He therefore compiled a fresh collection, here given.

From a French version of Homer.

The shouting army cry'd with joy extreme,
He sure must conquer, who himself can tame!

The Bee, 1759, p. 90.

The next is also from Homer, and is proposed as an improvement of Pope :—

They knew and own'd the monarch of the main :
The sea subsiding spreads a level plain :
The curling waves before his coursers fly :
The parting surface leaves his brazen axle dry.

Miscellaneous Works, 1801, iv. 410.

From the same source comes number three, a quatrain from
Vida's *Eclogues* :—

Say heavenly muse, their youthful frays rehearse ;
Begin, ye daughters of immortal verse ;
Exulting rocks have crown'd the power of song !
And rivers listen'd as they flow'd along.

Miscellaneous Works, 1801, iv. 427.

Another is a couplet from Ovid, the fish referred to being the
scarus or bream :—

Of all the fish that graze beneath the flood,
He, *only,* ruminates his former food.

History of the Earth, &c., 1774, iii. 6.

Bolton Corney also prints the translation from the *Spectator,*
already given at p. 94 of this volume. His last fragment is
from the posthumous translation of Scarron's *Roman Comique* :

Thus, when soft love subdues the heart
With smiling hopes and chilling fears,
The soul rejects the aid of art,
And speaks in moments more than years.

The Comic Romance of Monsieur Scarron, 1775, ii. 161.

It is unnecessary to refer to any other of the poems attributed
to Goldsmith. Mitford included in his edition a couple of
quatrains inserted in the *Morning Chronicle* for April 3, 1800,
which were said to be by the poet ; but they do not resemble
his manner. Another piece with the title of *The Fair Thief* was
revived in July, 1893, by an anonymous writer in the *Daily*

Chronicle, as being possibly by Goldsmith, to whom it was assigned in an eighteenth-century anthology (1789-80). Its discoverer, however, subsequently found it given in Walpole's *Noble Authors* (Park's edition, 1806) to Charles Wyndham, Earl of Egremont. It has no great merit ; and may safely be neglected as an important addition to Goldsmith's *Works,* already burdened with much which that critical author would never have reprinted.

APPENDIX E

GOLDSMITH ON POETRY UNDER ANNE AND GEORGE THE FIRST.

In Letter xvi, vol. ii. pp. 139-41, of *An History of England in a Series of Letters from a Nobleman to his Son,* 1764, Goldsmith gives the following short account of the state of poetry in the first quarter of the Eighteenth Century.

' But, of all the other arts, poetry in this age was carried to the greatest perfection. The language, for some ages, had been improving, but now it seemed entirely divested of its roughness and barbarity. Among the poets of this period we may place John Philips, author of several poems, but of none more admired than that humourous one, entitled, *The Splendid Shilling* ; he lived in obscurity, and died just above want. William Congreve deserves also particular notice ; his comedies, some of which were but coolly received upon their first appearance, seemed to mend upon repetition ; and he is, at present, justly allowed the foremost in that species of dramatic poesy. His wit is ever just and brilliant ; his sentiments new and lively ; and his elegance equal to his regularity. Next him Vanbrugh is placed, whose humour seems more natural, and characters more new ; but he owes too many obligations to the French, entirely to pass for an original ; and his total disregard to decency, in a great measure, impairs his merit. Farquhar is still more lively, and, perhaps more entertaining than either ; his pieces still continue the favourite performances of the stage, and bear frequent repetition without satiety ; but he often mistakes pertness for wit, and seldom strikes his characters with proper force or originality. However, he died very young ; and it is remarkable, that he continued to improve as he grew older ; his last play, entitled *The Beaux' Stratagem*, being the best of his productions. Addison, both as a poet and prose writer, deserves the highest regard and imitation. His *Campaign*, and *Letter to Lord Halifax from Italy*, are masterpieces in the former, and his *Essays* published in the *Spectator* are inimitable specimens of the latter. Whatever he treated of was handled with elegance and precision ; and that virtue which was taught in his writings, was enforced by his example. Steele was Addison's friend and admirer ; his comedies are perfectly polite, chaste, and genteel ; nor were his other works contemptible ; he wrote on several subjects, and yet it is amazing, in the multiplicity of his pursuits, how he found leisure for the discussion of any. Ever persecuted by creditors, whom his profuseness drew upon him, or pursuing impracticable schemes, suggested by ill-grounded ambition. Dean Swift was the professed antagonist both of Addison and him. He perceived that there was a spirit of romance mixed with all the works of the poets who preceded him ; or, in other words, that they had drawn nature on the most pleasing side. There still therefore was a place left for him, who, careless of censure, should describe it just as it was, with all its deformities ; he therefore owes much of his fame, not so much to the greatness of his genius, as to the boldness of it. He was dry, sarcastic, and severe ; and suited his style exactly to the turn of his thought, being concise and nervous. In this period also flourished many of subordinate fame. Prior was the first who adopted the French elegant easy manner of telling a story ; but if what he has borrowed from that nation be taken from him, scarce anything will be left upon which he can lay any claim to applause in poetry. Rowe was only outdone by Shakespeare and Otway as a tragic writer ; he has fewer absurdities than either ; and is, perhaps, as pathetic as they ; but his flights are not so bold, nor his characters so strongly marked. Perhaps his coming later than the rest may have contributed to lessen the esteem he deserves. Garth had success as a poet ; and, for a time, his fame was even greater than his desert. In his principal work, *The Dispensary*, his versification is negligent ; and his plot is now become tedious ; but whatever he may lose as a poet, it would be improper to rob him of the merit he deserves for having written the prose dedication, and preface, to the poem already mentioned ; in which he has shown the truest wit, with the most refined elegance. Parnell, though he has written but one poem, namely, *The Hermit*, yet has found a place among the English first rate poets. Gay, likewise, by his *Fables* and *Pastorals*, has acquired an equal reputation. But of all who have added to the stock of English Poetry, Pope, perhaps, deserves the first place. On him foreigners look as one of the most successful writers of his time ; his versification is the most harmonious, and his correctness the most remarkable of all our poets. A noted contemporary of his own calls the English the finest writers on moral topics, and Pope the noblest moral writer of all the English. Mr. Pope has somewhere named himself the last English Muse ; and, indeed, since his time, we have seen scarce any production that can justly lay claim to immortality ; he carried the language to its highest perfection ; and those who have attempted still farther to improve it, instead of ornament, have only caught finery.'

APPENDIX F

CRITICISMS FROM GOLDSMITH'S 'BEAUTIES OF ENGLISH POESY.'

To *The Beauties of English Poesy*, 2 vols., 1767, Goldsmith prefixed, in each case, ' short introductory criticisms.' They are, as he says, ' rather designed for boys than men ' ; and aim only at being ' obvious and sincere ' ; but they carry his views on the subject somewhat farther than the foregoing account from the *History of England*.

THE RAPE OF THE LOCK.

This seems to be Mr. Pope's most finished production, and is, perhaps, the most perfect in our language. It exhibits stronger powers of imagination, more harmony of numbers, and a greater knowledge of the world, than any other of this poet's works ; and it is probable, if our country were called upon to show a specimen of their genius to foreigners, this would be the work here fixed upon.

THE HERMIT.

This poem is held in just esteem, the versification being chaste, and tolerably harmonious, and the story told with perspicuity and conciseness. It seems to have cost great labour, both to Mr. Pope and Parnell himself, to bring it to this perfection.[1] It may not be amiss to observe that the fable is taken from one of Dr. Henry More's Dialogues.

IL PENSEROSO.

I have heard a very judicious critic say, that he had an higher idea of Milton's style in poetry, from the two following poems [*Il Penseroso* and *l'Allegro*], than from his *Paradise Lost*. It is certain the imagination shown in them is correct and strong. The introduction to both in irregular measure is borrowed from the Italian, and hurts an English ear.

AN ELEGY, WRITTEN IN A COUNTRY CHURCH YARD.

This is a very fine poem, but overloaded with epithet.[2] The heroic measure with alternate rhyme is very properly adapted to the solemnity of the subject, as it is the slowest movement that our language admits of. The latter part of the poem is pathetic and interesting.

LONDON. IN IMITATION OF THE THIRD SATIRE OF JUVENAL.

This poem of Mr. Johnson's is the best imitation of the original that has appeared in our language, being possessed of all the force and satirical resentment of Juvenal. Imitation gives us a much truer idea of the ancients than even translation could do.

THE SCHOOL-MISTRESS. IN IMITATION OF SPENSER.

This poem is one of those happinesses in which a poet excels himself, as there is nothing in all Shenstone which in any way approaches it in merit ; and, though I dislike the imitations of

[1] Parnell's *Poems*, 1770, xxiv.
[2] This is a strange complaint to come from Goldsmith, whose own *Hermit*, as was pointed out to the present Editor by the late Mr. Kegan Paul, is certainly open to this impeachment.

our old English poets in general, yet, on this minute subject, the antiquity of the style produces a very ludicrous solemnity.

COOPER'S HILL.

This poem, by Denham, though it may have been exceeded by later attempts in description, yet deserves the highest applause, as it far surpasses all that went before it : the concluding part, though a little too much crowded, is very masterly.

ELOISA TO ABELARD.

The harmony of numbers in this poem is very fine. It is rather drawn out to too tedious a length, although the passions vary with great judgement. It may be considered as superior to anything in the epistolary way ; and the many translations which have been made of it into the modern languages, are in some measure a proof of this.

AN EPISTLE FROM MR. PHILIPS [1] TO THE EARL OF DORSET.

The opening of this poem is incomparably fine. The latter part is tedious and trifling.

A LETTER FROM ITALY, TO THE RIGHT HONOURABLE CHARLES LORD HALIFAX.

In the Year MDCCI.

Few poems have done more honour to English genius than this. There is in it a strain of political thinking that was, at that time, new in our poetry. Had the harmony of this been equal to that of Pope's versification, it would be incontestably the finest poem in our language ; but there is a dryness in the numbers which greatly lessens the pleasure excited both by the poet's judgement and imagination.[2]

[1] Ambrose Philips.
[2] See introductory note to *The Traveller*, p. 162.

ALEXANDER'S FEAST; OR, THE POWER OF MUSIC. AN ODE, IN HONOUR OF ST. CECILIA'S DAY.

This ode [by Mr. Dryden] has been more applauded, perhaps, than it has been felt, however, it is a very fine one, and gives its beauties rather at a third, or fourth, than at a first perusal.

ODE FOR MUSIC ON ST. CECILIA'S DAY.

This ode [by Mr. Pope] has by many been thought equal to the former. As it is a repetition of Dryden's manner, it is so far inferior to him. The whole hint of Orpheus, and many of the lines, have been taken from an obscure Ode upon Music, published in Tate's Miscellanies.[1]

THE SHEPHERD'S WEEK. IN SIX PASTORALS.

These are Mr. Gay's principal performances. They were originally intended, I suppose, as a burlesque on those of [Ambrose] Philips; but, perhaps without designing it, he has hit the true spirit of pastoral poetry. In fact, he more resembles Theocritus than any other English pastoral writer whatsoever. There runs through the whole a strain of rustic pleasantry which should ever distinguish this species of composition; but how far the antiquated expressions used here may contribute to the humour, I will not determine; for my own part, I could wish the simplicity were preserved, without recurring to such obsolete antiquity for the manner of expressing it.

MAC FLECKNOE.

The severity of this satire, and the excellence of its versification give it a distinguished rank in this species of composition. At present, an ordinary reader would scarce suppose that Shadwell, who is here meant by Mac Flecknoe, was worth being chastised, and that Dryden's descending to such game was like an eagle's stooping to catch flies.[2] The truth however is, Shadwell, at one time, held divided reputation with this great poet. Every

---

[1] *A Pindaric Essay upon Musick*—says Gibbs—by 'Mr. Wilson,' which appears at p. 401 of Tate's Collection of 1685.

[2] 'Aquila non capit muscas' (Apostolius).

age produces its fashionable dunces, who, by following the transient topic, or humour, of the day, supply talkative ignorance with materials for conversation.

ON POETRY. A RHAPSODY.

Here follows one of the best versified poems in our language, and the most masterly production of its author. The severity with which Walpole is here treated, was in consequence of that minister having refused to provide for Swift in England, when applied to for that purpose in the year 1725 (if I remember right). The severity of a poet, however, gave Walpole very little uneasiness. A man whose schemes, like this minister's, seldom extended beyond the exigency of the year, but little regarded the contempt of posterity.

OF THE USE OF RICHES.

This poem, as Mr. Pope tells us himself, cost much attention and labour ; and, from the easiness that appears in it, one would be apt to think as much.

FROM THE DISPENSARY.

This sixth canto of the *Dispensary*, by Dr. Garth, has more merit than the whole preceding part of the poem, and, as I am told, in the first edition of this work it is more correct than as here exhibited ; but that edition I have not been able to find. The praises bestowed on this poem are more than have been given to any other ; but our approbation, at present, is cooler, for it owed part of its fame to party.[1]

ECLOGUE I.
SELIM : OR, THE SHEPHERD'S MORAL.

The following eclogues [2], written by Mr. Collins, are very pretty : the images, it must be owned, are not very local ; for the pastoral subject could not well admit of it. The description

[1] Cf. Dedication of *The Traveller*, ll. 34-45.
[2] i. e.—Selim, Hassan, Agib and Secander, and Abra. Goldsmith admired Collins, whom he calls in the *Enquiry*, 1759, p. 143, 'the neglected author of the Persian eclogues, which, however inaccurate, excel any in our language.' He borrowed freely from him in the *Threnodia Augustalis*, q.v.

of Asiatic magnificence, and manners, is a subject as yet un-
attempted amongst us, and I believe, capable of furnishing a great
variety of poetical imagery.

THE SPLENDID SHILLING.
By Mr. J. Philips.

This is reckoned the best parody of Milton in our language:
it has been an hundred times imitated, without success. The
truth is, the first thing in this way must preclude all future
attempts ; for nothing is so easy as to burlesque any man's
manner, when we are once showed the way.

A PIPE OF TOBACCO:
In Imitation of Six Several Authors.

Mr. Hawkins Browne, the author of these, as I am told, had
no good original manner of his own, yet we see how well he
succeeded when he turns an imitator ; for the following are
rather imitations than ridiculous parodies.

A NIGHT-PIECE ON DEATH.

The great fault of this piece, written by Dr. Parnell, is that
it is in eight-syllable lines, very improper for the solemnity of the
subject ; otherwise, the poem is natural, and the reflections just.

A FAIRY TALE.
By Dr. Parnell.

Never was the old manner of speaking more happily applied,
or a tale better told, than this.

PALEMON AND LAVINIA.[1]

Mr. Thomson, though, in general, a verbose and affected poet,
has told this story with unusual simplicity : it is rather given
here for being much esteemed by the public, than by the editor.

THE BASTARD.

Almost all things written from the heart, as this certainly was,
have some merit. The poet here describes sorrows and misfortunes which were by no means imaginary ; and, thus, there

---

[1] From *The Seasons*.

runs a truth of thinking through this poem, without which it would be of little value, as Savage is, in other respects, but an indifferent poet.

THE POET AND HIS PATRON.

Mr. Mo[o]re was a poet that never had justice done him while living ; there are few of the moderns have a more correct taste, or a more pleasing manner of expressing their thoughts. It was upon these fables [Nos. v, vi, and xvi of the *Fables for the Ladies*] he chiefly founded his reputation ; yet they are, by no means, his best production.

AN EPISTLE TO A LADY.

This little poem, by Mr. Nugent [afterwards Lord Clare] is very pleasing. The easiness of the poetry, and the justice of the thoughts, constitute its principal beauty.

HANS CARVEL.

This bagatelle, for which, by the by, Mr. Prior has got his greatest reputation, was a tale told in all the old Italian collections of jests, and borrowed from thence by Fontaine. It had been translated once or twice before into English, yet was never regarded till it fell into the hands of Mr. Prior. A strong instance how everything is improved in the hands of a man of genius.

BAUCIS AND PHILEMON.

This poem [by Swift] is very fine ; and though in the same strain with the preceding [Prior's *Ladle*] is yet superior.

TO THE EARL OF WARWICK, ON THE DEATH OF MR. ADDISON.

This elegy (by Mr. Tickell) is one of the finest in our language ; there is so little new that can be said upon the death of a friend, after the complaints of Ovid and the Latin Italians, in this way, that one is surprised to see so much novelty in this to strike us, and so much interest to affect.

COLIN AND LUCY.

Through all Tickell's works there is a strain of ballad-thinking, if I may so express it; and, in this professed ballad, he seems to have surpassed himself. It is, perhaps, the best in our language in this way.

THE TEARS OF SCOTLAND.

Written in the Year MDCCXLVI.

This ode, by Dr. Smollett, does rather more honour to the author's feelings than his taste. The mechanical part, with regard to numbers and language, is not so perfect as so short a work as this requires; but the pathetic it contains, particularly in the last stanza but one, is exquisitely fine.

ON THE DEATH OF THE LORD PROTECTOR.

Our poetry was not quite harmonized in Waller's time; so that this, which would be now looked upon as a slovenly sort of versification, was, with respect to the times in which it was written, almost a prodigy of harmony. A modern reader will chiefly be struck with the strength of thinking, and the turn of the compliments bestowed upon the usurper. Everybody has heard the answer our poet made Charles II; who asked him how his poem upon Cromwell came to be finer than his panegyric upon himself. 'Your majesty,' replies Waller, 'knows, that poets always succeed best in fiction.'

THE STORY OF PHOEBUS AND DAPHNE APPLIED.

The French claim this [by Mr. Waller] as belonging to them. To whomsoever it belongs the thought is finely turned.

NIGHT THOUGHTS.

By Dr. Young.

These seem to be the best of the collection; from whence only the two first are taken. They are spoken of differently, either with exaggerated applause or contempt, as the reader's disposition is either turned to mirth or melancholy.

SATIRE I.

Young's Satires were in higher reputation when published, than they stand in at present.   He seems fonder of dazzling than pleasing ;   of raising our admiration for his wit, than our dislike of the follies he ridicules.

A PASTORAL BALLAD.

These ballads of Mr. Shenstone are chiefly commended for the natural simplicity of the thoughts and the harmony of the versification.   However, they are not excellent in either.

PHOEBE. A PASTORAL.

This, by Dr. Byrom, is a better effort than the preceding [a ballad by Shenstone].

A SONG.

This [' Despairing beside a clear stream '] by Mr. Rowe, is better than anything of the kind in our language.

AN ESSAY ON POETRY.

This work, by the Duke of Buckingham, is enrolled among our great English productions.   The precepts are sensible, the poetry not indifferent, but it has been praised more than it deserves.

CADENUS AND VANESSA.

This is thought one of Dr. Swift's correctest pieces ; its chief merit, indeed, is the elegant ease with which a story, but ill-conceived in itself, is told.

ALMA : OR, THE PROGRESS OF THE MIND.

What Prior meant by this poem I can't understand ; by the Greek motto to it one would think it was either to laugh at the subject or the reader.   There are some parts of it very fine ; and let them save the badness of the rest.

OXFORD: HORACE HART
PRINTER TO THE UNIVERSITY